Condé Nast
Traveler

TRUTH IN TRAVEL

Caribbean Resort and Cruise Ship Finder 1996

GW00601932

Fodor's Travel Publications, Inc.
New York • Toronto • London • Sydney • Auckland

Text copyright © 1995 by Fodor's Travel Publications, Inc.

Survey results copyright © 1995 by the Condé Nast Publications, Inc.

Fodor's is a registered trademark of Fodor's Travel Publications, Inc.

Condé Nast Traveler is a registered trademark of Advance Magazine Publishers, Inc., published through its division, the Condé Nast Publications, Inc. All rights reserved.

All rights reserved under International and Pan-American Copyright Conventions. Published in the United States by Fodor's Travel Publications, Inc., a subsidiary of Random House, Inc., New York, and simultaneously in Canada by Random House of Canada Limited, Toronto. Distributed by Random House, Inc., New York.

No maps, illustrations, or other portions of this book may be reproduced in any form without written permission from the publisher.

ISBN 0–679–02999–0

Condé Nast Traveler Caribbean Resort and Cruise Ship Finder 1996

Condé Nast Traveler Project Editor: Cliff Hopkinson

Editors: David Low, Jennifer Paul
Editorial Contributors: Steven Amsterdam, Karen Cure, Debra Gach, Laura M. Kidder, Rebecca Miller
Creative Director: Fabrizio La Rocca
Cartographers: David Lindroth, Inc; Kris Tobiassen
Cover Photograph: Catherine Karnow/Woodfin Camp
Design: Tigist Getachew

Special Sales

Fodor's Travel Publications are available at special discounts for bulk purchases for sales promotions or premiums. Special editions, including personalized covers, excerpts of existing guides, and corporate imprints, can be created in large quantities for special needs. For more information, contact your local bookseller or Special Markets, Fodor's Travel Publications, 201 E. 50th Street, New York, NY 10022. Inquiries from Canada should be directed to your local Canadian bookseller or sent to Random House of Canada, Ltd., Marketing Dept., 1265 Aerowood Drive, Mississauga, Ontario L4W 1B9. Inquiries from the United Kingdom should be sent to Fodor's Travel Publications, 20 Vauxhall Bridge Road, London, England SW1V 2SA.

PRINTED IN THE UNITED STATES OF AMERICA

10 9 8 7 6 5 4 3 2 1

CONTENTS

Introduction *vi*

The Islands *1*

The Cruise Lines *219*

Directories

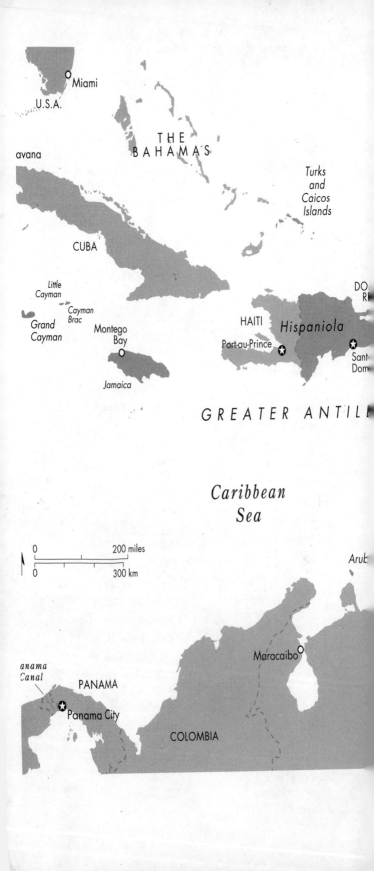

THE CARIBBEAN

ATLANTIC OCEAN

Turks and Caicos Islands

LEEWARD ISLANDS

DOMINICAN REPUBLIC

aniola

Santo Domingo

San Juan

Puerto Rico

St. Thomas

St. John

Virgin Gorda

Tortola

Anguilla

St. Maarten/ St. Martin

St. Barthélemy

Saba

Barbuda

St. Croix

St. Eustatius

St. Kitts

Nevis

Antigua

Montserrat

Guadeloupe

Marie Galante

ANTILLES

Dominica

Martinique

WINDWARD ISLANDS

St. Lucia

St. Vincent

Barbados

LESSER ANTILLES

Aruba

Bonaire

Curaçao

The Grenadines

Grenada

Tobago

Caracas

Trinidad

VENEZUELA

INTRODUCTION

Do you pin as many hopes on your vacation as I do? Then, like me, you probably plan your trip around the results of *Condé Nast Traveler*'s annual Readers' Choice Survey.

This is the largest and most prestigious travel poll in the world today, rating nearly 2,000 hotels, restaurants and cruise lines, and other travel services based on the votes of tens of thousands of *Condé Nast Traveler* subscribers.

If they rave about a ship or resort, I probably will too. If they say, "stay away," I do. And if their reactions are mixed, well, then I have the information I need to make my own choice, based on what I want from my moment in the sun.

Condé Nast Traveler is the country's most honest and respected travel magazine—and the most widely read. So when editor-in-chief Tom Wallace offered to team up with Fodor's, we jumped at the chance.

Together we produced something that's never been available before: the complete results of the Caribbean portion of the survey in book form, rating more than 150 island resorts, 80 cruise ships, and 28 islands, plus Bermuda and the Bahamas, along with the personal comments of hundreds of travelers who have stayed in these properties or sailed on these cruises, and who took vicarious delight in sharing their loves and hates with readers such as yourself. (To encourage respondents to be frank, they were offered anonymity. Comparatively few requested it.) We also added island maps locating all the resorts, and the detailed, practical service information that Fodor's is famous for. We don't just tell you whether rooms have TVs—we indicate how many channels they get, and whether VCRs are available. We don't just list tennis courts, we tell you whether or not they're lighted.

A word on the ratings

A 16-page questionnaire was sent to a random selection of subscribers receiving the May 1995 issue. Readers were asked to judge each resort, cruise line, etc., on a variety of criteria, such as service and facilities, using a scale of one to five ("excellent," "very good," "good," "fair," or "poor"). The responses were tabulated by an independent research firm, Mark Clements, Inc.

The numbers below each one of these criteria in our text represent the percentage of respondents who gave the facility a "very good" or "excellent" rating. These percentages were then averaged into an overall score, which is given under our "TOTAL" heading.

In order to qualify for a Readers' Choice Award in the magazine, an entry had to be evaluated by a minimum number of respondents. However, entries with fewer responses are still worth hearing about (some properties may simply be too small to garner a large response), so we've decided to include them as well.

Ratings for these spots are designated on our charts as "N/A."

A word on resort prices

Please note that hotel prices listed in the text do *not* include taxes and service charges, which could raise the nightly cost by 20% or more.

Room rates are given according to three plans—**AP,** or American Plan, with three meals; **MAP,** or Modified American Plan, with breakfast and dinner; **EP,** or European Plan, with no meals. We also indicate when full or Continental breakfast is included.

Unless we state otherwise, prices are always based on two guests sharing one room or suite.

Hurricanes

As we went to press in October 1995, hurricanes Luis and Marilyn had just ravaged the western Caribbean. Antigua and St. Martin/St. Maarten bore the brunt of Luis and St. Thomas of Marilyn, but Anguilla, the British Virgin Islands, Montserrat, Saba, and St. Barts were also hit by Luis and St. Croix and St. John were buffeted by Marilyn; several resorts on these islands sustained serious damage. At this writing, some are closed for repairs or slated to open behind schedule (noted in the text); most should be up and running by the holiday season, although some landscaping and other restoration work may still be underway. If you plan to vacation on any of the affected islands, make sure that any facilities you want to use will be available when you visit.

A brief disclaimer

All the service information in this guide was fact-checked for accuracy just before we went to press by all the relevant resorts, government tourist offices, and cruise lines. But time brings changes, so it's always wise to call ahead to verify that the facilities you expect to find will be available at the time you plan to visit. Fodor's cannot accept responsibility for errors that may occur.

Please feel free to write and share with us any comments you may have on this guide, or on the resorts or cruise ships listed. You can reach us at Fodor's Travel Publications, 201 E. 50th St., New York, New York 10022. We'll look forward to hearing from you.

Karen Cure

Karen Cure
Editorial Director

The Islands

ANGUILLA

69.0%	67.6%	46.9%	72.4%	**TOTAL** **69.2%**

Reader Report

"What struck me most about this poor island was its beautiful beaches. My favorite was Shoal Beach—the water was the bluest I have ever seen."

KATHY COAKLEY, WEST PALM BEACH, FLORIDA

"Good restaurants keep springing up like flowers—the fresh fish and lobsters are outstanding. Forget shopping, although you can hop the ferry to St. Martin if you experience shopper's withdrawal. If you want to decompress, this is the place!"

JOEL M. CHUSID, IRVING, TEXAS

"Unlike many islands, Anguilla remains safe, quiet, friendly. Come here if you're seeking peace, solitude, sun, and beautiful beaches."

JULIE DONOVAN, NEW YORK, NEW YORK

Islands. Anguilla is a 35-square-mile independent protectorate of the United Kingdom. The population is about 7,000.
Language. The official language is English.

Visitor Information

In the U.S. Contact the **Anguilla Tourist Information Office** (c/o Medhurst and Associates, the Huntington Atrium, 775 Park Ave., Suite 105, Huntington, NY 11743, tel. 516/271–2600 or 800/553–4939, fax 516/425–0903).
In Canada. There is no tourist office in Canada.
In the U.K. Contact the **Anguilla Tourist Information and Reservation Office** (Windotel, 3 Epirus Rd., London 3W6 7UJ, tel. 01/937–7725, fax 01/938–4793).
In Anguilla. Contact the **Anguilla Tourist Board** (The Valley, Anguilla, B.W.I., tel. 809/497–2451 or 809/497–2759, fax 809/497–3091).

CAP JULUCA

78.0%	91.5%	67.8%	96.6%	**TOTAL** **83.5%**

This 180-acre resort on the island's southwestern coast is a string of whitewashed two-story villas, punctuated with palm trees, private pools, and walled gardens. The hotel was built in 1988 and expanded in 1990.

ANGUILLA

Scrub Island

Little Scrub Island

Captain's Bay

ATLANTIC OCEAN

Savannah Bay

Scilly Cay

Island Harbor

Mimi Bay

Sea Feathers Bay

Island Harbour

Sandy Hill Bay

Shoal Bay

Long Salt Pond

MAP

The Valley

The Quarter

Forest Bay

Cinnamon Reef Beach Club

Little Bay

Flat Cap Point

Wallblake Airport

Little Harbour

North Hill

Blowing Point Harbour

Sandy Ground

Road Bay

Sandy Ground

Sandy Island

Rendezvous Bay

Casablanca Resort

Long Bay

Cove Bay

Malliouhana Hotel

Meads Bay

Maunday's Bay

Cap Juluca

Barnes Bay

Coccoloba

Shoal Bay West

West End

Anguillita Island

KEY

Beach

Hotel or Resort

N

4 miles

6 km

Reader Report

"Magnificent Moorish villas where private courtyards lead to warm sands and clear waters. Impeccable service, friendly atmosphere, casual dining. An expensive getaway—but so is heaven."

RANDEE LEVINE, PORT WASHINGTON, NEW YORK

"Very romantic—the bathrooms alone are worth the price! . . . Food is good, but the restaurant's location is what makes it special—it's a great place to watch the sun set."

CHRIS AND PAM CAVANAUGH, NASHVILLE, TENNESSEE

"The bathrooms are so incredible you'll consider spending more time there than usual—with 'tubs for two' with leather headrests, a private sun deck, and a glass shower open to the sky!"

JOEL M. CHUSID, IRVING, TEXAS

"This resort should be the yardstick by which others are judged! The decor was exotic, the beach the best I've seen (I've been to eight Caribbean islands) We'd go back in a minute."

KAREN ROBICHAUD, GREENWICH, CONNECTICUT

Address. Box 240, Maunday's Bay, Anguilla, B.W.I., tel. 809/497–6666 or 800/323–0139, fax 809/497–6617.

Rooms. 85 rooms and 13 suites, in all 12 villas. All have air-conditioning and ceiling fans. 6 villas with private bath. 7 rooms have showers only.

Facilities. 3 restaurants, 2 bars/lounges, 2 lighted tennis courts, freshwater pool, exercise room with weights and aerobic machines, massages, dry-cleaning, supervised children's program Mar 15–Apr 30 and July 1–Aug 31, sailboats, croquet.

TV and VCR. TV in public area and for rent, with 25 channels including CNN and cable movie channels. VCRs for rent.

No-smoking rooms. None.

Credit cards. AE, MC, V.

Restrictions. Min. 7 nights over Christmas, 7 nights over New Year's, or 14 nights over both. No children under 6 Dec 29–Mar 15.

Wheelchair accessibility. No accessible rooms.

Prices. Dec 16–Apr 1: doubles $455–$735; suites $1,050–$1,725; villas $2,775–$3,965. Low season: doubles $275–$425; suites $530–$800; villas $1,410–$2,085. All rates include Continental breakfast.

CASABLANCA RESORT

| 53.8% | 61.5% | 38.5% | 84.6% | **TOTAL** 59.6% |

Right on a beach at Anguilla's western end, this low-rise, pink-and-green, Moorish hotel is set on 10 acres and is the largest resort on the island. Built in 1992, the all-inclusive Casablanca has a 1,200-square-foot pool, water-sports instruction, tennis courts, and a fitness center. The resort sustained some serious damage during Hurricane Luis and its opening was delayed; it is scheduled to be up and running for the season by December.

Reader Report

*"Probably one of the most pristine places I've ever been to....
People bend over backwards for you—they're always happy
to help."*

TERESA BELCHER, ALEXANDRIA, VIRGINIA

Address. Box 444, Rendezvous Bay W, The Valley, Anguilla, B.W.I., tel. 809/497–6999 or 800/231–1945, fax 809/497–6899.

Affiliation. F.D.R. Jamaica/Braco Village Resort Jamaica.

Rooms. 88 rooms, 6 suites. All have air-conditioning, ceiling fans, and minibars.

Facilities. 2 restaurants, 2 bars/lounges, 2 lighted tennis courts nearby, freshwater pool, an exercise room with weights and aerobic machines, aerobic classes, conference center with business services, sailboats, windsurfing, snorkeling, kayaking.

TV and VCR. TVs in all rooms, with 33 channels including CNN and cable movie channels. TV in public areas. VCRs in rooms on request.

No-smoking rooms. 40 rooms, 3 suites.

Credit cards. AE, MC, V.

Restrictions. Min. 6 nights Dec. 22–Jan. 1. No children under 16.

Wheelchair accessibility. No accessible rooms.

Prices. Dec. 22–Apr. 5: doubles $390–$465 AP, $450–$700 EP; suites $465–$565 AP, $600–$700 EP. Low season: doubles $265–$365 AP, $255–$455 EP; suites $365–$465 AP, $405–$455 EP.

CINNAMON REEF BEACH CLUB

				TOTAL
76.2%	**66.7%**	**71.4%**	**76.2%**	**72.6%**

This 12-acre Mediterranean-style resort near the airport, built in 1984, is made up of split-level white stucco villas, mostly beachfront, with five others on a nearby blufftop. Note that the property sustained some superficial damage during Hurricane Luis.

Reader Report

*"Anguilla has many deluxe resorts to have lunch or dinner
at ...this resort is especially lovely."*

LESLEY HOHEB, PORT WASHINGTON, NEW YORK

*"The owners were really nice, and made me feel at home. The
accommodations were very clean, and the pillowcases, hand-
embroidered by local women, were a nice touch. The food*

was excellent...I could have sat there taking in the view from the dining room for the rest of my life."

BARBARA CHRISTENSON, LONG VALLEY, NEW JERSEY

Address. Box 141, Little Harbour, Anguilla, B.W.I., tel. 809/497–2727 or 800/346–7084, fax 809/497–3727.

Rooms. 22 suites. All have minibars and ceiling fans, and all with showers only.

Facilities. Restaurant, bar/lounge, freshwater pool, 2 unlighted tennis courts, sailboats, paddleboats, kayaks, windsurfing, fishing.

TV and VCR. TV in public area only, only one channel (CNN). VCR in public area only.

No-smoking rooms. None.

Credit cards. AE, D, MC, V.

Restrictions. No children under 6 in high season. No children under 10 in low season.

Wheelchair accessibility. No accessible rooms.

Prices. Dec 21–Apr 5: $300–$400. Low season: $150–$225. Rates include Continental breakfast. Add $50 per person for MAP.

COCCOLOBA

👷⚓	🛏	✕	☀	TOTAL
81.3%	56.3%	81.3%	100.0%	79.7%

The resort's West Indian-style villas and main house are set on 28 acres of gardens on a low bluff between two mile-long beaches near the island's western tip. The hotel was built in 1982.

Reader Report

"Individual units at Coccoloba stretch out along a wonderful white sand beach, where pelicans fly. The size of the property with respect to the number of rooms gives one a feeling of privacy, and wonderful food. An extremely helpful and friendly staff and many little extras make for low-key elegance."

PAT LAWRIE, STONINGTON, CONNECTICUT

"Service was good, the rooms and food excellent. The resort has a relaxing atmosphere."

NAME WITHHELD, BROOKLYN, NEW YORK

Address. Box 332, Barnes Bay, Anguilla, B.W.I., tel. 809/497–6871 or 800/982–7729, fax 809/497–6332.

Rooms. 5 rooms, 2 suites, 44 villas. All have minibars and air-conditioning. All suites and villas have ceiling fans.

Facilities. Restaurant, 2 bars/lounges, 2 lighted tennis courts, 2 freshwater pools, exercise room with weights and aerobic machines, massages, sailboats.

TV and VCR. VCR in public area only.

No-smoking rooms. None.
Credit cards. AE, MC, V.
Restrictions. Min. 10 nights Dec 20–Jan 5.
Wheelchair accessibility. No accessible rooms.
Prices. Dec 20–Apr 16: doubles $455–$655 MAP, $375–$575 with breakfast; suites $655–$755 MAP, $575–$675 with breakfast; villas $455–$655 MAP, $375–$575 with breakfast. Low season: doubles $305–$540 MAP, $225–$460 with breakfast; suites $540–$640 MAP, $460–$560 with breakfast; villas $305–$540 MAP, $225–$460 with breakfast.

MALLIOUHANA HOTEL

				TOTAL
82.4%	85.3%	82.4%	88.2%	84.6%

A two-story Mediterranean-style main building and a few scattered villas perch on a landscaped bluff. Stairs lead down to the two long beaches, on Meads Bay and Turtle Cove. Built in 1984, the hotel was expanded in 1986 and renovated in 1995. The resort sustained some serious damage during Hurricane Luis and has closed for repairs; it is scheduled to be opened for the season on November 17.

Reader Report

"This has to be one of the two or three most exclusive, sophisticated, and expensive hotels in the Caribbean! No gold chains in sight."

HENRY BIBBER, MANASSAS, VIRGINIA

"Akin to driving in the middle of the Sahara Desert and suddenly coming across the Ritz Hotel in Paris. It's one of the finest resorts in the world. The rooms are beautiful, and it has fine European service but with a nice Caribbean character and flavor. I'm convinced that there's no better dining room in the Caribbean than at this particular hotel."

STEVE STANDISH, SYRACUSE, NEW YORK

"Travel guides and people's comments had led me to believe this was a glitzy place—LIES! It oozes understated class. Hard to find, as it doesn't even have a sign."

CAROL BLODGETT, NEW RICHMOND, OHIO

Address. Box 173, Meads Bay, Anguilla, B.W.I., tel. 809/497–6111 or 800/835–0796, fax 809/497–6011.
Affiliation. Insignia Resorts.
Rooms. 35 rooms, 19 suites. All have minibars, private terraces or patios, and ceiling fans. 29 rooms and 16 suites have air-conditioning. 1 suite has a private pool, 3 have Jacuzzis.
Facilities. Restaurant, 2 bars/lounges, 3 lighted tennis courts, 1 unlighted, 2 freshwater pools, exercise room with weights and aerobic machines, massages, salon, boutique, drug store, library, supervised children's program and playground, sail-

boats, windsurfing.

TV and VCR. TV in public area only, with 30 channels including CNN, and cable movie channels. VCRs in public area, and in rooms on request.

No-smoking rooms. None.

Credit cards. None accepted.

Restrictions. Min. 7 nights Dec 18–Mar 5.

Wheelchair accessibility. No accessible rooms.

Prices. Dec 18–Mar 31: doubles $480–$575 EP; suites $660–$1,600 EP. Low season: doubles $240–$270 EP; suites $380–$1,000 EP.

ANTIGUA

| 62.7% | 43.0% | 45.4% | 49.3% | **TOTAL** 53.7% |

Reader Report

"I could move here and never have another thought other than lying on the beaches. Antigua was my favorite of the islands we visited on our cruise because the people were so pleasant and friendly. I am planning a two-week holiday there next year."

CHRISTOPHER D. BASS, ALEXANDRIA, VIRGINIA

"The prettiest and most unspoiled island. Nelson's Dockyard is spectacular. The views from the mountains are next to heaven."

BILL AND LINDA QUICK, ANCHORAGE, KENTUCKY

"There are 365 white sand beaches, some of the best I have ever seen, and you can stay at renovated hotels dating back to the 1700s. The people are friendly and helpful. And it's no problem dining at hotels or local eateries."

ILENE SMITH, TRENTON, MICHIGAN

"Brand-new port, brand-new resorts, brand-new casino—old beaches and charm disappearing."

JOHN T. RICE, CHATTANOOGA, TENNESSEE

Islands. Antigua is a 171-square-mile independent nation with a population of about 67,000. It includes the island of Barbuda (population 1,200), which is 25 miles to the east.

Language. Antigua's official language is English, though local English dialects are spoken by some islanders.

Visitor Information

In the U.S. Contact the **Antigua and Barbuda Department of Tourism** (610 5th Ave., Suite 311, New York, NY 10020, tel. 212/541–4117, fax 212/757–1607;25 S.E. Second Ave., Suite 300, Miami, FL 33131, tel. 305/381–6762, fax 305/381–7908).

In Canada. Contact the **Antigua and Barbuda Department of Tourism and Trade** (60 St. Clair Ave. E, Suite 304, Toronto, Ont. M4T 1N5, tel. 416/961–3085, fax 416/961–7218).

In the U.K. Contact the **Antigua and Barbuda Department of Tourism** (Antigua House, 15 Thayer St., London W1M 5LD, tel. 0171/486–7073, fax 0171/486–9970).

In Antigua. Contact the **Antigua and Barbuda Department of Tourism** (Box 363, Long and Thames Sts., St. John's, Antigua, W.I., tel. 809/462–0480, fax 809/462–2483).

BLUE WATERS BEACH HOTEL

👤 **55.0%**	🛏 **45.0%**	🍴 **25.0%**	☀ **60.0%**	**TOTAL** **46.3%**

Two-story hotel blocks and a few outlying villas are set on 14 acres along a cove, a short drive north of St. John's on the leeward side of the island. The resort was built in 1964 and renovated in 1986. During Hurrican Luis, the hotel sustained some serious damage and was closed for repairs; it is scheduled to reopen in February.

Reader Report

"A relaxing resort with a delightful staff, ready to grant any request. It's on the north (and hence cooler) side of the island.

NAME WITHHELD, BERNARDSVILLE, NEW JERSEY

"Really beautiful, with great accommodations. I can't complain about a thing. They took very good care of me—in fact, I think they spoiled me."

JAMES STEWART, OCALA, FLORIDA

Address. Box 256, Soldier's Bay, St. John's, Antigua, W.I., tel. 809/462–0290 or 800/223–6510, fax 809/462–0293.
Rooms. 46 rooms in main building, and 8 villas with 13 rooms and 8 suites. All have minibars and air-conditioning. 8 villa suites have Jacuzzis.
Facilities. 2 restaurants, 2 bars/lounges, lighted tennis court, 18-hole golf course nearby, freshwater pool, massages, conference center with business services, dive center, sailboats, windsurfing.
TV and VCR. TV in public area only, with about 12 channels including CNN and cable movie channels. VCR in public area.
No-smoking rooms. None.
Credit cards. AE, D, MC, V.
Restrictions. None.
Wheelchair accessibility. No accessible rooms.
Prices. Dec 16–Apr 15: doubles $245–$295 EP; entire villas $380–$810 EP. Low season: doubles $147–$185 EP; entire villas $240–$525 EP. Add $48 per person and $36 per child-for MAP.

CURTAIN BLUFF RESORT

👤 **85.3%**	🛏 **76.5%**	🍴 **88.2%**	☀ **88.2%**	**TOTAL** **84.6%**

A low-rise contemporary Caribbean-style building accommodates guests at this 20-acre resort. The setting is a bluff right where the Atlantic and the Caribbean meet, on the island's southwest coast. Built in 1962 and most recently renovated in

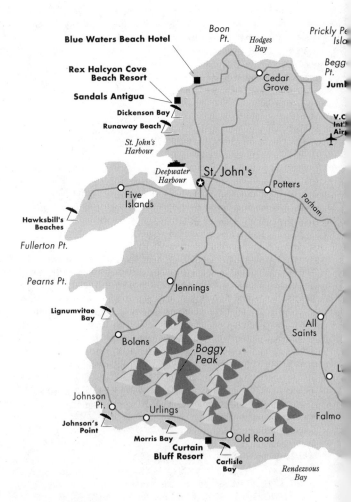

ANTIGUA

TO
BARBUDA

*Boon
Pt.*

*Hodges
Bay*

*Prickly Pe
Isla*

Blue Waters Beach Hotel

Cedar
Grove

*Begg
Pt.*

Jum

**Rex Halcyon Cove
Beach Resort**

Sandals Antigua

**V.C
Int'l
Airp**

Dickenson Bay

Runaway Beach

*St. John's
Harbour*

*Deepwater
Harbour*

St. John's

Potters

Parham

Five
Islands

**Hawksbill's
Beaches**

Fullerton Pt.

Pearns Pt.

Jennings

**Lignumvitae
Bay**

All
Saints

Bolans

*Boggy
Peak*

L.

Johnson
Pt.

Urlings

Falmo

**Johnson's
Point**

Morris Bay

Old Road

**Curtain
Bluff Resort**

**Carlisle
Bay**

*Rendezvous
Bay*

*Caribbean
Sea*

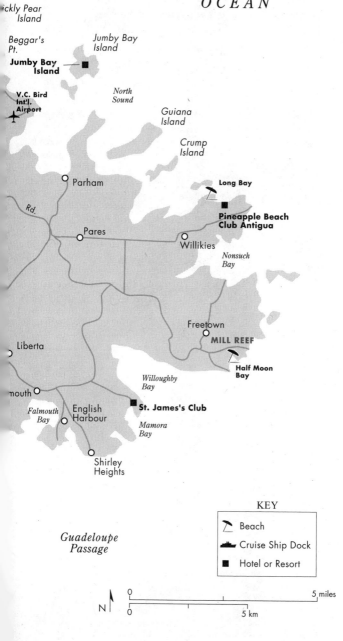

ATLANTIC
OCEAN

Prickly Pear
Island

Beggar's
Pt.

Jumby Bay
Island

**Jumby Bay
Island** ■

North
Sound

V.C. Bird
Int'l.
Airport ✈

Guiana
Island

Crump
Island

Parham ○

Rd.

Pares ○

Long Bay ☂
■
**Pineapple Beach
Club Antigua**

Willikies ●

Nonsuch
Bay

Freetown ○

MILL REEF

Liberta ○

Half Moon
Bay ☂

Willoughby
Bay

Falmouth ○

Falmouth
Bay

English
Harbour ●

■ **St. James's Club**

Mamora
Bay

Shirley
Heights ●

Guadeloupe
Passage

KEY

☂ Beach

⛴ Cruise Ship Dock

■ Hotel or Resort

N ↑

0 ————————————— 5 miles

0 ————————————— 5 km

1994, the resort will be closed for further renovations between May and October 1995. Note that the hotel sustained some superficial damage during Hurricane Luis.

Reader Report

"One of the finest resorts anywhere, with two beaches—one with surf and one with quiet water—and attractive beachfront rooms . . . Top quality service, food, and amenities. Not inexpensive, but there is no tipping allowed here."

NAME WITHHELD, PROVIDENCE, RHODE ISLAND

"I'd highly recommend it—the setting is beautiful and the staff very pleasant. A wonderful experience."

MAUREEN LARROUX, INDIAN ROCKS BEACH, FLORIDA

Address. Box 288, St. John's, Antigua, W.I, tel. 809/462–8400, 212/289–8888 in NY, fax 809/462–8409.
Rooms. 51 rooms, 12 suites. All have ceiling fans. 7 suites have minibars. After October 1995, every room and suite will have a tub and a shower.
Facilities. 2 restaurants, 2 bars/lounges, 4 lighted tennis courts, exercise room with weights and aerobic machines, aerobics classes, massages, salon, dive center, sailboat.
TV and VCR. No TV.
No-smoking rooms. None.
Credit cards. AE.
Restrictions. No children under 12 Jan 10–Mar 10.
Wheelchair accessibility. No accessible rooms.
Prices. Dec 19–Apr 14: doubles $625; suites $695–$1,550. Low season: doubles $495; suites $595–$1,350. All rates are all-inclusive.

JUMBY BAY ISLAND

👔	🛏	🍴	☀	**TOTAL**
90.3%	**87.1%**	**87.1%**	**96.8%**	**90.3%**

This resort, accessible by launch from Antigua's east coast (10 minutes away), is on a 300-acre private island with four beaches; guests stay in cottages, villas, or the Pond Bay House. The hotel was built in 1983. During Hurricane Luis, the hotel sustained some serious damage and its opening was delayed; it is scheduled to reopen by December 1.

Reader Report

"This is by far the finest resort we have been to . . . the only negative is the airplane engine noise."

NAME WITHHELD, PURCHASE, NEW YORK

"Convenient to St. John's, with tiki bars on the small but pretty white-sand beach."

GAIL GILLEN DE HAAS, SMITHTOWN, NEW YORK

Address. Box 243, St. John's, Antigua, W.I., tel. 809/462–6000 or 800/421–9016, fax 809/462–6020.

Rooms. 38 suites, 17 villas. All have shower only. All suites have ceiling fans.

Facilities. 2 restaurants, 2 bars/lounges, 2 lighted tennis courts, 1 unlighted, fresh- and saltwater pools (only for guests in some of the villas), massages, supervised children's program (Jul–Sep), dive center nearby, sailboats, croquet, putting green, waterskiing.

TV and VCR. No TV.

No-smoking rooms. None.

Credit cards. AE, MC, V.

Restrictions. Min. 10 nights mid-Dec–early Jan. No children under 8 except Jul–Sep.

Wheelchair accessibility. No accessible rooms.

Prices. Dec 15–Apr 6: suites $990–$1100; villas $1,575–$1,650. Low season: suites $645–$775; villas $1,195–$1,325. All rates are all-inclusive.

PINEAPPLE BEACH CLUB ANTIGUA

👔	🛏	✕	☀	**TOTAL**
60.5%	**42.1%**	**55.3%**	**71.1%**	**57.2%**

At this 25-acre resort on the Long Bay beach, on the windward side of the island, guests stay in two-story pink structures done in a contemporary version of Caribbean gingerbread style. Built in 1986, the hotel was expanded in 1994.

Reader Report

"A beautiful all-inclusive resort on a wonderful beach. The menu is limited—grouper is the catch of the day every day."

NAME WITHHELD, TOLEDO, OHIO

"Beach is nice, though the water is calmer next door at Long Bay. Activities are very limited—my husband asked about playing volleyball and was told to form his own group. Food good-to-adequate."

DONNA L. BUDKA, ROTTERDAM, NEW YORK

Address. Box 54, St. John's, Antigua, W.I., tel. 809/463–2006 or 800/345–0356, fax 809/463–2452. U.S. office: 6401 Congress Ave., Suite 100, Boca Raton, FL 33487, tel. 407/994–5640, fax 407/994–6344.

Affiliation. Pineapple Beach Clubs.

Rooms. 133 rooms, 83 with showers only. All have air-conditioning; most have ceiling fans.

Facilities. 2 restaurants, 3 bars/lounges, 4 unlighted tennis courts, oceanfront freshwater pool, casino, exercise room with weights and aerobic machines, sailboats, windsurfing, kayaking, snorkeling.

TV and VCR. TV in public area only, with only one channel (CNN). No VCR.

No-smoking rooms. None.
Credit cards. AE, MC, V.
Restrictions. Min. 8 nights Dec 22—29, 7 nights Feb 11—25, 3 nights all other times. No children under 6 except during holidays.
Wheelchair accessibility. No accessible rooms.
Prices. Dec 21–Mar 31: $390–$460. Low season: $320–$390. Rates are all-inclusive.

REX HALCYON COVE BEACH RESORT

				TOTAL
46.8%	42.6%	31.9%	68.1%	47.3%

A lively half-mile of white sand on Dickenson Bay, just north of St. John's, is the focus of this large, busy resort with its own water-sports center. The hotel was built in 1959 and renovated in 1992. Rooms were added to the hotel in 1993. The resort sustained some serious damage during Hurricane Luis and will be closed for repairs until further notice.

Reader Report

"It was a delight to take one of the complimentary pedal boats out around the cove to 'discover' our own secluded beach. The view from the lounge and restaurant overlooking the beach is stupendous."

DAVID CONLEY, TULSA, OKLAHOMA

"On a long stretch of beach with plenty to do—waterskiing, scuba diving expeditions, jet-skiing. It seems to attract a big international crowd, with lots of British and Germans."

GAIL GILLEN DE HAAS, SMITHTOWN, NEW YORK

Address. Box 251, Dickenson Bay, St. John's, Antigua, W.I., tel. 809/462–0256 or 800/255–5859, fax 809/462–0271.
Affiliation. Rex Resorts.
Rooms. 210 rooms, 17 suites. All suites and 186 rooms have air-conditioning; the remaining rooms and all but 1 suite have ceiling fans.
Facilities. 3 restaurants, 4 bars/lounges, coffee shop, 4 lighted tennis courts, freshwater pool, aerobics classes, salon, conference center with business services, supervised children's program, dive center, sailboats.
TV and VCR. TVs in public area and in some rooms, with 15 channels including CNN and cable movie channels. No VCRs.
No-smoking rooms. None.
Credit cards. AE, DC, D, MC, V.
Restrictions. None.
Wheelchair accessibility. 2 rooms.
Prices. Nov 1–Apr 15: doubles $190–$426 EP; suites $380–$523 EP. Low season: doubles $130–$337 EP; suites $315–$433 EP. $50 per person for MAP. Meal reductions for children.

ST. JAMES'S CLUB

👨‍🍳	🛏️	🍴	🏖️	TOTAL
76.1%	63.0%	58.7%	78.3%	69.0%

This resort, built in 1961 and renovated in 1991, fills a 100-acre spit of land along Mamora Bay, on the island's southeast corner. Accommodations are in two-story hotel blocks and a hillside villa village; the newest rooms were added in 1984. There are two beaches and a casino. The hotel sustained some serious damage during Hurricane Luis and its opening was delayed; it is scheduled to be up and running by December 1.

Reader Report

"The staff is very concerned about its guests. I was injured and they were right there to take care of me. The service was superb. The rooms were only average."

HOWARD TAVEL, DENVER, COLORADO

"We have been there a couple of times. The service was attentive without being intrusive. The facilities were great; they have everything—croquet, scuba, horseback riding. Tennis matches were arranged, and they offered lessons. Rooms very just fair."

DONN M. GORDON, NESHANIC, NEW JERSEY

"We found this place charming—service was excellent."

CHARLES GEO. AND JUDY DONDERO, OAKLAND, CALIFORNIA

Address. Box 63, Mamora Bay, Antigua, W.I., tel. 809/460–5000 or 800/274–0008, fax 809/460–3015.

Rooms. 85 rooms, 20 suites, 73 villas. All have air-conditioning and ceiling fans. All rooms and suites have minibars.

Facilities. 6 restaurants, 7 bars/lounges, coffee shop, 5 lighted tennis courts, 2 unlighted, 3 freshwater pools, horseback riding, small casino, exercise room with weights and aerobic machines, aerobics classes, massages, sauna, salon, 24-hr room service, conference center with business services, supervised children's program, dive center, sailboats.

TV and VCR. TVs in all rooms, with 12 channels including CNN and cable movie channels. VCRs for rent.

No-smoking rooms. None.

Credit cards. AE, DC, MC, V.

Restrictions. Min. 7 nights Dec 20–Jan 2. MAP mandatory Dec 20–Jan 2.

Wheelchair accessibility. 3 accessible rooms.

Prices. Dec 20–Mar 31: doubles $650–$840; suites $640–$840; villas $810–$1,130. Low season: doubles $390–$440; suites $490; villas $600–$660. Rates are all-inclusive. EP plan available.

SANDALS ANTIGUA

 58.1%	 62.8%	 48.8%	 69.8%	**TOTAL** **59.9%**

This all-inclusive resort for couples only accommodates guests in circular, one-room guest bungalows called rondevals and in two-story hotel blocks. It's on the northwest coast, on Dickenson Bay. The hotel was built in 1957, renovated in 1991, and expanded in 1994. Note that the property sustained some superficial damage during Hurricane Luis.

Reader Report

"A fantastic, extremely long, white-sand beach with calm waters—and rooms with tropical decor are just steps away. All-inclusive means that everything, from scuba diving to the best liquor and late-night snacks, is part of the package. You want for nothing."

CHUCK AND PHYLLIS BLOODGOOD, MANALAPAN, NEW JERSEY

"One of the best reasons to visit is the water sports—unlimited and included in the price. Our last three days we spent waterskiing all day long. The entertainment was not too entertaining; I was pleasantly surprised when I found there were satellite TVs in the rooms. The one thing that bothered me was that the restaurants were right on the beach."

ANNE SHEEHAN, STATEN ISLAND, NEW YORK

Address. Box 147, Dickerson Bay, Antigua, W.I., tel. 809/462–0267 or 800/726–3257, fax 809/462–4135.
Affiliation. Sandals Resorts International.
Rooms. 102 rooms, 61 suites. All have air-conditioning and ceiling fans. All suites have minibars.
Facilities. 4 restaurants, 4 bars/lounges, 2 lighted tennis courts, 4 freshwater pools, exercise room with weights and aerobic machines, aerobics classes, massages, sauna, salon, dry-cleaning, conference center with business services, dive center, sailboats.
TV and VCR. TVs in all rooms, with 9 channels including CNN and cable movie channels. VCRs in public area and in rooms on request.
No-smoking rooms. None.
Credit cards. AE, MC, V.
Restrictions. Min. 3 nights. Couples 18 and older only; no gay couples or singles.
Wheelchair accessibility. No accessible rooms.
Prices. Dec 22–Mar 29: doubles $1,700–$1,980; suites $2,140–$2,460. Low season: doubles $1,620–$1,880; suite $2,040–$2,340. Prices are per couple for 3 nights all-inclusive.

ARUBA

				TOTAL
56.8%	60.9%	55.0%	64.2%	62.6%

Reader Report

"With a yearly average temperature of 82°F and with nearly daily sunshine, beautiful beaches, the world's largest mini-golf course, casinos, international dining, and a host of celebrities on vacation, Aruba has something for everyone."

CHARLES AND GEORGINA HEINKEL, NEVADA CITY, CALIFORNIA

"A delightful Dutch oasis in the lower Caribbean, this upscale, hassle-free, and virtually crime-free island is a rarity in these contemporary times. Plan on leaving a contribution in one of its several casinos, however."

BILLY HANCOCK, ST. PETERSBURG, FLORIDA

"Not for anyone who expects something other than a good beach. Hotels are expensive, there's very little of interest historically or culturally—and the island is barren of vegetation other than cactus. Too far to travel for so little reward."

VAL CHERNI, BRANFORD, CONNECTICUT

"By far our favorite island ...inhabited by courteous multicultural folks who attempt to sell you nothing but friendship, sunshine, and safe beautiful beaches."

DARRELL REED AND FAMILY, PITTSBURGH, PENNSYLVANIA

Islands. Aruba is a 75-square-mile protectorate of the Netherlands, with a population of about 66,000.

Language. Aruba's official language is Papiamento—a mixture of Dutch, Spanish, Portuguese, English, and French. English and Spanish are spoken throughout the island.

Visitor Information

In the U.S. Contact the **Aruba Tourism Authority** (1000 Harbor Blvd., ground level, Weehawken, NJ 07087, tel. 201/330–0800 or 800/TO-ARUBA, fax 201/330–8757; 2344 Salzedo St., Miami, FL 33134, tel. 305/567–2720, fax 305/567–2721).

In Canada. Contact the **Aruba Tourism Authority** (86 Bloor St. West, Suite 204, Toronto, Ont., M5S 1M5, tel. 416/975–1950, fax 416/975-1947).

In the U.K. There is no tourist office in the U.K.

In Aruba. Contact **Public Relations** (J.E. Irausquin Blvd., Oranjestad, Aruba, tel. 297/8–60242, fax 297/8–60975).

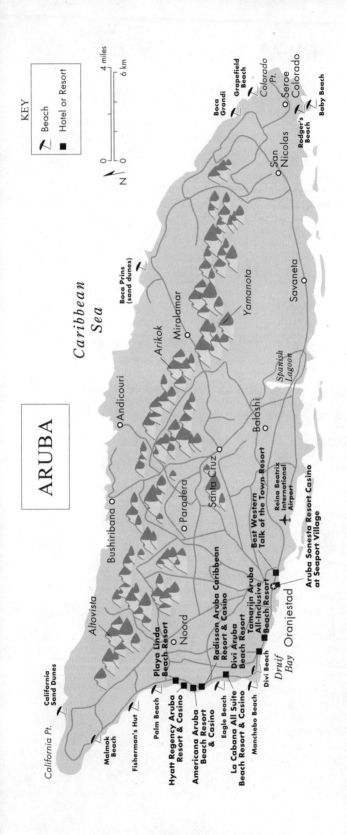

ARUBA

KEY

⚲ Beach

■ Hotel or Resort

Caribbean Sea

California Pt.

California Sand Dunes

Malmok Beach

Fisherman's Hut

Palm Beach

Playa Linda Beach Resort

Altovista

Noord

Hyatt Regency Aruba Resort & Casino

Americana Aruba Beach Resort & Casino

Eagle Beach

Radisson Aruba Caribbean Resort & Casino

La Cabana All Suite Beach Resort & Casino

Manchebo Beach

Divi Aruba Beach Resort

Tamarijn Aruba All-Inclusive Beach Resort

Divi Beach

Druif Bay

Bushiribana

Andicouri

Arikok

Miralamar

Paradera

Santa Cruz

Balashi

Spanish Lagoon

Savaneta

Boca Prins (sand dunes)

Yamanota

Oranjestad

Best Western Talk of the Town Resort

Reina Beatrix International Airport

Aruba Sonesta Resort Casino at Seaport Village

San Nicolas

Boca Grandi

Grapefield Beach

Colorado Pt.

Seroe Colorado

Baby Beach

Rodger's Beach

4 miles

6 km

N

AMERICANA ARUBA BEACH RESORT & CASINO

52.0%	40.0%	41.3%	76.0%	**TOTAL** 52.3%

The resort's two modern, nine-story buildings occupy six acres on the west coast's Palm Beach, on the leeward side of the island. The hotel was built in 1972 and expanded and renovated in 1987.

Reader Report

"Everything but the dining was great. There is a terrific beach and pool area, and the casino is friendly and fun, though it needs a late-night snack restaurant and bar."

H. R. BLAY, NOVI, MICHIGAN

"The beach was crowded (it reminded me of Coney Island), and the casino is dark. But the pool is nice and so is the open lobby."

NAME WITHHELD, ST. JAMES, NEW YORK

Address. J. E. Irausquin Blvd. #83, Palm Beach, Aruba, Dutch Caribbean, tel. 297/8–64500 or 800/203–4475, fax 297/8–63191 or 203/866–7307.
Rooms. 386 rooms, 33 suites. All have air-conditioning. 5 suites have Jacuzzis.
Facilities. 3 restaurants, 4 bars/lounges, 2 unlighted tennis courts, freshwater pool, casino, exercise room with weights and aerobic machines, salon, supervised children's program, dive center.
TV and VCR. TVs in all rooms, with 5 channels including CNN and pay movies. No VCRs.
No-smoking rooms. None.
Credit cards. AE, DC, MC, V.
Restrictions. Min. 7 nights Dec 25–Jan 2.
Wheelchair accessibility. 2 rooms.
Prices. Dec 19–Apr 6: doubles $310–$365 EP; suites $500–$1,150 EP. Low season: doubles $180–$190 EP; suites $325–$600 EP.

ARUBA SONESTA RESORT CASINO AT SEA PORT VILLAGE

60.3%	55.2%	51.7%	65.5%	**TOTAL** 58.2%

A canal runs through the lobby of this modern seven-story atrium hotel. Boats use it to ferry guests to the main beach club, which is on a 40-acre island 10 minutes away. The hotel was built in 1990.

Reader Report

*"It has a beautiful private island with terrific sandy beaches,
one for families and one that's quieter with inviting paths.
The hammock on that island was perfect for sharing romantic
sunsets with my boyfriend."*

ALICIA N. WORRELL, BEDFORD, TEXAS

*"The Sonesta is comparable with higher priced hotels such as
the Hyatt. It's close to everything you need and want."*

DAVID ANDERSON, NATICK, MASSACHUSETTS

Address. L. G. Smith Blvd. #82, Aruba, Dutch Caribbean, tel.
297/8–36000 or 800/766-3782, fax 297/8–34389.

Affiliation. Sonesta International.

Rooms. 299 rooms, 15 suites. All have minibars and air-conditioning.

Facilities. 3 restaurants, 4 bars/lounges, unlighted tennis court,
freshwater pool, casino, exercise room with weights and aerobic
machines, salon, dry-cleaning, conference center with business
services, supervised children's program, dive center.

TV and VCR. TVs in all rooms, with 7 channels including CNN
and cable movie channels. No VCR.

No-smoking rooms. None.

Credit cards. AE, DC, MC, V.

Restrictions. Must be 18 or older to enter casino and to drink
alcoholic beverages.

Wheelchair accessibility. No accessible rooms.

Prices. Dec 23–Apr 12: doubles $260–$380 EP; suites
$440–$660 EP. Low season: doubles $165–$215 EP; suites
$315–$540 EP. Add $62 per person for AP, $44 for MAP,
$14.50 for breakfast, $8.50 for Continental breakfast.

BEST WESTERN TALK OF THE TOWN RESORT

				TOTAL
37.5%	37.5%	31.3%	68.8%	43.8%

This two-story low-rise on the outskirts of Oranjstad surrounds a
pool and is across the street from a beach; guests have
exchange privileges at the two Best Westerns on Manchebo
Beach. The hotel was built in 1964, and rooms were added in
1974. It was last renovated in 1993.

Reader Report

*"While not directly on the beach, Talk of the Town offers a
great setting, outstanding food and service, and a quiet charm
not easily found in the larger hotel-casinos."*

RICHARD HUGGINS, LAKELAND, FLORIDA

*"Great location in the heart of Aruba's shopping district. The
casino is the island's most popular with the cruise ship
crowd, yet it's friendly."*

TOM BENISH, FRIESLAND, WISCONSIN

Address. L.G. Smith Blvd. #2, Oranjestad, Aruba, Dutch Caribbean, tel. 297/8–23380 or 800/528–1234, fax 297/8–20327.

Affiliation. Best Western International.

Rooms. 51 rooms, 12 suites. All have air-conditioning, direct dial telephones, microwaves, refrigerators, and ceiling fans.

Facilities. 3 restaurants, 3 bars/lounges, 2 freshwater pools, conference center with business services, dive center.

TV and VCR. TVs in all rooms, with 5 channels including CNN and cable movie channels. No VCRs.

No-smoking rooms. None.

Credit cards. AE, DC, MC, V.

Restrictions. Children under 18 must be under adult supervision. Min. 7 nights during high season.

Wheelchair accessibility. No accessible rooms.

Prices. Dec 22–Apr 16: doubles $125–$173 EP; suites $180–$220 EP. Low season: doubles $94–$114 EP; suites $115–$147 EP. Add $39 per person for MAP, $9 for breakfast.

DIVI ARUBA BEACH RESORT

| 47.5% | 33.8% | 40.0% | 62.5% | **TOTAL** 45.9% |

This low-rise resort with rooms and bungalows, built in 1969 and renovated in 1992, sits on Divi Beach. Guests have exchange privileges with Tamarijn Aruba Beach Resort.

Reader Report

"The beach was gorgeous, the rooms well-equipped. But it used to be better than it was—we were disappointed."

WENDY WILLIAMS, LARCHMONT, NEW YORK

"A small, friendly hotel, not fancy but comfortable—like an old shoe."

MARY-ALICE DENNY, FT. LAUDERDALE, FLORIDA

"A good option for visitors with disabilities; the pool has a ramp and steps with a center rail."

EILEEN KEARNEY, HYDE PARK, NEW YORK

"The beach is one of the finest, but the room was a disapointment. Although we paid top dollar, the furniture was shabby."

G. AL CHIZ, MUNH ALL, PENNSYLVANIA

Address. J.E. Irausquin Blvd. #45, Oranjestad, Aruba, Dutch Caribbean, tel. 297/8–33000 or 800/554–2008, fax 297/8–31940.

Affiliation. Doral Hospitality Company Hotels & Resorts.

Rooms. 203 rooms, 3 suites. All have air-conditioning and ceiling fans. All suites have minibars.

Facilities. 2 restaurants, 2 bars/lounges, unlighted tennis court, 2 freshwater pools, salon, nightly entertainment, shopping cen-

ter, supervised children's program, watersports.
TV and VCR. TVs in all rooms, with 12 channels including CNN and cable movie channels. No VCR.
No-smoking rooms. None.
Credit cards. AE, DC, D, MC, V.
Restrictions. None.
Wheelchair accessibility. 2 rooms.
Prices. Dec 23–Apr 19: doubles $360–$480 EP; suites $400–$600 EP. Low season: doubles $330–$400 EP; suites $180–$400 EP. Add $50 per person for MAP.

HYATT REGENCY ARUBA RESORT & CASINO

| 82.9% | 81.9% | 73.3% | 81.0% | **TOTAL** 79.8% |

A nine-story pink tower is flanked by two low-slung wings at this 12-acre resort on Palm Beach, built in 1990. It has its own casino and a big free-form pool.

Reader Report

"The grounds were beautiful, the room was fair, and the price high. Excellent service, nice people, good food."

NAME WITHHELD, BASKING RIDGE, NEW JERSEY

"It was lovely, a really nice resort, with all of the amenities you would expect. Camp Hyatt is a nice option for families with children."

MARK MORROW, TULSA, OKLAHOMA

Address. J. E. Irausquin Blvd. #85, Palm Beach, Aruba, Dutch Caribbean, tel. 297/8–61234 or 800/233–1234, fax 297/8–65478.
Affiliation. Hyatt Hotels and Resorts.
Rooms. 360 rooms, 18 suites. All have minibars, air-conditioning, and ceiling fans. 1 suite has a Jacuzzi.
Facilities. 4 restaurants, 4 bars/lounges, 2 lighted tennis courts, freshwater pool, casino, exercise room with weights and aerobic machines, aerobics classes, massages, sauna, salon, 24-hr room service, dry-cleaning, conference center, supervised children's program, dive center, sailboat.
TV and VCR. TVs in all rooms, with 9 channels including CNN and cable movie channels. VCRs in rooms on request.
No-smoking rooms. 43 rooms.
Credit cards. AE, DC, D, MC, V.
Restrictions. Min. 10 nights Dec 22–Jan 1.
Wheelchair accessibility. 7 rooms.
Prices. Dec 22–Apr 16: doubles $350–$465 EP; suites $650–$1,180 EP. Low season: doubles $185–$305 EP; suites $390–$1,085 EP.

LA CABANA ALL SUITE BEACH RESORT & CASINO

				TOTAL
52.5%	67.8%	32.2%	62.7%	53.8%

All accommodations are suites at this five-story, horseshoe-shape Mediterranean-style complex. It has 3 free-form pools and a casino and is right across the street from Eagle Beach, on Aruba's west coast. The hotel was built in 1991 and expanded in 1994 with an additional wing around a landscaped courtyard.

Reader Report

"The resort was beautiful, and the suites were spacious and well-equipped. The restaurants were disappointing."

V. V. BOLZA, ALLENTOWN, PENNSYLVANIA

"I thoroughly enjoyed the island, the people, the resort, and the beaches."

GERALD KRAMER, VENICE, FLORIDA

Address. J.E. Irausquin Blvd. #250, Aruba, Dutch Caribbean, tel. 297/8–79000 or 800/835–7193, fax 297/8–77208.
Rooms. 803 suites. All have air-conditioning, ceiling fans, whirlpool tubs, kitchenettes, and a balcony or patio.
Facilities. 4 restaurants, 4 bars/lounges, 5 lighted tennis courts, 3 freshwater pools, casino, exercise room with weights and aerobic machines, aerobics classes, massages, sauna, salon, dry-cleaning, supervised children's program, shopping arcade.
TV and VCR. TVs in all rooms, with 13 channels including CNN and cable movie channels.
No-smoking rooms. None.
Credit cards. AE, DC, MC, V.
Restrictions. Min. 7 nights Dec 24–31.
Wheelchair accessibility. No accessible rooms.
Prices. Dec 22–Apr 16: suites $190–$300 EP. Low season: suites $100–$175 EP. Add $49 per person for AP, $39 for MAP, $11 for breakfast. Prices are per suite.

PLAYA LINDA BEACH RESORT

				TOTAL
66.7%	74.4%	64.1%	84.6%	72.4%

This all-suite timeshare resort property, built in 1983, has a terra-cotta and off-white main building in a ziggurat shape, with levels of balconies stepped back from each other.

Reader Report

"A deluxe resort on Palm Beach. All units have kitchens and

*terraces, and there is a waterfall swimming pool. It's a great
value, good for all ages."*

DIANE ASCIONE HOROWITZ, BLOOMFIELD, NEW JERSEY

*"The pools were beautiful, as were the hot tubs, and there was
a lovely beach. As scuba divers, we found the dive facility
within walking distance to be very convenient. The service
was very good, and the ambience in the restaurants was
lovely."*

PHYLLIS PRAGER, SUDBURY, MASSACHUSETTS

Address. J.E. Irausquin Blvd. #87, Oranjestad, Aruba, Dutch
Caribbean, tel. 297/8–61000 or 800/223–6510, fax 297/8–
63479.
Rooms. 194 suites. All have air-conditioning, ceiling fans, balconies or terraces, and full kitchens.
Facilities. 2 restaurants, 4 bars/lounges, 3 lighted tennis courts,
golf course nearby freshwater pool (plus freshwater children's
pool), horseback riding nearby, exercise room with weights and
aerobic machines, aerobics classes (occasionally), massages,
sauna, salon, dry-cleaning, conference center with business services, supervised children's program, shopping arcade, dive
center nearby, sailboats nearby.
TV and VCR. TVs in all rooms, with 15 channels including CNN
and cable movie channels. VCRs in rooms on request.
No-smoking rooms. None.
Credit cards. AE, DC, D, MC, V.
Restrictions. None.
Wheelchair accessibility. 4 suites.
Prices. Dec 18–Apr 9: $220–$650 EP. Low season: $170–
$420 EP.

RADISSON ARUBA CARIBBEAN
RESORT & CASINO

🍸	🛏	✕	☀	**TOTAL**
65.9%	**53.7%**	**53.7%**	**73.2%**	**61.6%**

The former Golden Tulip is set on Palm Beach, about five miles
northwest of Oranjestad. When the resort was built in 1959, it
was the island's first high-rise. There are three hotel towers and
a casino. The hotel was renovated in 1993.

Reader Report
"Very nice hotel. Good eats, et cetera."

ELWOOD AND MARION HANSEN, MINNEAPOLIS, MINNESOTA

*"It was great. The staff was nice, and the room was very good.
Not one of those loud resorts, this is more relaxing, for
families."*

JOHN R. MCCONNELL, SUN CITY CENTER, FLORIDA

Address. J.E. Irausquin Blvd. #81, Aruba, Dutch Caribbean, tel. 297–8/66555 or 800/333–3333, fax 297–8/63260.
Affiliation. Radisson Hotels International.
Rooms. 387 rooms, 19 suites. Most have refrigerators and air-conditioning; all have balconies or patios.
Facilities. 2 restaurants, 3 bars/lounges, coffee shop, 4 lighted tennis courts, freshwater pool, casino, exercise room with weights and aerobic machines, steam cabinet, massages, salon, dry-cleaning, daily activities program.
TV and VCR. TVs in all rooms, with 11 channels including CNN. VCRs in rooms on request.
No-smoking rooms. None.
Credit cards. AE, CB, DC, D, MC, V.
Restrictions. Children under 18 must be accompanied by an adult.
Wheelchair accessibility. 1 room.
Prices. Dec 22–Apr 23: doubles $260–$350 EP; suites $500–$800 EP. Low season: doubles $155–$240 EP; suites $300–$525 EP.

TAMARIJN ARUBA ALL-INCLUSIVE BEACH RESORT

57.5%	32.5%	35.0%	65.0%	TOTAL 47.5%

Accommodations at this all-inclusive resort on Divi Beach, west of Oranjestad, are in two-story, white stucco, cottage-style structures. It's a sister property to the Divi Aruba Beach Resort. The Tamarijn Aruba was built in 1963 and renovated in 1990.

Reader Report

"We were very happy with the resort. The beach was right outside our back door. We plan on going back again in a few months."

RUTH FURTADO, SWANSEA, MASSACHUSETTS

"I was disappointed in the rather stony beach (though the Divi next door has a much better beach that guests here may use). It is an older resort that has been fairly well maintained. There is a nice breakfast buffet."

NAME WITHHELD, OLD LYME, CONNECTICUT

Address. J.E. Irausquin Blvd. #41, Oranjestad, Aruba, Dutch Caribbean, tel. 297/8–24150 or 800/554–2008 for reservations, fax 297/8–34002.
Affiliation. Doral Hospitality Company Hotels & Resorts.
Rooms. 236 rooms, all with air-conditioning.
Facilities. 5 restaurants, 4 bars/lounges, 2 lighted tennis courts, freshwater pool, exercise room with weights and aerobic machines, aerobics classes, dry-cleaning, supervised children's program, nightly entertainment, watersports.

TV and VCR. TVs in all rooms, with 12 channels including CNN and cable movie channels. No VCRs.

No-smoking rooms. None.

Credit cards. AE, DC, D, MC, V.

Wheelchair accessibility. No accessible rooms.

Prices. Dec 23–Apr 19: doubles $330–$400 AP. Low season: doubles $300–$320 AP.

BAHAMAS

60.0% | **46.9%** | **51.0%** | **42.3%** | **TOTAL** **53.0%**

Reader Report

"What the country lacks in historical value, culture, arts, et cetera, is made up for by the kindness and warmth of the people. The kindness, however, has a price . . . so bring lots of money."

RON LORILLA, SAN JOSE, CALIFORNIA

"We began traveling to Nassau when it was British, and liked it enough to buy property on Eleuthera. After independence, Nassau became a slum. Our daughter's purse was snatched . . . the police did nothing. We will sell our lot."

MARY BRITTEN LYNCH, CHATTANOOGA, TENNESSEE

"The 'out' islands are the way to go for true Bahamian flavor and culture."

GARY W. VAUGHN, ARLINGTON, TEXAS

"On Grand Bahama island, dine and drink where the natives hang out for much more cultural diversity and fresh authentic food. People are friendly and very helpful."

MARY NIEHAUS, VAN NUYS, CALIFORNIA

"Eleuthera is a great place for a peaceful vacation with friendly people and beautiful, almost deserted beaches."

BILL AND LAURA IVES, MARBLEHEAD, MASSACHUSETTS

Islands. The Bahamas are a 5,382-square-mile, independent group of islands, with a population of about 243,000.
Language. The official language is English.

Visitor Information

In the U.S. Contact the **Bahamas Tourist Office** (2957 Clairmont Rd., Suite 150, Atlanta, GA 30329, tel. 404/633–1793, fax. 404/633–1575; 8600 W. Bryn Mawr Ave., Suite 820, Chicago, IL 60631, tel. 312/693–1111, fax 312/693–1114; 2050 Stemmons Fwy., Suite 186, World Trade Center, Dallas, TX 75258, tel. 214/742–1886, fax 214/741–4118; 3450 Wilshire Blvd., Suite 206, Los Angeles, CA 90010, tel. 213/385–0033, fax 213/383–3966; 19495 Biscayne Blvd., Miami, FL 33180, tel. 305/932–0051, fax 305/682–8758; 150 E. 52nd St., New York, NY 10022, tel. 212/758–2777, fax 212/ 753–6531; or by calling 800/422–4262).
In Canada Contact the **Bahamas Tourist Office** (121 Bloor St. E, Suite 1101, Toronto, Ont. M4W 3M5, tel. 416/968–2999, fax 416/968–6711).
In the U.K. Contact the **Bahamas Tourist Office** (10 Chesterfield St., London W1X 8AH, tel. 071/629–5238, fax 071/491–9311).

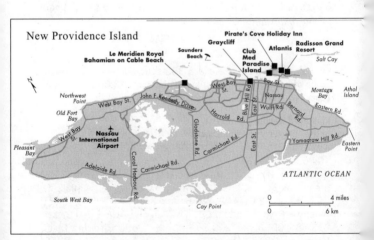

BAHAMAS

KEY

- Beach
- Cruise Ship Dock
- Hotel or Resort

0   50 miles
0   75 km

N

*ATLANTIC
OCEAN*

Med
era

Arthur's Town
Cat I.

Port Howe

**Club Med
Columbus Isle**

San Salvador

Rum Cay

George
Town

Stella Maris

*Great
Exuma I.*

Long I.

Samana Cay

Crooked I.

*Crooked
Island
Passage*

*Mayaguana
Passage*

Mayaguana I.

Acklins I.

*Caicos
Passage*

*Little
Inagua I.*

Great Inagua I.

*Lake
Windsor*

Matthew Town

In the Bahamas Contact the **Ministry of Tourism** (Market Square, tel. 809/322–7500, fax 809/328–0945; Rawson Sq., tel. 809/326–9772 or 809/326–9781, no fax).

ATLANTIS

👨‍💼	🛏️	🍴	〰️	**TOTAL**
47.7%	**47.7%**	**61.4%**	**72.7%**	**57.4%**

After a $250-million renovation of the former Paradise Island Resort & Casino, this 14-acre resort reopened in December 1994. It has two high-rise towers amid an elaborate waterscape with lagoons, more than 40 waterfalls, underground grottoes, and an underwater glass tunnel, which allows observation of sharks and barracuda. The 30,000-square-foot casino provides an abundance of games and more than 800 slot machines.

Reader Report

"It was fabulous. I couldn't speak highly enough of [our cleaning lady]. I told my children to take their children there. The swimming pool is endless."

MARGARET BAIRD, VIRGINIA BEACH, VIRGINIA

"You don't even have to leave [the resort], there's so much to do. It's a great place for kids, and they have employees stationed every few feet to look out for them."

JOANNE CILENTO, WALL, NEW JERSEY

Address. Box N-4777, Nassau, Bahamas, tel. 809/363–3000 or 800/821–3000, fax 809/363–3524.
Affiliation. Sun International.
Rooms. 1,147 rooms, 62 suites. All have air-conditioning and minibars. 86 rooms have ceiling fans. 2 suites have Jacuzzis.
Facilities. 12 restaurants, 6 bars/lounges, coffee shop, 9 lighted tennis courts nearby, 18-hole golf-course, 5 freshwater pools, casino, exercise room with weights and aerobic machines, massages, salon, dry-cleaning, 24-hour room service, conference center with business services, supervised children's program, dive center, sailboats.
TV and VCR. TVs in all rooms, with 12 channels including CNN. VCRs in rooms on request (at a fee).
No-smoking rooms. 128 rooms.
Credit cards. AE, DC, MC, V.
Restrictions. Min. 6 nights Dec. 28–Jan. 1. Guests must be 18 years to gamble in the casino.
Wheelchair accessibility. 4 rooms.
Prices. Dec. 22–Apr. 20: doubles $185–$365 EP; suites $420–$2,500 EP. Low season: doubles $130–$325 EP; suites $320–$2,500 EP. Three kinds of meal plans (none include lunch).

BAHAMAS PRINCESS RESORT & CASINO

| 52.4% | 43.7% | 49.8% | 60.2% | TOTAL 51.5% |

This complex on Grand Bahamas Island includes the Moorish-style 10-story Princess Tower, which has a casino, and the tropical low rise Princess Country Club; there's a shuttle to the beach. The hotel was built in 1968; renovations have been ongoing.

Reader Report

"A great place to get away for three or four days at a great price—most of all a great place for rest and relaxation. Enjoy the beaches, the snorkeling, and the water sports."

KERRY PEELER, CARY, NORTH CAROLINA

"Very nice, though the food was not so hot. There are better places to eat outside the hotel."

MATILDA D'ALTO, BROOKLYN, NEW YORK

"It's a nice hotel, with good service, right next to the casino. It was Christmas when we were there, and there were poinsettias everywhere, making us feel right at home."

DAVID AND MARY EILEENE BEER, SANDY, UTAH

Address. Box F–4207, Freeport, Grand Bahama, tel. 809/352–6721 or 800/223–1818, fax 809/352–2542.
Affiliation. Princess Hotels International.
Rooms. 965 rooms, 39 suites. All have air-conditioning.
Facilities. 7 restaurants, 4 bars/lounges, 2 coffee shops, 6 lighted tennis courts, 3 unlighted tennis courts, 2 golf courses, 2 freshwater pools, casino, exercise room with weights and aerobic machines, massages, salon, dry-cleaning, conference center with business services, supervised children's program.
TV and VCR. TVs in all rooms with 8 channels including CNN. No VCRs.
No-smoking rooms. None.
Credit cards. AE, D, DC, JCB, MC, V.
Restrictions. No pets.
Wheelchair accessibility. 3 rooms.
Prices. Dec 17–Apr 6: doubles $120–$170 EP; suites $200–$950 EP. Low season: doubles $95–$150 EP; suites $180–$700 EP. Add $29–$54 per person for MAP.

CLUB MED COLUMBUS ISLE

| 68.8% | 75.0% | 62.5% | 81.3% | TOTAL 71.9% |

Set on 80 acres, this all-inclusive resort village on the island of San Salvador opened in 1992. Accommodations are in bunga-

33

lows painted in bright colors. There's a large active dive center. The village was built in 1991.

Reader Report

"Its magnificent beach, uncrowded diving, snorkeling, tennis, cycling, and Far Eastern works of art make this a truly luxurious resort. It's tranquil and has very comfortable rooms (with TV and phone!) and an accommodating staff who never make you to do anything you don't want to do. If you like the hectic atmosphere at some other Club Meds, you'll be disappointed—this is a great place to read a good book or have a romantic interlude."

JOEL M. CHUSID, IRVING, TEXAS

"The scuba diving was excellent—there were beautiful reefs that were not 'overdived,' as so many are. The facilities are the best Club Med has to offer anywhere. You don't go to Club Med for gourmet dining, but the food here was very good. Good spot for couples, less so for singles."

DANIEL JOHNSON, ST. LOUIS, MISSOURI

Address. Columbus Isle, San Salvador, Bahamas, tel. 809/331–2000 or 800/258–2633, fax 809/331–2222.
Affiliation. Club Med.
Rooms. 296 rooms. All have minibars and air-conditioning.
Facilities. 3 restaurants, 3 bars/lounges, 4 lighted tennis courts, 5 unlighted tennis courts, freshwater pool, nightclub, theater, exercise room with weights and aerobic machines, aerobics classes, massages, swimming pool, kayaking, snorkeling, bicycling, volleyball, basketball, waterskiing, arts and crafts, dive center, sailboats.
TV and VCR. TVs in all rooms, with CNN. No VCRs.
No-smoking rooms. None.
Credit cards. AE, MC, V.
Restrictions. No children under 12.
Wheelchair accessibility. No accessible rooms.
Prices. Year-round: $150–$210 all-inclusive. Prices are per person.

CLUB MED ELEUTHERA

🕴️	🛏️	✖️	🌅	**TOTAL**
51.6%	**9.7%**	**48.4%**	**58.1%**	**41.9%**

This all-inclusive resort in Governor's Harbor on Eleuthera has an Atlantic beach on one side and a marina on the other. Rooms are in two-story structures that face the beach or the gardens. The hotel was built in 1979 and last renovated in 1989.

Reader Report

"Too many bugs when we were there (August), but otherwise perfect in every way."

MURRAY LAUREN, NEW YORK, NEW YORK

"Rooms were minimal, but the philosophy here is that you shouldn't spend much time in your room. Beaches were beautiful, and the staff was wonderful—they kept the children busy and taught them things."

LISA LANIER, LAKE ZURICH, ILLINOIS

Address. French Leave, Box 80, Governor's Harbour, Eleuthera, Bahamas, tel. 809/332–2270 or 809/332–2271 or 800/258-2633, fax 809/332–2691.
Affiliation. Club Med.
Rooms. 288 rooms, all with air-conditioning and showers only.
Facilities. 3 restaurants, bars/lounge, nightclub, theater, 2 lighted tennis courts, 6 unlighted tennis courts, freshwater pool, aerobics classes, supervised children's program, scuba diving school, circus workshops, snorkeling, volleyball, basketball, softball, soccer, sailboats.
TV and VCR. TV in public area only, with 35 channels including CNN. VCR in public area.
No-smoking rooms. None.
Credit cards. AE, MC, V.
Restrictions. Mini Club for children 12 months to 5 years.
Wheelchair accessibility. No accessible rooms.
Prices. Year-round: $130–$155 all-inclusive. Prices are per person.

CLUB MED PARADISE ISLAND

| 47.9% | 21.1% | 53.5% | 57.7% | **TOTAL** 45.1% |

This 21-acre all-inclusive resort is on the grounds of a colonial estate a ferry ride away from Nassau. Rooms face the beach or the gardens. The hotel was built in 1977.

Reader Report

"Great for couples. There were people there from all over the world. It's within walking distance of the casinos. It didn't seem like a typical Club Med—it was really more like a hotel."

LAUREL GLICKMAN, CHICAGO, ILLINOIS

"The rooms are spartan, but with so many beach activities to choose from, time spent in the room is minimal. The buffet-style food tends to get boring over a week but Club Med adds specialty nights to liven things up."

DAVID ARIAS, LOS ANGELES, CALIFORNIA

"It had a great tennis program and many optional side trips.

You never have to leave the resort, though, and you don't have to spend a penny while you're there. It's convenient to the U.S.—and great for short vacations."

JAY VICTOR, BLOOMFIELD HILLS, MICHIGAN

Address. Box N 7137, Nassau, tel. 809/363–2640, 809/363–2644, or 800/258–2633, fax 809/363–3496.
Affiliation. Club Med.
Rooms. 312 rooms. All have air-conditioning, but with showers only.
Facilities. 3 restaurants, 2 bars/lounges, nightclub, theater, 8 lighted tennis courts, 12 unlighte, saltwater pool, exercise room with weights and aerobic machines, aerobics classes, conference center with business services, sailboats, kayaking, windsurfing, snorkeling, volleyball, basketball, golf package available.
TV and VCR. TV in public area only, with VCR.
No-smoking rooms. None.
Credit cards. AE, MC, V.
Restrictions. No children under 12.
Wheelchair accessibility. No accessible rooms.
Prices. Dec 10–Apr 30: $118–$150. Low season: $120–$127. Rates are all-inclusive and per person.

GRAYCLIFF

72.2%	44.4%	66.7%	44.4%	**TOTAL** 56.9%

This renovated 18th-century Georgian mansion, a national monument, sits on three acres near Nassau's harbor; guests stay in the main house or in a garden annex. Built in 1726, the hotel was expanded on 1982 and most recently renovated in 1988.

Reader Report

"It's the most famous mansion in Nassau, originally built by a famous pirate. My favorite room is the Woodes-Rodgers room, which has total charm. You hate to leave it for reality. Graycliff certainly beats the commercial hotels for charm and personal service, but if you want glitter, head elsewhere, and just come here for the best meal in Nassau."

PATRICIA NEISSER, NEWPORT BEACH, CALIFORNIA

"Probably the finest service and food in Nassau—we loved the lobster bisque and conch chowder. You may find yourself dining next to James Bond, Richard Harris, or a member of British royalty."

H. KANE, OLDSMAR, FLORIDA

"Service is the most attentive I have ever experienced, without being worrisome. There is no better wine selection in the

Caribbean. The ambience is Old World, with a real sense of history."

RICHARD JACOBS, JACKSON, TENNESSEE

"We stayed in the honeymoon suite, which was large and very Victorian. Great location downtown, and the beach is wonderful. Fabulous facilities, but very expensive—be prepared to tip everyone."

RENEE ELLIOTT, MARIETTA, OHIO

Address. W. Hill St, Nassau, Bahamas, tel. 809/322–2797 or 800/633–7411, fax 809/326–6110.
Rooms. 9 rooms, 5 suites. All rooms and suites have minibars and air-conditioning. 4 rooms have ceiling fans. 2 suites have Jacuzzis. 1 suite has shower only.
Facilities. Restaurant, bar/lounge, freshwater pool, exercise room with weights and aerobic machines, sauna, massages, 24-hr room service, dry-cleaning, conference center with business services.
TV and VCR. TVs in all rooms, with 4 channels including CNN and cable movie channels. VCRs in rooms on request.
No-smoking rooms. None.
Credit cards. AE, DC, D, MC, V.
Restrictions. Min. 3 nights during major holidays.
Wheelchair accessibility. 1 room.
Prices. Nov. 16–Apr 30: doubles $215–$265 EP; suites $265–$365 EP. Low season: doubles $140–$195 EP; suites $165–$235 EP.

PIRATE'S COVE HOLIDAY INN

				TOTAL
49.3%	31.3%	31.3%	61.2%	43.3%

Situated in a lagoonlike setting on a crescent-shape private beach, this 16-story contemporary resort has a 10-acre recreational area and rooms with private balconies. Built in 1973 and renovated in 1993, the Pirate's Cove Holiday Inn is 5 minutes from the Atlantis resort and casino.

Reader Report

"Absolutely beautiful. We had a suite on the 16th floor, with breathtaking views—one side overlooked the ocean; the other side overlooked the harbor with all the cruise ships.... A lot was within walking distance—like beautiful flower gardens with waterfalls."

MARIE ROELSE, SHEBOYGAN, WISCONSIN

"A good experience, in fact, the only good experience I had on the island was at [Pirate's Cove]."

CURTIS REEVES, TULSA, OKLAHOMA

Address. Box 6214 Casaurina Dr., Nassau, Bahamas, tel. 809/363–2100 or 800/23–HOTEL, fax 809/363–3386.
Affiliation. Holiday Inn.
Rooms. 564 rooms, 80 suites. All have air-conditioning.
Facilities. 3 restaurants, 2 bars/lounges, coffee shop, freshwater pool, 2 hot tubs, lighted tennis court, 2 unlighted tennis courts, 18-hole golf course nearby, exercise room with weights and aerobic machines, massages, dry-cleaning, conference center with business services, supervised children's program, dive center.
TV and VCR. TVs in all rooms, with 9 channels including CNN and cable movie channels. VCR in public area.
No-smoking rooms. 74 rooms.
Credit cards. AE, D, DC, MC, V.
Wheelchair accessibility. No accessible rooms.
Prices. Feb. 15–Apr. 13: doubles $110–$165 EP; suites $188–$243 MAP. Low season: doubles $85–$120 EP; suites $163–$198 MAP.

RADISSON GRAND RESORT

43.9%	39.4%	34.8%	43.9%	**TOTAL** 40.5%

This 15-story contemporary-style high-rise on Paradise Island—the former Sheraton Grand—is right on the beach, next door to the Atlantis casino and very near the bridge to Nassau. The hotel was built in 1982 and renovated in 1992.

Reader Report

"Comfortable rooms, spotlessly maintained and well-equipped, and a courteous, accommodating staff. Great beach! Food in the main restaurant was a good value. There are also well-supervised activities for children. We would choose it again."

PAIGE WHITECAR, WASHINGTON, DC

"The beach was great, and the service excellent. I was really happy with the location."

ANNAMARIA GERASIMOU, JAMAICA HILLS, NEW YORK

Address. Paradise Island (mailing address: 1 Turnberry Pl., Suite 601, 19495 Biscayne Blvd., Aventura, FL 33180), tel. 809/363–3500, 305/931–7646, or 800/333–3333, fax 305/363–3900.
Affiliation. Radisson Hotels Worldwide.
Rooms. 347 rooms, 33 suites. All have minibars and air-conditioning.
Facilities. 4 restaurants, 4 bars/lounges, coffee shop, 4 lighted tennis courts, freshwater pool, casino nearby, aerobics classes, dry-cleaning, supervised children's program in high season, dive center, sailboats.
TV and VCR. TVs in all rooms, with 19 channels including CNN and cable movie channels. VCRs in rooms on request.

No-smoking rooms. 120 rooms, 12 suites.
Credit cards. AE, CB, D, DC,, MC, V.
Wheelchair accessibility. No accessible rooms.
Prices. Dec 22–Apr 19: doubles $200–$230 EP; suites $250–$600 EP. Low season: doubles $145–$190 EP; suites $185–$600 EP. Add $37 per person for MAP.

BARBADOS

				TOTAL
67.3%	50.8%	49.5%	42.3%	53.0%

Reader Report

"People are extremely friendly and accommodating. They really like Americans, especially African-Americans. The best of the Caribbean islands by far!"

CALVIN R. SWINSON, SAN JOSE, CALIFORNIA

"The best way to see the island is by car. If you're up to the challenge of driving on the left and navigating without road signs, rent a car. Otherwise, taxi cabs are for hire, and usually the driver is enthusiastic and full of interesting information."

DEANNE M. RYMAROWICZ, WEST DES MOINES, IOWA

"The beaches on the Caribbean side were wonderful, but to get to the best ones you really need to stay at a beachside hotel. Off-season in May is nice and quiet with plenty of sun. I loved the rum factory tour."

JAN SMITH, SARATOGA, CALIFORNIA

"The Bajans' love of life shines in the sparkling beaches, rhythmic music, colorful homes, happy cafés, and tasty fresh fish. There are fine local artists—and they'll ship to the USA."

MARY LEE GWIZDALA, ORCHARD LAKE, MICHIGAN

Islands. Barbados is an independent 166-square-mile nation, with a population of about 260,000.
Language. The official language is English.

Visitor Information

In the U.S. Contact the **Barbados Tourism Authority** (800 2nd Ave., New York, NY 10017, tel. 212/986–6516, fax 212/573–9850; 3440 Wilshire Blvd., Suite 1215, Los Angeles, CA 90010, tel. 213/380–2199, fax 213/384–2763).
In Canada. Contact the **Barbados Board of Tourism** (5160 Yonge St., Suite 1800, N. York, Ont. M2N 6L9, tel. 416/512–6569, fax 416/512–6581; 615 Dorchester, Suite 960, Montreal, Que. H3B 1P5, tel. 514/861–0085, fax 514/861–7917).
In the U.K. Contact the **Barbados Board of Tourism** (263 Tottenham Court Rd., London W1P 9AA, tel. 4471/636–9448, fax 4471/637–1496).
In Barbados. Contact the **Barbados Board of Tourism** (Box 242, Prescod Blvd. and Harbor Rd., Bridgetown, Barbados, W.I., tel. 809/427–2623, fax 809/426–4080).

ALMOND BEACH CLUB

| 69.2% | 61.5% | 76.9% | 69.2% | TOTAL 69.2% |

The former Divi St. James Beach Resort is located on the west coast, about three miles north of Bridgetown. This all-inclusive offers low-rise plantation-style accommodations on four-and-a-half-acres. The hotel was built in 1984, expanded in 1991, and renovated in 1992.

Reader Report

"The room was just not up to par."

AARON JACOVIS, LOS ANGELES, CALIFORNIA

"One of the drawbacks is that it is on the reef and doesn't have its own beach, though it is within walking distance of a really beautiful beach, Sandy Lane. However, there was a wreck on the reef in front of us, which made for great snorkeling. The room was nice, not spectacular. It's a really nice place for a honeymoon."

CAROLE AND TIM REHAK, BALTIMORE, MARYLAND

Address. Vauxhall, St. James, Barbados, W.I., tel. 809/432–7840 or 800/425–6663, fax 809/432–2115.
Affiliation. Barbados Shipping & Trading Resorts Ltd.
Rooms. 151 rooms including 55 suites. All have air-conditioning and ceiling fans.
Facilities. 2 restaurants, 4 bars/lounges, lighted tennis court, exercise room with weights and aerobic machines, aerobics classes, massages, sauna, dry cleaning, sailboats.
TV and VCR. TVs in all rooms, with 7 channels including CNN and cable movie channels. No VCRs.
No-smoking rooms. None.
Credit cards. AE, DC, D, MC, V.
Restrictions. No children under 6.
Wheelchair accessibility. No accessible rooms.
Prices. Dec 18–Mar 31: doubles $430–$460 AP; suites $475–$560 AP. Low season: doubles $315–$380 AP; suites $380–$475 AP.

COBBLERS COVE

| 77.8% | 100.0% | 77.8% | 55.6% | TOTAL 77.8% |

At this all-suite resort on the west coast, two-story villas surround a turn-of-the-century pink stone mansion with crenellated towers. The shore is rocky, but there's a seaside pool and a beach nearby. The hotel was built in 1969 expanded in 1989.

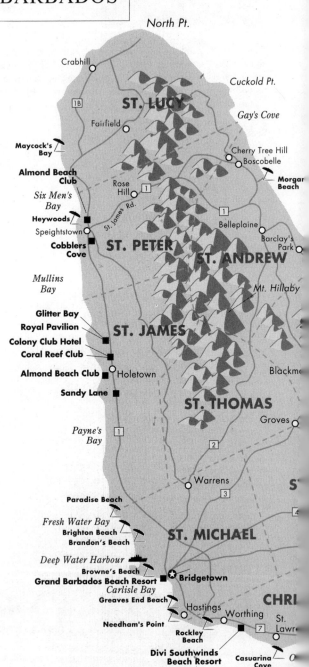

BARBADOS

North Pt.

Crabhill

ST. LUCY

Cuckold Pt.

Gay's Cove

Fairfield

Maycock's Bay

Cherry Tree Hill
Boscobelle

Almond Beach Club

Rose Hill

Morgan Beach

Six Men's Bay

St. James Rd.

Belleplaine

Heywoods
Speightstown

ST. PETER

Barclay's Park

Cobblers Cove

ST. ANDREW

Mullins Bay

Mt. Hillaby

Glitter Bay
Royal Pavilion
Colony Club Hotel
Coral Reef Club

ST. JAMES

Almond Beach Club

Holetown

Blackm

Sandy Lane

ST. THOMAS

Groves

Payne's Bay

Warrens

S'

Paradise Beach

Fresh Water Bay
Brighton Beach
Brandon's Beach

ST. MICHAEL

Deep Water Harbour

Browne's Beach
Grand Barbados Beach Resort
Carlisle Bay
Greaves End Beach

Bridgetown

CHRI

Hastings
Worthing

St. Lawre

Needham's Point

Rockley Beach

Divi Southwinds Beach Resort

Casuarina Cove

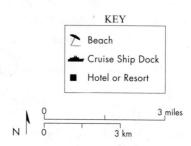

KEY

↗ Beach

⛴ Cruise Ship Dock

■ Hotel or Resort

N

0 ——————————— 3 miles

0 ——————————— 3 km

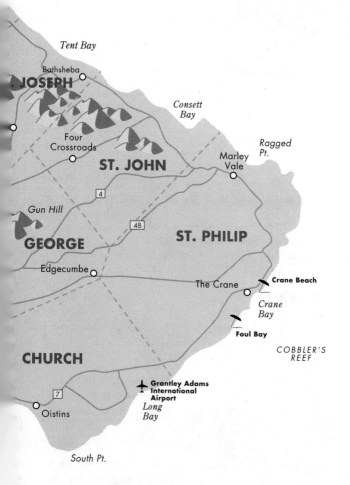

ewis

ATLANTIC OCEAN

Tent Bay

Bathsheba

JOSEPH

Consett Bay

Four Crossroads

ST. JOHN

Marley Vale

Ragged Pt.

4

Gun Hill

4B

GEORGE

ST. PHILIP

Edgecumbe

The Crane

Crane Beach

Crane Bay

Foul Bay

COBBLER'S REEF

CHURCH

7

Grantley Adams International Airport

Long Bay

Oistins

South Pt.

Reader Report

"There was a certain European flavor, but you always knew you were in the tropics; the buildings were very open and inviting. We liked the kitchenette in the room."

SARAH ANDERSON, ALBUQUERQUE, NEW MEXICO

"The pool area and restaurant were excellent, the beach very good. English tea is served around four o'clock. The rooms were nice but could be better. They need to add more facilities. I enjoyed it."

ARLENE SHAPIRO, BROOKLYN, NEW YORK

Address. Road View, St. Peter, Barbados, W.I., tel. 809/422–2291 or 800/223–6510, fax 809/422–1460.

Affiliation. Relais & Châteaux.

Rooms. 40 suites. All have minibars, air-conditioning, direct-dial telephones, hair dryers, safes, and ceiling fans. 1 has a Jacuzzi.

Facilities. Restaurant, bar/lounge, lighted tennis court, freshwater pool, horseback riding nearby, massages, dry-cleaning, watersports.

TV and VCR. No TVs or VCRs.

No-smoking rooms. None.

Credit cards. MC, V.

Restrictions. No children under 12 mid-Jan–mid-Mar.

Wheelchair accessibility. 19 rooms.

Prices. Dec 22–Apr 14: suites $450–$1,400 MAP. Low season: suites $330–$710 MAP, $150–$580 EP. Prices are per suite.

COLONY CLUB HOTEL

70.0%	60.0%	55.0%	85.0%	**TOTAL** 67.5%

Built in 1953 and renovated in 1995, this seven-acre resort consists of a main house and two- and three-story-high bungalows with red tile roofs, in Colonial Caribbean style. There are waterfalls and pools throughout the resort.

Reader Report

"Day began with a full breakfast served on our balcony at the precise time requested. A large pool was available but we preferred the sea, where swimming was excellent."

FRANK R. WEGNER, LAKEHURST, NEW JERSEY

"It's a reasonable taxi ride from good shopping in the town. The rooms are large and sparsely furnished, and the hotel is on a beautiful sandy beach. The food is excellent and the staff very friendly."

VIOLA STEWART, SYLVANIA, OHIO

"Things have brightened up considerably since I last visited, and the new additions—particularly the water gardens and

an ocean terrace restaurant—will go a long way to re-establishing Colony Club as a favorite."

PATRICIA NEISSER, NEWPORT BEACH, CALIFORNIA

"Well situated, with pleasant rooms and a great beach. I'll go back anytime."

E. PALMER TAYLOR, WILLIAMSBURG, VIRGINIA

Address. Porters, St. James, Barbados, W.I., tel. 809/422–2335, fax 809/422–0667.
Affiliation. St. James Beach Hotels.
Rooms. 64 rooms, 34 suites. All have air-conditioning, hair dryers, minibars and balconies or patios.
Facilities. 2 restaurants, 2 bars/lounges, 2 lighted tennis courts, 4 freshwater pools, fitness center, massages, salon, 24-hr room service, dry-cleaning, 2 boutiques, watersports.
TV and VCR. TV in public area only, with 5 channels including CNN. VCR in public area.
No-smoking rooms. None.
Credit cards. AE, DC, D, MC, V.
Restrictions. Min. 12 nights mid-Dec–early Jan. No children under 12 in Feb.
Wheelchair accessibility. 10 rooms.
Prices. Dec 19–Apr 23: doubles $365–$435 MAP; suites $430–$495 MAP. Low season: doubles $260–$310 MAP; suites $300–$340 MAP.

CORAL REEF CLUB

| 56.3% | 56.3% | 43.8% | 68.8% | **TOTAL** 56.3% |

This low-rise resort, built in 1954 and renovated in 1993, is spread out over 12 acres of gardens on the west coast overlooking the Caribbean. There's a main house and coral-stone cottages.

Reader Report

"Coral Reef is stress-free, and they treat you wonderfully."

DAVID ANDERSON, NATICK, MASSACHUSETTS

"A wonderful choice, even though we stayed there in August, the first week they were open after their summer break. Warm, welcoming family and staff—the big chains just can't compete with a place like this with its caring, on-the-spot owners. Wonderful beach and food."

J.R. DAVIDSON, HANOVER, NEW HAMPSHIRE

Address. Porters, St. James, Barbados, W.I., tel. 809/422–2372, fax 809/422–1776.
Affiliation. Small Luxury Hotels of the World.
Rooms. 69 rooms. All have air-conditioning and ceiling fans.
Facilities. Restaurant, bar/lounge, 2 lighted tennis courts, fresh-

water pool, horseback riding, massages, salon, dry-cleaning, dive center, sailboats.

TV and VCR. TVs and VCRs in rooms on request.

No-smoking rooms. None.

Credit cards. AE, MC, V.

Restrictions. Min. 14 nights during the Christmas season. No children under 12 during Feb.

Wheelchair accessibility. 1 room fully equipped, half accessible.

Prices. Dec 16–Apr 16: doubles $362–$485 MAP. Low season: doubles $300–$350 MAP, $200–$250 EP.

DIVI SOUTHWINDS BEACH RESORT

🍸	🛏	✕	☀	TOTAL
69.2%	50.0%	34.6%	76.9%	57.7%

This resort's two-story beachfront units and its six-story hotel tower set among gardens next to a pool occupy 18 acres on St. Lawrence Beach, on the island's south coast. The hotel was built in 1981 and was renovated in 1988.

Reader Report

"The accommodations are spacious, clean, and adequately furnished. The beach and pool are fine, but the hotel should have a better selection of restaurants."

NAME WITHHELD, ARLINGTON, VIRGINIA

"We paid top dollar to stay in one of the oceanfront rooms, and we never felt comfortable there, especially at night. The window shutters had to be kept closed for privacy—we might as well have been staying in a dark cave."

J. R. DAVIDSON, HANOVER, NEW HAMPSHIRE

Address. St. Lawrence, Christ Church, Barbados, W.I., tel. 809/428–7181 or 800/367–3484, fax 305/633–1621.

Affiliation. Divi Resorts.

Rooms. 34 rooms, 116 suites. All have air-conditioning. All suites have ceiling fans and refrigerators.

Facilities. 2 restaurants, 2 bars/lounges, 2 lighted tennis courts, 2 unlighted, 9-hole golf course nearby, 3 freshwater pools, salon, dry-cleaning, dive center nearby.

TV and VCR. TVs in all rooms, with 7 channels including CNN and cable movie channels. No VCRs.

No-smoking rooms. 30 suites.

Credit cards. AE, CB, DC, D, MC, V.

Restrictions. Min. 7 nights during Christmas and New Year's.

Wheelchair accessibility. No accessible rooms.

Prices. Dec 23–Apr 7: doubles $185–$200 EP; suites $200–$355 EP. Low season: doubles $110 EP; suites $125–$200 EP. Add $60 per person for all-inclusive, $40 for MAP.

GLITTER BAY

👔	🛏	✕	☀	**TOTAL**
70.6%	**73.5%**	**64.7%**	**85.3%**	**73.5%**

This 10-acre condo resort on the west coast grew out of an estate built in the 1930s for Sir Edward Cunard. Lodging is in three-story white buildings done in Spanish style with red tile roofs. The hotel was renovated in 1982, and is affiliated with the Royal Westmoreland Golf & Country Club.

Reader Report

"We were so unhappy with where we were staying that at 10 PM we went to Glitter Bay, without reservations. They gave us a one-bedroom suite on the water, and it was great. The staff couldn't have been nicer. My wife and I travel only deluxe, and Glitter Bay fits our plans for the future."

KEN BRAUDE, HIGHLAND PARK, ILLINOIS

"A very well-maintained property, with a great beach area, away from the noise of the crowds. The food is above average."

NAME WITHHELD, LEWISBURG, PENNSYLVANIA

"A tropical village in miniature, Glitter Bay draws an elite crowd. I prefer the rooms with views of the lush gardens, which cost less than seaview rooms."

PATRICIA NEISSER, NEWPORT BEACH, CALIFORNIA

Address. Porters, St. James, Barbados, W.I., tel. 809/422–4111 or 800/283–8666, fax 809/422–3940.
Affiliation. Pemberton Hotels.
Rooms. 75 rooms and suites, and 1 villa with 5 individual suites. All have minibars, air-conditioning, and ceiling fans.
Facilities. Restaurant, 2 bars/lounges, 2 lighted tennis courts, 18-hole golf course nearby, 2 freshwater pools (1 for children), exercise room with weights and aerobic machines, aerobics classes, salon, 24-hr room service, afternoon tea, dry-cleaning, conference center with business services, supervised children's program during holidays, dive center, sailboats.
TV and VCR. TV in public area and for rent, with 5 channels including CNN and cable movie channels. VCRs in public area and for rent.
No-smoking rooms. None.
Credit cards. AE, DC, D, MC, V.
Restrictions. Min. 10 nights Dec 17–Jan 2.
Wheelchair accessibility. 2 rooms.
Prices. Dec 17–Mar 29: doubles $395–$415 EP; suites $485–$1,450 EP. Low season: doubles $215 EP; suites $250–$995 EP. For MAP, add $60 per person Dec 17–Nov 10, $40 at other times.

GRAND BARBADOS BEACH RESORT

💼	🛏	🍴	🌅	TOTAL
81.3%	81.3%	75.0%	68.8%	76.6%

This modern seven-story high-rise, built in 1969 and renovated in 1986, is located on four acres a mile from Bridgetown on Carlisle Bay. It has its own 260-foot pier.

Reader Report

"A very nice property, convenient to historical sites. The beach is small but adequate, but there is sometimes a slight odor from the nearby oil refineries and storage tanks."

ALICE R. LUCAS, GRANITE CITY, ILLINOIS

"There was a real nice, private beach. Everyone on Barbados is very friendly, very helpful. We received excellent service."

ANTIONETTE KIWACKA, HUBER HEIGHTS, OHIO

Address. Box 639, Bridgetown, Barbados, W.I., tel. 809/426–0890 or 800/227–5475, fax 809/436–9823.
Rooms. 128 rooms, 5 suites. All have minibars and air-conditioning. All suites have ceiling fans.
Facilities. 2 restaurants, 2 bars/lounges, 4 lighted tennis courts, 18-hole golf course nearby, freshwater pool, horseback riding nearby, exercise room with weights and aerobic machines, aerobics classes, massages, sauna, salon, dry-cleaning, conference center with business services nearby, dive center nearby, sailboats.
TV and VCR. TVs in all rooms, with 8 channels including CNN and cable movie channels. VCRs in rooms on request.
No-smoking rooms. 14 rooms.
Credit cards. AE, DC, D, MC, V.
Wheelchair accessibility. 5 rooms.
Prices. Dec 15–Apr 15: doubles $150–$270 EP; suites $450–$600 EP. Low season: doubles $110–$190 EP; suites $230–$310 EP. Add $46 per person for MAP.

ROYAL PAVILION

💼	🛏	🍴	🌅	TOTAL
72.7%	86.4%	77.3%	77.3%	78.4%

Sharing gardens with its sister property, Glitter Bay, this 10-acre resort on the west coast consists of a three-story Moorish-style building on the beach and one villa fronting the gardens. The hotel was built in 1987 and is affiliated with the Royal Westmoreland Golf & Country Club.

Reader Report

"What a view! An oversized lanai with a crisp white latticed deck rail turned the room into a suite. Seersucker bathrobes,

*inviting us into coolness after a day on the beach, completed
the sense of luxury."*

JUDE E. KEAN, SARATOGA SPRINGS, NEW YORK

*"Peaceful, quiet, and beautiful...a personal experience, where
the manager takes time to meet all the guests. Breakfast and
lunch are served outside. Great location."*

BARBARA DANNENBERG, PURCHASE, NEW YORK

*"Rooms couldn't be nicer. The gold courses are great, too—
and I'm spoiled, coming from California.*

GUS ALBERS, FALLBROOK, CALIFORNIA

Address. Porters, St. James, Barbados, W.I., tel. 809/422–
5555 or 800/283–8666, fax 809/422–3940.

Affiliation. Pemberton Hotels.

Rooms. 72 suites and 1 villa with 3 suites. All have minibars
and air-conditioning.

Facilities. 2 restaurants, 2 bars/lounges, 2 lighted tennis courts,
18-hole golf course nearby, horseback riding nearby, efitness-
room with weights and aerobics machines, aerobics classes,
massages, salon, 24-hr room service, dry-cleaning, afternoon
tea, conference center with business services, dive center, sailboats, watersports.

TV and VCR. TVs for rent and in public area, with 5 channels
including CNN, and cable movie channels. VCRs for rent and in
public area.

No-smoking rooms. None.

Credit cards. AE, DC, D, MC, V.

Restrictions. Min. 10 nights Dec 18–Jan 2. No children under
12 Dec 18–Jan 1 and Feb 3–Mar 2.

Wheelchair accessibility. 2 rooms.

Prices. Dec 17–Mar 29: suites $485–$545 EP; villa suites
$480–$1,060 EP; villa $1,430–$1,595 EP. Low season:
suites $250–$365 EP; villa suites $245–$720 EP; villa
$715–$1,070 EP. Prices are per villa or suite. For MAP, add
$60 per person; $40 in summer.

SANDY LANE

👔	🛏	🍴	☀	**TOTAL**
72.3%	**66.0%**	**72.3%**	**76.6%**	**71.8%**

A four-story, white coral-stone Palladian structure, built in
1961 and renovated in 1991, is the centerpiece of this
380-acre west coast resort. Stairs lead down to the beach.

Reader Report

*"Dining on the veranda next to the beautiful Caribbean is as
close to heaven as you can imagine! The wide, smooth beach
leads to a wonderful swimming area. The golf course is
unbelievable, with long, beautifully cared-for fairways and
greens. The staff is pleasant and prompt."*

J. MILTON HUTSON, NEW YORK, NEW YORK

"Whispered elegance. I found the older part of the hotel most charming, including the toaster in the room—the newer rooms are larger, but the ocean view suffers."

SEAN O'HARA, PHOENIX, ARIZONA

"Fabulous beach, food, and accommodations—very expensive but most definitely worth it."

RICHARD VAN CLEEF, OKLAHOMA CITY, OKLAHOMA

Address. St. James, Barbados, W.I., tel. 809/432–1311 or 800/225–5843, fax 809/432–2954.

Affiliation. Forte Hotels.

Rooms. 120 rooms, 90 suites. All have minibars, air-conditioning, and ceiling fans.

Facilities. 2 restaurants, 5 bars/lounges, 4 lighted tennis courts, 1 unlighted, 18-hole golf course, freshwater pool, horseback riding nearby, exercise room with weights and aerobic machines, aerobics classes, massages, salon, 24-hr room service, dry-cleaning, conference center with business services, supervised children's program, watersports.

TV and VCR. TVs in all rooms, with 11 channels including CNN and cable movie channels. No VCRs.

No-smoking rooms. None.

Credit cards. AE, DC, MC, V.

Restrictions. Min. 14 nights Dec 22–Jan 6.

Wheelchair accessibility. No accessible rooms.

Prices. Jan 6–Apr 20: doubles $765–$1,150 MAP; suites $1,000–$2,100 MAP. Low season: doubles $545–$695 MAP, $485–$635 with breakfast; suites $645–$945 MAP, $585–$885 with breakfast.

BERMUDA

| 90.3% | 80.5% | 73.9% | 79.8% | **TOTAL** 81.0% |

Reader Report

"Bermuda is almost too good to be true. We have wonderful memories of blue water, pink beaches, and pastel dwellings."

ROBERTA SANDRIN, DERWOOD, MARYLAND

"Without question, Bermuda is one of the most civilized paradises there is. Although it is more geared to polite adults, there is loads for kids to do. St. Georges seems a little less stuffy than Hamilton and the resorts."

MAGGIE STEVENS, CUMBERLAND FORESIDE, MAINE

"A scenic, friendly, and crime-free paradise for golfers and water sports enthusiasts. Diverse resorts and smaller hotels for all budgets."

JOAN JOHNSON, VIENNA, VIRGINIA

"Hospitable islanders and warm breezes that caress colorful flowers around limestone houses. Expensive, but worth it."

NANETTE MACASINAG, MYRTLE BEACH, SOUTH CAROLINA

"Bermuda regularly inspires love at first sight. The sparkling beaches, pastel houses, and British accents will enchant and charm you. A cruise makes it affordable to vacation on this otherwise expensive island."

MARIE AYERS, SUMMERVILLE, GEORGIA

Islands. Bermuda is a 21-square-mile protectorate of the United Kingdom, with a population of about 56,000.
Language. The official language is English.

Visitor Information

In the U.S. Contact the **Bermuda Department of Tourism** (310 Madison Ave., Suite 201, New York, NY 10017, tel. 212/818–9800 or 800/223–6106, fax 212/983–5289; 245 Peachtree Center Ave., Suite 803, Atlanta, GA 30303, tel. 404/524–1541, fax 404/586–9933; 44 School St., Suite 1010, Boston, MA 02108, tel. 617/742–0405, fax 617/723–7786; 150 N. Wacker Dr., Suite 170, Chicago, IL 60606, tel. 312/782–5486, fax 312/704–6996; 3151 Cahuenga Blvd., Suite 111, Los Angeles, CA 90068, tel. 213/436–0744, 800/421–0000, fax 213/436–0750).
In Canada. Contact the **Bermuda Department of Tourism** (1200 Bay St., Suite 1004, Toronto, Ont. M5R 2A5, tel. 416/923–9600 or 800/387–1304, fax 416/923–4840).
In the U.K. Contact the **Bermuda Department of Tourism** (BCB Ltd., 1 Battersea Church Rd., London SW11 3LY, tel. 071/734–8813, fax 071/352–6501).
In Bermuda. Contact the **Bermuda Visitors Service Bureaus**

BERMUDA

ATLANTIC OCEAN

N

KEY

⚓ Cruise Ship Dock
⚓ Ferry Route
—— Railway Route
—
■ Hotel or Resort

0   2 miles
0   3 km

Fort St. Catherine
St. Catherine Beach
Town of St. George
St. David's Lighthouse
St. George's Island
Tobacco Bay
Mullet Bay Rd.
St. George's Harbour
St. David's Rd.
St. David's Island
Sea Gardens
Castle Harbour
Kindley Field Rd.
The Causeway
Coney Island
Grotto Bay Beach Hotel & Tennis Club
Harrington Sound Rd.
Blue Hole
TUCKER'S TOWN
Marriott's Castle Harbour Resort
Pink Beach Club
John Smith's Bay
Sea Gardens
Church Bay
HARRINGTON
Crow Hill North
Harrington Sound
HAMILTON
SMITH'S
Harrington Sound Rd.
Ariel Sands Beach Club
North Shore Rd.
DEVONSHIRE
South Rd.
White Sands Hotel
PAGET
Stonington Beach Hotel
Devonshire Dock
Hamilton
Waterloo House
The Princess
Newcastle
Egan St.
Middle Rd.
The
Harmony Club
Horizons & Cottages
WARWICK
Harbour Rd.
Southampton Princess
Warwick Long Bay
Middle Rd.
South Rd.
Horseshoe Bay
Gibbs Hill Lighthouse
Sea Gardens
Belmont Hotel, Golf & Country Club
Hamilton Harbour
Hawkins Island
Little Sound
Great Sound
Cobbler's Island
Clarence Cove
Spanish Pt. Rd.
Spanish Point
PEMBROKE
The Reefs
Sonesta Beach Hotel & Spa
SOUTHAMPTON
West Whale Bay
Pompano Beach Club
Spring Benny's Bay
Middle Rd.
SANDYS
Lantana Colony Club
Somerset Island
Somerset Bridge
Cambridge Beaches
Sea Gardens
Somerset
Waterford I.
Watford Bridge
Boaz I.
Malabar Rd.
Ireland Island South
Ireland Island North

(Hamilton Ferry Terminal Building., 8 Front St., tel. 441/295–1480 or 441/295–4201; Civil Air Terminal-Airport, 2 Kindley Field Rd., tel. 441/293–0736), the **Bermuda Visitor's Information Centres** (Royal Naval Dockyard, The Cooperage, tel. 441/234–3824; 7 King's Sq., next to Town Hall, St. Georges, tel. 441/297–1642; 86 Somerset Rd., near St. James Church, Somerset, tel. 441/234–1388), or the **Bermuda Department of Tourism** (43 Church St., Hamilton, tel. 441/292–0023, fax 441/292–7537).

ARIEL SANDS BEACH CLUB

👤	🛏	✕	≈	**TOTAL**
77.8%	**38.9%**	**55.6%**	**61.6%**	**58.3%**

This cottage colony on the south coast, in Devonshire Parish, has a one-story, white limestone clubhouse and white cottages around the grounds; each containing between two and eight units. Built in 1955, the hotel was renovated in 1993.

Reader Report

"Its biggest asset, in my opinion, is the natural saltwater ocean pool carved out of rock next to the beach—great for families with children. Dining was the other area of note—the Swiss chef prepared delectable meals, among the best I've had on that island."

MICHAEL A. FREIBAND, ARLINGTON, VIRGINIA

"In our small cottage the little second bedroom was perfect for our teenage son—it gave all of us just enough privacy. Very friendly staff, lovely beach views."

EDWARD FLEISCHMAN, WASHINGTON, DC

"Food in the main dining area was very good (and fattening!). Good beach for snorkeling and swimming."

MARGOT BIANCHI, WILMINGTON, NORTH CAROLINA

"I have stayed there twice and would happily stay there again and again! The rooms are large and well-appointed, the service is excellent, the setting (right on the beach) is gorgeous. Bermuda is one of my favorite spots, and the Ariel Sands is more Bermudian to me than the big resort hotels like the Princesses, Marriott's Castle Harbour, and the Sonesta."

PHIL BENNIS, LYNBROOK, NEW YORK

Address. Box HM 334, Hamilton HM BX, Bermuda, tel. 441/236–1010 or 800/468–6610, fax 441/236–0087.
Rooms. 49 rooms, 3 suites. All have air-conditioning. 10 rooms and 2 suites have ceiling fans.
Facilities. Restaurant, bar/lounge, 2 lighted tennis courts, unlighted tennis court, saltwater pool, freshwater pool, exercise room with weights and aerobic machines, aerobics classes, conference center with business services, supervised children's program.

TV and VCR. TVs in public area and for rent, with 2 channels. VCR in public area and for rent.

No-smoking rooms. None.

Credit cards. AE, MC, V.

Wheelchair accessibility. 6 rooms.

Prices. Apr 15–Nov 14: doubles $268–$356 MAP, $248–$3336 with breakfast, $218–$306 EP; suites $356 MAP, $326 with breakfast, $306 EP. Low season: doubles $198–$270 MAP, $178–$250 with breakfast, $148–220 EP; suites $270 MAP, $240 with breakfast, $220 EP.

BELMONT HOTEL, GOLF & COUNTRY CLUB

				TOTAL
60.0%	50.0%	53.3%	63.3%	56.7%

This four-story pink hotel, built in 1898 and renovated regularly ever since, is on 115 acres across the harbor from Hamilton, with its own ferry dock. It's two miles from the beach.

Reader Report

"A nice old hotel with a dock where you can catch the ferry to downtown—a nice touch."

NAME WITHHELD, CHAMPAIGN, ILLINOIS

"It's one of the older hotels on the island, but rooms were nice and clean. The location is fine, with a ferry landing and bus stop right in front. The golf course was interesting and playable but not plush—I'd give it a 6 or 7 on a scale of 10 (we played in the off-season)."

HOWARD B. ADAIR, GREENSBORO, NORTH CAROLINA

Address. Box WK 251, Warwick WK BX, Bermuda, tel. 441/236–1301 or 800/225–5843, fax 441/236–6867.

Affiliation. Forte Hotels.

Rooms. 151 rooms, 1 suite. All accommodations have air-conditioning, and the suite also has a ceiling fan.

Facilities. Restaurant, bar/lounge, 3 lighted tennis courts, 18-hole golf course, saltwater pool, supervised children's program.

TV and VCR. TVs in public area and in 1 room, with 43 channels including CNN. No VCRs.

No-smoking rooms. None.

Credit cards. AE, DC, MC, V.

Wheelchair accessibility. No accessible rooms.

Prices. Apr 1–Oct 31: doubles $225–$250 MAP, $165–$190 with breakfast, $135–$160 EP; suite $270 MAP, $210 with breakfast, $180 EP. Low season: doubles $210–$235 MAP, $150–$175 with breakfast, $120–$145 EP; suite $255 MAP, $195 with breakfast, $165 EP.

CAMBRIDGE BEACHES

				TOTAL
83.0%	78.7%	80.9%	93.6%	84.0%

Near Somerset Village in the West End, this cottage colony dates from 1900. Its single-story clubhouse and cottages sit on a 25-acre peninsula with six beaches and a dock for the hotel's own ferry.

Reader Report

"Lovely, lovely property—wonderful and romantic. I was exceedingly impressed. Excellent service, absolutely top-notch."

NAME WITHHELD, DALLAS, TEXAS

"The resort is far from town and everything else, but the quiet is beautiful and the beaches and grounds are lovely. The staff seems proud to serve the devoted group of clientele."

CAROL BLODGETT, NEW RICHMOND, OHIO

Address. 30 Kings Point Rd., Somerset MA02, Bermuda, tel. 441/234–0331 or 800/468–7300, fax 441/234–3352.
Affiliation. None.
Rooms. 82 rooms, including 30 suites and 2 2-bedroom cottages. All have air-conditioning and ceiling fans. All suites and villas and some 39 rooms have whirlpool tubs. All rooms and suites have tub only.
Facilities. 3 restaurants, 3 bars/lounges, lighted tennis court, 2 unlighted, saltwater pool, exercise room with weights and aerobic machines, aerobics classes, health and beauty spa with over 100 treatments, dry-cleaning, conference center with business services, marina, putting green, golf course nearby.
TV and VCR. TVs in public area and in some rooms, with 40 channels including CNN and cable movie channels. VCRs in public area and in rooms on request.
No-smoking rooms. None.
Credit cards. No credit cards.
Restrictions. Min. 5 nights May–Oct. Children under 5 must be under adult supervision at all times.
Wheelchair accessibility. No accessible rooms.
Prices. Apr 4–Nov 15: doubles $335–$475 MAP; suites $510–$550 MAP; cottages $1075 MAP. Low season: doubles $230–$315 MAP; suites $340–$370 MAP; cottages $720 MAP.

GROTTO BAY BEACH HOTEL & TENNIS CLUB

👷	🛏️	🍴	〰️	**TOTAL**
63.3%	**34.7%**	**46.9%**	**69.4%**	**53.6%**

This 21-acre beach resort has a private dock on enclosed Grotto Bay, at the west end of the causeway from the airport. Guests stay in three-story lodges. The hotel was built in 1973, expanded in 1989, and renovated in 1995.

Reader Report

"It is nice for families—informal, quiet, and reasonably priced (for Bermuda), with a small but good and protected beach. Rooms are of adequate size for a family and brightly decorated, with private balconies."

JAMES R. SANDERS, PLAINWELL, MICHIGAN

"Very handy to the airport—yet little jet noise. Well-kept grounds and very good tennis courts. About as 'un-Hamilton' as you can get. Would go back—very nice!"

NAME WITHHELD, EAST ORLEANS, MASSACHUSETTS

"The resort is very low-key with a friendly staff. The dining package is adequate, but doesn't inspire you to ask for the recipes. The tiny beach is upstaged by the terrific pool-bar area."

JUDY DeBOARD, ORLANDO, FLORIDA

Address. 11 Blue Hole Hill, Hamilton Parish CR 04, Bermuda, tel. 441/293–8333 or 800/582–3190, fax 441/293–2306.
Rooms. 201 rooms, 3 suites. All have air-conditioning. All rooms have refrigerators, in-room safes, coffee makers, 1 has a Jacuzzi. All suites have minibars, 1 has a Jacuzzi.
Facilities. 2 restaurants, 2 bars/lounges, 2 lighted tennis courts, 2 unlighted, freshwater pool, exercise room with weights and aerobic machines, dry-cleaning, conference center with business services, supervised children's program, dive center, sailboats.
TV and VCR. TVs in all rooms, with 4 channels and cable. VCR in public area and in rooms on request.
No-smoking rooms. None.
Credit cards. AE, MC, V.
Wheelchair accessibility. No accessible rooms.
Prices. Apr 1–Oct 31: doubles $281–$294 MAP, $215–$228 with breakfast, $185–$198 EP; suites $446–$596 MAP, $380–$530 with breakfast, $350–$500 EP. Low season: doubles $206–$226 MAP, $140–$170 with breakfast, $110–$130 EP; suites $446–$596 MAP, $380–$530 with breakfast, $350–$500 EP.

THE HARMONY CLUB

👔	🛏	✕	☀	TOTAL
80.0%	60.0%	53.3%	60.0%	63.3%

This two-story pink-and-white hotel has an all-inclusive, adults-only policy; it's in three acres of gardens, in Paget, half a mile from a beach. Built in the 1890s, the hotel was renovated during the 1930s and expanded in 1967.

Reader Report

"An all-inclusive resort where the value received is tops. The staff is friendly and helpful, the food very good, and the mood relaxing, although the facilities are limited (the swimming pool is great, but the beach is a bus ride away)."

JOHN H. MYERS, DALLAS, TEXAS

"Tops, the best on the island. I've been there four times. A full-service resort, for couples only. The service is perfect."

JEAN MARTIN, WOONSOCKET, RHODE ISLAND

Address. Box PG 299, Paget PG BX, Bermuda, tel. 441/236–3500 or 800/225–5843, fax 441/236–2624.
Affiliation. Forte Hotels.
Rooms. 71 rooms. All with air-conditioning.
Facilities. Restaurant, bar/lounge, 2 unlighted tennis courts, freshwater pool, horseback riding, aerobics classes, massages, dry-cleaning.
TV and VCR. TVs in all rooms, with 4 channels including CNN and cable movie channels. VCR in public area.
No-smoking rooms. None.
Credit cards. AE, DC, MC, V.
Restrictions. No children under 18.
Wheelchair accessibility. No accessible rooms.
Prices. Apr 15–Oct 15: doubles $470. Low season: doubles $365. Rates are all-inclusive.

HORIZONS & COTTAGES

👔	🛏	✕	☀	TOTAL
82.4%	64.7%	70.6%	82.4%	75.0%

At this cottage colony with an 18th-century main house, guests stay in various cottages dating from around 1950, set on 25 acres in Paget, a quarter-mile from the south shore beaches. The newest rooms date from 1987.

Reader Report

"Bermuda is one of our favorite spots in the world, and we strongly prefer cottage-type places over hotels, where you have dinner at a scheduled time with six hundred of your

closest friends. Horizons is our first choice. The staff is especially accommodating, the central location makes either end of the island accessible, and the scenery and beaches are breathtakingly beautiful. The decor is typical Bermuda: antiques, colorful prints."

NORMA AND JERRY NOELL, MOUNT AIRY, NORTH CAROLINA

"Rooms are large and beautiful with great views of the ocean, and there's a terrace, a pool, and very good food. The only negative is that you're not on the beach, but it is a very short walk. As is typical in Bermuda, guests tend to be a mixture of honeymooners and retirees, so no one is up very late."

WENDY ZINN, CLEVELAND HEIGHTS, OHIO

Address. Box PG 198, South Shore Rd., Paget PG BX, Bermuda, tel. 441/236–0048, 800/468–0022, fax 441/236–1981.
Affiliation. Horizons Ltd., Relais & Châteaux.
Rooms. 44 rooms, 3 suites, 2 villas. All have air-conditioning. All suites and villas and 32 rooms have ceiling fans. Both villas, 6 rooms, and 2 suites have Jacuzzis.
Facilities. 2 restaurants, bar/lounge, 2 unlighted tennis courts, 4 lighted and 4 unlighted tennis courts nearby, 9-hole golf course, freshwater pool, horseback riding, exercise room with weights and aerobic machines.
TV and VCR. TVs in rooms on request. VCRs for rent.
No-smoking rooms. None.
Credit cards. No credit cards.
Restrictions. Min. 5 nights year-round. No children under 3 in one restaurant.
Wheelchair accessibility. No accessible rooms.
Prices. Mar 15–Nov 30: doubles $300–$500 MAP; suites $520 MAP; villas $700 MAP. Low season: doubles $260–400 MAP; suites $460 MAP; villas $500 MAP.

LANTANA COLONY CLUB

👤	🛏	✗	☀	TOTAL
80.0%	56.0%	76.0%	76.0%	72.0%

Located on the West End near the Somerset Bridge, this cottage colony has extensive gardens and its own dock; guests stay in a variety of suites and cottages around the 20-acre grounds. The hotel was built in 1958, renovated in 1985, and expanded in 1987.

Reader Report

"A beautiful property with a small but adequate beach (pool, too), within a half-mile of the ferry to Hamilton. It's delightful and relaxing, and quieter than the big hotels. But it's not for people with mobility problems—there's too much walking and too many steps."

DIANE ASCIONE HOROWITZ, BLOOMFIELD, NEW JERSEY

"Very luxurious, with excellent food and wonderful yet discreet service. It's especially great if you play croquet."

BERNARD FENSTERWALD, RESTON, VIRGINIA

Address. 53 Railway Trail, Box SB 90, Somerset Bridge SB BX, Bermuda, tel. 441/234–0141, 800/468–3733, fax 441/234–2562.

Affiliation. Insignia Resorts and The Bermuda Collection.

Rooms. 64 rooms, 19 suites, 6 villas. All have air-conditioning. All suites and villas and 24 rooms have minibars and refrigerators.

Facilities. 2 restaurants, 2 bars/lounges, 2 unlighted tennis courts, 18-hole golf course nearby, 2 croquet lawns, freshwater pool, massages by appointment, salon nearby, horseback riding nearby, dry-cleaning, dive center nearby, sailboats.

TV and VCR. TVs for rent, with 3 channels including CNN. VCRs for rent.

No-smoking rooms. None.

Credit cards. AE, MC, V.

Restrictions. No children under 3. Min. 4 nights May 1–Oct 31.

Wheelchair accessibility. No accessible rooms.

Prices. May 1–Oct 31: doubles $300—$465 MAP; suites $400–$445 MAP; villas $300—$465 MAP. Low season: doubles $210–$315 MAP; suites $290–$315 MAP; villas $210–$290 MAP.

MARRIOTT'S CASTLE HARBOUR RESORT

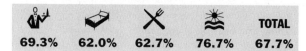

69.3%	62.0%	62.7%	76.7%	**TOTAL** 67.7%

A main building, constructed in 1931, with three modern wings added in 1986, sits on 250 hilltop acres on a strip of land between Harrington Sound and Castle Harbour. The hotel was most recently renovated in 1991.

Reader Report

"A top-notch luxury resort in a magnificent setting; everyone strives to please. Food prices were the only shocker."

C. C. MILLER, MIDLAND, MICHIGAN

"Excellent in terms of service, food, and comfort. Really a 'white glove' property."

NAME WITHHELD, PALM BEACH GARDENS, FLORIDA

Address. 2 Paynters Rd., Tuckers Town (mailing address: Box HM 841, Hamilton HM CX, Bermuda), tel. 441/293–2040 or 800/223–6388 for reservations, fax 441/293–8288.

Affiliation. Marriott.

Rooms. 384 rooms, 18 suites. All have air-conditioning, hair dryers, ironing supplies. Many have a balcony or terrace.

Facilities. 3 restaurants, 3 bars/lounges, 2 beaches, 6 unlighted tennis courts, 18-hole golf course, 3 freshwater pools, exercise room with weights and aerobic machines, sauna, salon, special-ty shops, moped rental, conference center with business ser-vices, supervised children's program.

TV and VCR. TVs in all rooms, with 10 channels including CNN. VCRs in rooms on request.

No-smoking rooms. 128 rooms.

Credit cards. AE, DC, MC, V.

Wheelchair accessibility. 4 rooms.

Prices. Apr 1–Nov 10: $344–$479 MAP, doubles $270–$405 with breakfast, $240–$375 EP; suites $540–$1,075 MAP, $480–$1,015 with breakfast, $450–$985 EP. Low season: doubles $226–$281 MAP, $157–$212 with breakfast, $130–$185 EP.

NEWSTEAD

👤	🛏	✕	🌅	**TOTAL**
76.9%	**61.5%**	**76.9%**	**69.2%**	**71.2%**

The two-story colonial manor house here, built in 1850 and regularly renovated since then, has been expanded by the addi-tion of poolside units and cottages. The four-acre property over-looks Hamilton Harbor and has its own swimming dock.

Reader Report

"One of the grande dames of Bermuda, but she's a little frayed around the edges. Although the common rooms were stunning, many of the guest rooms were in need of paint and dusting. The hotel was elegant and formal—more utensils were set out at breakfast than I knew what to do with."

MATTIE HENDRICK, NARBERTH, PENNSYLVANIA

"Rooms were small but beautiful, the gardens lovely, and the atmosphere gracious, quite formal, and very British—with mostly English guests. The swimming pool is on a hilltop. Activities were very limited, but the food was good."

NAME WITHHELD, DENVER, COLORADO

Address. Box PG 196, 27 Harbour Rd., Paget PG 02, Bermuda, tel. 441/236–6060 or 800/468–4111, fax 441/236–7454.

Affiliation. Horizons Ltd.

Rooms. 50 rooms, 2 suites. All accommodations have air-condi-tioning, and all rooms have ceiling fans.

Facilities. 2 restaurants, 2 bars/lounges, 2 unlighted tennis courts, 4 lighted and 4 unlighted tennis courts nearby, freshwa-ter pool, exercise room with weights and aerobic machines nearby, sauna, dry-cleaning, conference center with business services.

TV and VCR. TVs in public area and in some rooms, with 30 channels including CNN and cable movie channels. VCRs in rooms on request.

No-smoking rooms. None.

Credit cards. AE, MC, V.

Wheelchair accessibility. No accessible rooms.

Prices. May 1–Oct 31: doubles $266–$348 MAP; suites $355–$375 MAP. Low season: doubles $230–$280 MAP; suites $290–$305 MAP. For breakfast only, deduct $50 per couple.

PINK BEACH CLUB

| 90.0% | 86.7% | 63.3% | 86.7% | TOTAL 81.7% |

This 16 1\2-acre cottage colony on the eastern end of the south coast consists of a variety of low-rise pink cottages, a clubhouse dating from 1947, and two private beaches. The hotel was expanded in 1970 and renovated in 1995.

Reader Report

"A well-run resort, with fine service, excellent food, and beautiful views. It's close to a bus line, so it's easy to get to any part of the island. Breakfast is served on your patio if you wish, overlooking the ocean—a treat."

NAME WITHHELD, SUMMIT, PENNSYLVANIA

"Excellent location, right on the ocean and next to the Mid-Ocean Golf Course."

RICHARD BLAIR, GREAT MEADOWS, NEW JERSEY

Address. Box HM 1017, Hamilton HM DX, Bermuda, tel. 441/293–1666 or 800/355–6161, fax 441/293–8935.
Affiliation. Elite Hotels Inc.
Rooms. 41 executive suites, 46 deluxe rooms, 2 studios, all in 25 cottages. All have air-conditioning.
Facilities. 2 restaurants, bar/lounge, 2 unlighted tennis courts, 2 18-hole golf courses nearby, mixed freshwater/saltwater pool, entertainment 7 nights a week, small meeting room, exercise room with weights, dry-cleaning.
TV and VCR. TVs for rent; cable TV with 50 channels including CNN available in club house. VCRs for rent.
No-smoking rooms. None.
Credit cards. AE, MC, V.
Restrictions. Min. 5 nights during holidays. Some restrictions for children under 5.
Wheelchair accessibility. No accessible rooms.
Prices. Apr 15–Oct 31: doubles $330–$355 MAP, $290–$315 with breakfast; suites $340–$380 MAP, $300–$340 with breakfast. Low season: doubles $220–$237 MAP, $180–$197 with breakfast; suites $227–$253 MAP, $187–$213 with breakfast.

POMPANO BEACH CLUB

| 76.2% | 42.9% | 66.7% | 81.0% | TOTAL 66.7% |

The two-story, pink-and-white stone main building and the smaller guest-room buildings here are set on 12 acres in Southampton, on the west coast. The hotel was built in 1956, expanded in 1975, and renovated in 1994.

Reader Report

"The perfect little getaway, perched on a mountain with a beautiful view of the Atlantic. Casual dining, friendly atmosphere, relaxed service—all the qualities that make Bermuda so special."

RANDEE LEVINE, PORT WASHINGTON, NEW YORK

"Very laid-back and relaxed, with friendly people. Tea is served every afternoon. The breakfasts and dinners were the best I've ever eaten—every night! The golf course can be seen off your balcony, and it's right on the ocean. "

MADELINE WEBB, MEMPHIS, TENNESSEE

"I can't say enough good things about [the resort]. It's as quiet as you want it to be, or you can find nightlife...The food is incredible!"

MRS. ELLIOTT PRATT, BOSTON, MASSACHUSETTS

Address. 36 Pompano Beach Rd., Southampton SB 03, Bermuda, tel. 441/234–0222 or 800/343–4155, fax 441/234–1694.
Affiliation. The Bermuda Collection.
Rooms. 52 rooms, 20 suites. All have air-conditioning and refrigerators.
Facilities. Restaurant, 2 bars/lounges, unlighted tennis court, 18-hole golf course, freshwater pool, exercise room with weights and aerobic machines, dry-cleaning, conference center with business services, sunfish sailboats, 2 outdoor Jacuzzis.
TV and VCR. TV in public area only, with 35 channels including CNN. VCRs in public area, and in rooms on request.
No-smoking rooms. None.
Credit cards. AE, MC,V as of Apr 1 1996.
Restrictions. Min. 4–5 nights during major U.S. holidays.
Wheelchair accessibility. No accessible rooms.
Prices. May 1–Nov 14: doubles $335–$360 MAP, $305–$330 with breakfast; suites $345 MAP, $315 with breakfast. Low season: doubles $220–240 MAP, $190–$210 with breakfast; suites $230 MAP, $200 with breakfast.

THE PRINCESS

👤	🛏	🍴	🌅	TOTAL
68.1%	52.4%	57.8%	75.9%	63.6%

This seven-story, pink Victorian hotel, which opened in 1884 and was completely rebuilt after a fire in 1930, occupies about seven acres right on Hamilton Harbor with its own ferry dock. Facilities at the sister hotel, the Southampton Princess, 20 minutes away by ferry, are available for guests. There's no beach.

Reader Report

"It continues to be a fine hotel, within easy walking distance of downtown Hamilton. You also get dining privileges at the Southampton Princess, which is on the beach in a lovely setting."

ELSIE AND JACK HAAG, GLEN ROCK, NEW JERSEY

"Bermuda has friendly people and a beautiful climate; it's a fabulous vacation spot—especially because of the Princess Hamilton and our waiter, Romeo. We are going back."

MARY JANE MUNCEY, WILLIAMSTOWN, NEW JERSEY

Address. 76 Pitts Bay Rd., Hamilton (mailing address: Box HM 837, Hamilton HM CX, Bermuda), tel. 441/295–3000 or 800/223—1818, fax 441/295–1914.
Affiliation. Princess Hotels International.
Rooms. 446 rooms, 26 suites. All have air-conditioning and voice mail.
Facilities. 3 restaurants, 2 bars/lounges, saltwater pool, freshwater pool, exercise room with weights and aerobic machines, massages, sauna, salon, dry-cleaning, conference center with business services, dive center. For facilities at the Southampton Princess, see below.
TV and VCR. TVs in all rooms, with 13 channels including CNN. VCRs in rooms on request.
No-smoking rooms. 50 rooms.
Credit cards. AE, DC, MC, V.
Wheelchair accessibility. 2 accessible rooms.
Prices. Apr 12–Nov 16: doubles $310–$420 MAP, $240–$350 with breakfast, $210–$320 EP; suites $450–$1,250 MAP, $380–$1,180 with breakfast, $350–$1,150 EP. Low season: doubles $234–$244 MAP, $174–$234 with breakfast, $150–$210 EP; suites $304–$929 MAP, $244–$869 with breakfast, $220–$845 EP.

THE REEFS

73.7%	55.3%	63.2%	81.6%	TOTAL 68.4%

At this 7-acre resort on the western end of the south shore, guests stay in the pink Bermuda cottage-style clubhouse, in private cottages, and in poolside or hillside rooms with balconies, known as lanais. The hotel was built in 1947, expanded in 1984 and 1985, and renovated in 1994.

Reader Report

"A delightful hideaway with extremely personal service, nothing at all like the too-large and glitzy superhotels. A real find!"

REV. JOHN M. SCHULTZ, OIL CITY, PENNSYLVANIA

"We recommend it highly. Service was great—they knew our names everywhere we went. We had everything we needed right there."

BRAD AND DEANNA WADDELL, MARTINEZ, GEORGIA

Address. 56 South Shore Rd., Southampton SN 02, Bermuda, tel. 441/238–0222 or 800/742–2008, fax 441/238–8372.
Rooms. 59 rooms, 8 suites. All have air-conditioning. 7 suites and 49 rooms have ceiling fans.
Facilities. 2 restaurants, 2 bars/lounges, 2 unlighted tennis courts, freshwater pool, exercise room with weights and aerobic machines, massages, dry-cleaning.
TV and VCR. TVs in public area and in 8 suites, with 42 channels including CNN. VCRs in public area and in 8 suites.
No-smoking rooms. None.
Credit cards. No credit cards.
Restrictions. Min. 5 nights Apr 15–Nov 10.
Wheelchair accessibility. No accessible rooms.
Prices. Apr 14–Nov 10: doubles $336–$396 MAP; suites $366–$926 MAP. Low season: doubles $220–$280 MAP; suites $250–$630 MAP.

SONESTA BEACH RESORT BERMUDA

68.8%	58.8%	58.8%	85.0%	TOTAL 67.8%

This contemporary, four-story hotel on the western end of the south shore, sits on a low 25-acre promontory above three beaches. The hotel was built in 1961, expanded in 1982, and most recently renovated in 1994.

Reader Report

"Although not very wide, the pink-sand, crescent-shape beach, just steps from the hotel, is beautiful. Service is very friendly."

CHRISTINA BRAUN, OCEANSIDE, NEW YORK

"Excellent food."

NAME WITHHELD, BRANT BEACH, NEW JERSEY

"The staff was amazingly helpful. Several different restaurants were open, with different dress codes and food, and all were included in the meal plan. The location was good—not far from downtown but also on the beach."

SUSAN AND CHRIS RAND, WALLINGFORD, CONNECTICUT

Address. South Shore Rd., Southampton (mailing address: Box HM 1070, Hamilton HM EX, Bermuda), tel. 441/238–8122 or 800/766-3782, fax 441/238–8463.
Affiliation. Sonesta International.
Rooms. 400 rooms, 35 suites. All have air-conditioning.
Facilities. 5 restaurants, 2 bars/lounges, coffee shop, 2 lighted tennis courts, 4 unlighted, 2 18-hole golf courses nearby, 2 freshwater pools, exercise room with weights and aerobic machines, aerobics classes, massages, sauna, salon, room service, dry-cleaning, conference center with business services, supervised children's program, dive center.
TV and VCR. TVs in all rooms, with 18 channels including CNN. Movies upon request.
No-smoking rooms. 170 rooms.
Credit cards. AE, MC, V.
Wheelchair accessibility. 6 rooms.
Prices. Apr 16–Nov 12: doubles $198–$385 EP; suites $535–$980 EP. Low season: doubles $118–$178 EP; suites $260–$380 EP. Add $50 per person for MAP, $15 for breakfast.

SOUTHAMPTON PRINCESS

				TOTAL
83.6%	73.0%	74.3%	80.3%	77.8%

This contemporary nine-story tower sits on a hilltop near Gibb's Hill Lighthouse, on the western south shore. The resort complex, built in 1972 and renovated in 1989, covers 100 acres and has two beaches.

Reader Report
"Service was wonderful—the beach and the launch to town were only a short walk downstairs. The best vacation I ever had!"

RANDALL BAILEY, ATLANTA, GEORGIA

"On the beach in a lovely setting."

ELSIE AND JACK HAAG, GLEN ROCK, NEW JERSEY

Address. Box HM 1379, Hamilton HM FX, Bermuda, tel. 441/238–8000 or 800/223–1818, fax 441/238–8968.
Affiliation. Princess Hotels International.
Rooms. 600 rooms, 36 suites. All have air-conditioning.

Facilities. 6 restaurants, 2 bars/lounges, coffee shop, 3 lighted tennis courts, 8 unlighted, 18-hole golf course, 2 freshwater pools, exercise room with weights and aerobic machines, aerobics classes, massages, sauna, salon, dry-cleaning, conference center with business services, supervised children's activities, dive center.

TV and VCR. TVs in all rooms, with 13 channels including CNN and pay movies. VCRs in rooms on request.

No-smoking rooms. 100 rooms, 6 suites.

Credit cards. AE, DC, MC, V.

Wheelchair accessibility. 5 rooms.

Prices. Nov 26–Apr 11: doubles $150–$185 EP; suites $335–$1,000 EP. Low season: doubles $319–$519 MAP; suites $590–$2,600 MAP.

STONINGTON BEACH HOTEL

				TOTAL
80.8%	**57.7%**	**88.5%**	**80.8%**	**76.9%**

This modern, 15-acre, low-rise complex—a hotel of the Hospitality and Culinary Institute of Bermuda—sits in the middle of the south shore. Guest quarters are terraced down to a beach. Built in 1980, the hotel was renovated in 1994.

Reader Report

"Expensive, but joyful, relaxing, and home-like. The dining room is run by the Bermuda School of Culinary Arts— the food is excellent and the service superb."

HELEN HUGHES, DUBOIS, PENNSYLVANIA

"We often stay here. It's friendly, and the food is excellent."

JANELLE G. SHAW, NORTH CONWAY, NEW HAMPSHIRE

Address. Box HM 523, Hamilton HM CX, Bermuda, tel. 441/236–5416 or 800/447–7462, fax 441/236–0371.

Affiliation. Hospitality and Culinary Institute of Bermuda.

Rooms. 64 rooms. All with air-conditioning and ceiling fans.

Facilities. Restaurant, bar/lounge, 2 unlighted tennis courts, freshwater pool, dry-cleaning.

TV and VCR. TVs in all rooms, with 42 channels including CNN and cable movie channels. VCR in public area only.

No-smoking rooms. None.

Credit cards. AE, CB, DC, MC, V.

Restrictions. No children under 3.

Wheelchair accessibility. 1 room.

Prices. May 1–Oct 31: $365–$405 MAP. Low season: $228–$260 MAP.

WATERLOO HOUSE

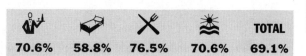

🍸	🛏	🍴	🌅	TOTAL
70.6%	58.8%	76.5%	70.6%	69.1%

A two-story, white-columned town house built in 1815 is the centerpiece of this inn on five acres in Hamilton; guests also stay in pink, two-story stone buildings beside the pool and patio. Rooms were added to the hotel in 1992 and renovation has been ongoing.

Reader Report

"A lovely small English hotel. It's perfect off-season, as it is close to shopping—nice at Christmas. Good service and food."

PHYLLIS WIENBERG, NEW YORK, NEW YORK

"A dining high point of our Bermuda stay."

JEAN L. COBB, WINTHROP, MASSACHUSETTS

"A very good place, especially for a woman traveling alone, because it's so close to downtown Hamilton, so you don't always need an escort. Very quaint—it's decorated as if it were someone's private home. The only thing the least bit negative is that the swimming pool is quite small, but they can arrange transportation to a beach."

ELIZABETH McHUGH, QUINCY, MASSACHUSETTS

"Charming—the location is great for evening walks in Hamilton, and it's one of the few places to dine right on the harbor. It has reciprocal beach arrangements and lovely cool gardens."

SUSAN BUCKLEY, POTOMAC, MARYLAND

Address. Box HM 333, Hamilton HM BX, Bermuda, tel. 441/295–4480 or 800/468–4100, fax 441/295–2585.
Affiliation. Horizons Ltd., Relais & Châteaux
Rooms. 31 rooms, 8 suites. All have air-conditioning. All suites and 22 rooms have ceiling fans. 10 rooms and 7 suites have Jacuzzis.
Facilities. 2 restaurants, 2 bars/lounges, 4 lighted and 4 unlighted tennis courts nearby, 18-hole golf course nearby, freshwater pool, exercise room with weights and aerobic machines nearby, aerobics nearby (with advance notice), dive center, sailboats.
TV and VCR. TVs in some rooms and in public area, with 30 channels including CNN and cable movie channels. VCRs in some rooms and in other rooms on request.
No-smoking rooms. None.
Credit cards. AE, MC, V.
Wheelchair accessibility. No accessible rooms.
Prices. Apr. 1–Nov. 30: doubles $300–$400 MAP, $270–$340 with breakfast; suites $410–$510 MAP, $350–$450 with breakfast. Low season: doubles $250–$330 MAP, $190–$270 with breakfast; suites $320–$400 MAP, $260–$370 with breakfast.

WHITE SANDS HOTEL

| 77.8% | 55.6% | 55.6% | 55.6 % | TOTAL 61.1% |

Located mid-island, in Paget, this two-story guest house was built in 1952, with a terraced wing added in 1970; it's set on six acres, and most rooms are some 250 yards from a beach.

Reader Report

"The excellent location above Grape Bay Beach is minutes from the shore. The restaurant is the best of the hotel's facilities, with excellent food and service. Opt for the MAP meal plan."

CARLOS M. SANTOYO, ARLINGTON, VIRGINIA

"The dining room staff was exceptionally friendly and helpful."

NAME WITHELD, GREENSBURG, PENNSYLVANIA

Address. 55 White Sands Rd., Box PG 174, Paget PG BX, Bermuda, tel. 441/236–2023 or 800/548–0547, fax 441/236–2023.
Rooms. 40 rooms, 3 cottages. All have air-conditioning.
Facilities. Restaurant, 2 bars/lounges, coffee shop, heated fresh-water pool.
TV and VCR. TVs in all rooms, with 12 channels including cable. VCRs for rent with advance notice.
No-smoking rooms. None.
Credit cards. AE, MC, V.
Restrictions. Min. 5 nights Memorial Day weekend.
Wheelchair accessibility. No accessible rooms.
Prices. Apr 1–Nov 15: doubles $250–$290 MAP, $190–$230 EP; cottages $300—$450 EP. Low season: doubles $174–$204 MAP, $114–$144 EP; cottages $250–$375 EP.

BONAIRE

				TOTAL
69.1%	55.6%	65.4%	61.7%	63.2%

Reader Report

"Bonaire is a desert island like Aruba—its beauty is under the sea. It has better snorkeling than any other island I've visited."

ILENE SMITH, TRENTON, MICHIGAN

"No beaches to speak of—coral everywhere—but the beauty is spectacular, and the diving world-class. Don't go for good food unless you like fish!"

MARIANNE REDER, AKRON, OHIO

"Fantastic diving—perfect for beginners. The current is nonexistent, and there are plenty of shallow pristine diving sites. The island is quiet and not very developed."

NAME WITHHELD, PITTSTOWN, NEW JERSEY

Islands. Bonaire is a 122-square-mile independent protectorate of the Netherlands, with a population of about 10,000.
Language. The official language of Bonaire is Dutch, though Papiamento—a mixture of Dutch, Spanish, Portuguese, English, and French—is spoken by the islanders.

Visitor Information
In the U.S. Contact the **Bonaire Tourism Office** (10 Rockefeller Plaza, Suite 900, New York, NY 10020, tel. 212/956–5911 or 800/U–BONAIR, fax 212/956–5913).
In the U.K. There is no tourist office in the U.K.
In Bonaire. Contact the **Tourism Corporation Bonaire** (Kaya Simon Bolivar 12, Kralendijk, Bonaire, Netherlands Antilles, tel. 599/7–8322, fax 599/7–8408).

DIVI FLAMINGO BEACH RESORT & CASINO

				TOTAL
48.3%	27.6%	37.9%	48.3%	40.5%

This all-inclusive resort just north of the airport has a two-story layout, a newer timeshare complex with studio apartments, and the island's only casino. Built in the 1950s the hotel was renovated during the 1960s and expanded in 1974.

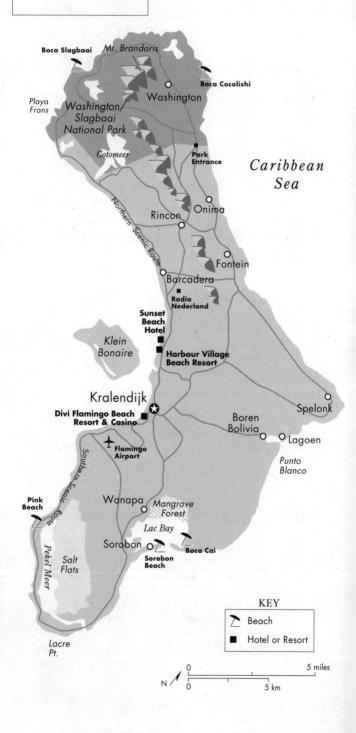

BONAIRE

Boca Slagbaai
Mt. Brandaris
Boca Cocolishi
Washington
Playa Frans
Washington/
Slagbaai
National Park
Gotomeer
Park Entrance

Caribbean Sea

Rincon
Onima
Fontein
Barcadera
Radio Nederland
Sunset Beach Hotel
Klein Bonaire
Harbour Village Beach Resort
Kralendijk
Divi Flamingo Beach Resort & Casino
Spelonk
Boren Bolivia
Lagoen
Flamingo Airport
Punto Blanco
Pink Beach
Wanapa
Mangrove Forest
Lac Bay
Sorobon
Boca Cai
Sorobon Beach
Pekel Meer
Salt Flats
Northern Scenic Route
Southern Scenic Route
Lacre Pt.

KEY

➤ Beach

■ Hotel or Resort

N

| 0 | | 5 miles |
| 0 | | 5 km |

Reader Report

"Excellent dive operation; their dive staff was very accommodating. We were really pleased. The rooms could use some renovation, but overall, no complaints."

IRENE PEARMAN, ST. LOUIS, MISSOURI

"The Flamingo is first-class all the way—the dive center even caters to divers with disabilities."

PAT SKEELE, COLUMBUS, OHIO

"Not a bargain."

MARIANNE REDER, AKRON, OHIO

Address. J. A. Abraham Blvd. (mailing address: Box 43), Bonaire, Netherlands Antilles, tel. 599/7–8285 or 800/367–3484, fax 599/7–8238.
Affiliation. Divi Resorts.
Rooms. 145 rooms. All have air-conditioning. 113 have showers only.
Facilities. 2 restaurants, 2 bars/lounges, coffee shop, lighted tennis court, freshwater pool, horseback riding, 2 dive centers, sailboats.
TV and VCR. TVs in some rooms, with 12 channels including CNN and cable movie channels. No VCRs.
No-smoking rooms. None.
Credit cards. AE, MC, V.
Wheelchair accessibility. 8 rooms.
Prices. Dec 18–Apr 1: $150–$215 MAP. Low season: $84–$125 MAP.

HARBOUR VILLAGE BEACH RESORT

| 50.0% | 57.1% | 42.9% | 71.4% | **TOTAL** 55.4% |

Built in 1990 in Spanish colonial style, this low-rise resort just north of Kralendijk encompasses eight two-story buildings spread out among gardens. It has its own marina.

Reader Report

"By far the best on the island. You have a beautiful beach with palm trees at your doorstep, gorgeous flowers, and manicured grounds. It's very relaxed—you don't feel crowded, only pampered."

BETTY INGRISH, ALEXANDRIA, LOUISIANA

"Lovely, well-appointed rooms, but the property had hardly any guests both times I stayed—rather spooky. I think it's a bit too formal and pricey for Bonaire, an island that attracts primarily divers."

CATHERINE PENNER, ADDRESS WITHHELD

"The room was a bit small but neat and on the beach. Excellent facilities—the restaurant was fine, and there was a nice outdoor bar with a large deck overlooking water. Friendly atmosphere."

ANGELO BELLINI, RINGWOOD, NEW JERSEY

Address. Kaya Gob, N. Debrot 71, Bonaire, Netherlands Antilles, tel. 599/7–7500 or 800/424–0004, fax 599/7–7507.
Rooms. 64 rooms, 10 suites. All have minibars, terraces or decks, ceiling fans, and air-conditioning.
Facilities. 2 restaurants, 2 bars/lounges, freshwater pool, full-service spa and fitness center, excercise classes, dry-cleaning, conference center with business services, dive center, sailboats.
TV and VCR. TVs in all rooms, with 22 channels including CNN and cable movie channels. VCRs for rent.
No-smoking rooms. None.
Credit cards. AE, DC, MC, V.
Wheelchair accessibility. No accessible rooms.
Prices. Dec 17–Jan 7: doubles $295–$325 EP; suites $315–$725 EP. Low season: doubles $265–$295 EP; suites $285–$695 EP. Add $85 per person for AP.

SUNSET BEACH HOTEL

| 33.3% | 20.0% | 33.3% | 53.3% | **TOTAL** 35.0% |

Covered walkways link outlying structures to the central building of this 12-acre low-rise resort on the west coast, a half-mile north of Kralendijk. Built in 1962, the property will finish renovations in Dec 1995.

Reader Report

"Standard rooms but a lovely resort complex. You can't beat the package deal, which includes rooms, tax, and a daily breakfast buffet. Meals at the beach hut are also excellent."

CHARISSE P. RUDOLPH, CAPE MAY, NEW JERSEY

"Very laid-back, restful and peaceful. I liked the outdoor restaurant. There's plenty to do there, even if you don't dive."

ED DZURKO, SOLON, OHIO

"For divers, it is really excellent—they really cater to them (non-divers might want to consider going elsewhere). There is really nice diving right off the beach in front of the hotel. Food was mediocre, rooms were moderately comfortable."

MARILYN SUZUKI-DAY, NEW CARROLLTON, MARYLAND

Address. Box 333, Kaya Gouveneur Debrot 75, Bonaire, Netherlands Antilles, tel. 599/7–5300 or 599/7-8291 for reservations, fax 599/7–8118.
Affiliation. Sunset Resorts.
Rooms. 142 rooms, 3 suites. All have air-conditioning, safes,

refrigerators and direct-dial telephones. 27 rooms have showers only, 115 rooms and all suites have bathtubs only.

Facilities. Restaurant, 2 bars/lounges, 2 lighted tennis courts, dive center, watersports, freshwater pool, 3 whirlpool spas, fitness center, sailboats.

TV and VCR. TVs in all rooms, with 22 channels including CNN and cable movie channels. VCR in public area.

No-smoking rooms. None.

Credit cards. AE, DC, MC, V.

Wheelchair accessibility. 3 rooms.

Prices. Dec 20–Apr 15: doubles $125–$155 EP; suites $185 EP. Low season: doubles $95–$115 EP; suites $155 EP.

THE BRITISH VIRGIN ISLANDS
Virgin Gorda

				TOTAL
87.7%	**54.0%**	**57.2%**	**82.5%**	**69.2%**

Reader Report

"Very interesting rock formations and great snorkeling [on Virgin Gorda]."

MARY K. ELLENWOOD, FORT WORTH, TEXAS

"Virgin Gorda is like a boring version of Tortola. There's not enough here to spend a week. If you're staying on St. Thomas, you might come over for a day to Tortola or Virgin Gorda."

CHERI ALBERT, NEW YORK, NEW YORK

Tortola

				TOTAL
75.7%	**37.7%**	**47.8%**	**60.1%**	**58.1%**

Reader Report

"On a 13-day cruise, Tortola was the only island that we enjoyed. We found more than enough to do right in town at the wharf . . . friendly people, good scenery. Great island."

VEL LITT, CLEVELAND, OHIO

"Tortola recently built a cruise ship dock, but it's too small for most liners—this is typical of the ingenuous mindset of Torotolians, who remain charming and helpful despite an increase in tourism. An ideal island for a getaway, with much to explore."

JUDY WADE, VAN NUYS, CALIFORNIA

"Dining was overpriced in the well known restaurants and the service slow. The people were friendly and courteous, but drive like madmen on the mountain roads. Beautiful greenery with wonderful vistas in the mountains and beaches that looked like postcards with no one on them."

RUSSELL L. DUNFEE, JR., SMITHVILLE, NEW JERSEY

Peter Island

				TOTAL
85.5%	73.7%	52.6%	59.2%	70.3%

Reader Report

"Beautiful, nearly deserted beaches, traffic-free roads with gorgeous hilltop views, and startlingly blue waters.

MELANIE ROTH, NEW YORK, NY

Islands. The British Virgin Islands, or B.V.I., as they're common-ly called, are a 59-square-mile group of 36 islands and islets with a population of about 13,000. The group is a territory con-trolled by the United Kingdom, whose largest islands are Tortola and Virgin Gorda.

Language. English is the official language.

Visitor Information

In the U.S. Contact the **British Virgin Islands Tourist Board** (370 Lexington Ave., Suite 313, New York, NY 10017, tel. 212/696–0400, fax 212/949–8254) or the **British Virgin Islands Information Office** (1804 Union St., San Francisco, CA 94123, tel. 415/775–0344, fax 415/775–2554. 800/835–8530 can be called for both cities).

In Canada. There is no tourist office in Canada.

In the U.K. Contact the **British Virgin Islands Information Office** (110 St. Martin's La., London WC2N 4DY, tel. 071/240–4259, fax 071/240–4270).

In the B.V.I. Contact the **British Virgin Islands Tourist Board** (Box 134, Road Town, Tortola, B.V.I., tel. 809/494–3134, fax 809/494–3866).

BIRAS CREEK

64.7%	70.6%	82.4%	82.4%	TOTAL 75.0%

Set on the east end of Virgin Gorda on a high isthmus between North Sound and the Caribbean Sea, this 140-acre resort is reachable only by launch. Guests stay in single-story cottages. Note: Serious hurricane damage delayed opening.

Reader Report

"A low-key resort, with wonderful food and a friendly staff. Bike at your door—the beach is half a mile away. It's a little too isolated, but perfect for honeymooners."

JUDY F. OLIPHANT, LAFAYETTE, CALIFORNIA

"Accommodations are private and romantic, and meals served

VIRGIN GORDA

KEY

⅄ Beach
⬤━ Ferry Route
■ Hotel or Resort

N

0   2 miles
0   3 km

TO ANEGADA

Parjaros Pt.

Eustatia Island

Prickly Pear Island

Deep Bay
Berchers

Berchers Bay

Berchers Bluff

Bitter End Yacht Club

Biras Creek

North Sound

Joe Bay

Mosquito Island

Blunder Bay

Gun Creek

South Sound

Valley Hill

Sound Bluff

Leverick Bay

South Sound Bluff

Caribbean Sea

Mountain Pt.

Long Bay

Savannah Bay

Pond Bay

Handsome Bay

Sir Francis Drake Channel

Little Dix Bay

Virgin Gorda Airport

Copper Mine Bay

Copper Mine Pt.

Little Dix Bay

Colison Pt.

St. Thomas Bay

Spanish Town

Little Trunk Bay

Crook's Bay

George Dog

Great Dog

Cockroach Island

West Dog

Fort Pt.

Valley Trunk Bay

The Crawl

Spring Bay

Stoney Bay

Fallen Jerusalem

TO TORTOLA

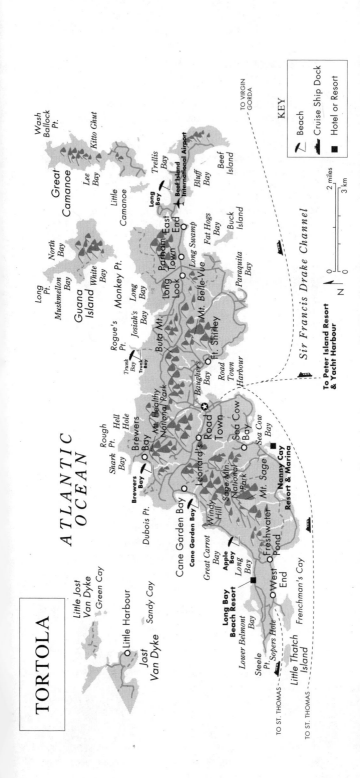

TORTOLA

ATLANTIC OCEAN

Sir Francis Drake Channel

KEY

≈ Beach
⚓ Cruise Ship Dock
■ Hotel or Resort

N

0   2 miles
0   3 km

TO VIRGIN GORDA

Little Jost Van Dyke
Green Cay
Little Harbour
○ Little Harbour
Sandy Cay
Jost Van Dyke

Wash Ballock Pt.
Kitto Ghut
Lee Bay
Little Camanoe
Great Camanoe
Trellis Bay
Long Bay Beef Island International Airport
Bluff Bay
Beef Island

Long Pt.
North Bay
Mushmellon Bay
White Bay
Guana Island
Monkey Pt.
Little Camanoe
Rogue's Pt.
Josiah's Bay
Long Bay
Buta Mt.
Long Look
Long Swamp
Parham Town
East End ○
Fat Hogs Bay
Buck Island
Mt. Belle-Vue
Ft. Shirley
Paraquita Bay

Trunk Bay Trunk Bay
Baughter's Bay
Road Town Harbour
To Peter Island Resort & Yacht Harbour

Mt. Healthy National Park
Hell Hole
Rough Bay
Shark Bay
Brewers ○ Bay
Brewers Bay
Dubois Pt.
Leonard's ○
Road Town
Sea Cow ○
Sea Cow Bay
Nanny Cay Resort & Marina ■

Cane Garden Bay ○
Cane Garden Bay
Great Carrot Bay
Windy Hill
Sage Mtn. National Park
Mt. Sage
Apple Bay Long Bay
Freshwater ○ Pond
Long Bay

Long Bay Beach Resort ■
○ West End
Lower Belmont Bay
Steele Pt.
⚓ Sopers Hole
Frenchman's Cay
Little Thatch Island

TO ST. THOMAS
TO ST. THOMAS

with care. The beach is beautiful, but entertainment is limited to the companion you bring. A great getaway."

GARRY WRIGHT, NORTH CALDWELL, NEW JERSEY

Address. Box 54, Virgin Gorda, B.V.I., tel. 809/494–3555 or 800/223–1108, fax 809/494–3557.

Rooms. 32 suites, 1 villa. All have ceiling fans. 16 suites have air-conditioning. 30 suites have showers only. All suites have minibars.

Facilities. Restaurant, 2 bars/lounges, 2 lighted tennis courts, freshwater pool, activities room, sailboats.

TV and VCR. TV in public area only, with over 50 channels including CNN and cable movie channels. VCR in public area.

No-smoking rooms. None.

Credit cards. AE, D, MC, V.

Restrictions. Min. 7 nights Dec 20–Jan 2. No children under 6.

Wheelchair accessibility. No accessible rooms.

Prices. Dec 17–Mar 31: suites $395–$595 AP; villa $695 AP. Low season: suites $350–$550 AP; villa $575 AP.

BITTER END YACHT CLUB

| 70.4% | 56.8% | 72.8% | 92.6% | TOTAL 73.1% |

Two-room single-story bungalows spread over 87 acres with three beaches on Virgin Gorda's North Sound. Guests arrive by launch—some stay on yachts—and there's a sailing school on site. The hotel was built in 1974, and rooms were added in 1987. Note that the resort sustained some superficial damage during hurricanes Luis and Marilyn.

Reader Report

"If you love sailing and other water sports, you'll be in heaven here. Unless you can fall asleep to the music of a steel band and like to wake at the crack of dawn, stay away from the beach bungalows; try the large, spacious ones on the hillside—they have spectacular views. Food is very good although not great. Visiting yachtsmen from faraway ports give this intimate resort a special flair."

MARY THOMPSON DENEWELLIS, JOLIET, ILLINOIS

"The best rooms are Swiss-Family-Robinsonesque, clinging to cliffs reached by weathered wood stairways. It's all very rustic, with hammocks strung on balconies and louvered bathrooms open to the sea. These rooms are not air-conditioned (happily!), so prevailing breezes can do their job."

JUDY WADE, VAN NUYS, CALIFORNIA

Address. Box 46, North Sound, Virgin Gorda, B.V.I., tel. 809/494–2745 or 800/872–2392, fax 809/494–4756.

Rooms. 92 rooms, and 8 sailboats with on-board accommodations for 2 people. 40 rooms have air-conditioning. All have ceiling fans and small refrigerators.

Facilities. 2 restaurants, 2 bars/lounges, freshwater pool, conference center with business services, supervised children's program, sailing school, sailboats, kayaks, snorkeling.

TV and VCR. TV in public area only, with about 60 channels including CNN and cable movie channels. VCRs in public area, and in some rooms (hooked up to monitors, not TVs).

No-smoking rooms. None.

Credit cards. AE, DC, MC, V.

Restrictions. Min. 7 nights Dec 23–Jan 7. Children under 4 not encouraged.

Wheelchair accessibility. No accessible rooms.

Prices. Dec 23–Apr 13: doubles $500–$595 AP; sailboats $450 AP. Low season: doubles $420–$470 AP; sailboats $420 AP.

LITTLE DIX BAY

| 84.4% | 77.1% | 78.9% | 87.2% | TOTAL 81.9% |

Much of this 500-acre low-rise resort on Virgin Gorda, just north of Spanish Town, is nature preserve. Guests stay in cottages (some on stilts). The hotel was built in 1964, expanded in 1973, and renovated in 1993. Note that the property sustained superficial damage during hurricanes Luis and Marilyn.

Reader Report

"Quiet, laid-back, casual—perfect for a few days of R&R or romance."

HILARY GRANT, LANCASTER, PENNSYLVANIA

"A pretty resort with terrific service. Meals are delicious, and the staff is very helpful. The large, airy rooms with balconies provide lots of privacy."

LESLEY HOHEB, PORT WASHINGTON, NEW YORK

Address. Box 70, The Valley, Virgin Gorda, B.V.I., tel. 809/495–5555 or 800/928–3000, fax 809/495–5661.

Affiliation. Rosewood Hotels and Resorts.

Rooms. 98 rooms, 4 suites. All have minibars and ceiling fans. 40 rooms and all suites have air-conditioning. 94 rooms have showers only; all suites have tubs and showers.

Facilities. 3 restaurants, 2 bars/lounges, 7 unlighted tennis courts, aerobics classes, massages, dry-cleaning, conference center with business services, dive center, beach and boat activities center.

TV and VCR. TV in public area only, with 32 channels including CNN and cable movie channels.

No-smoking rooms. None.

Credit cards. AE, DC, MC, V.

Restrictions. Min. 10 nights over Christmas.

Wheelchair accessibility. 4 accessible rooms.

Prices. Dec 20–Mar 31: doubles $450–$650 EP; suites $1,100 EP. Low season: doubles $250–$350 EP; suites $450 EP. Meal plans and vacation packages available upon request.

LONG BAY BEACH RESORT

50.0%	50.0%	52.3%	72.7%	**TOTAL** 56.3%

Sloping down to a mile-long white sand beach on Tortola's western end, this 52-acre estate has hillside rooms and studios, a beachfront low rise, cabanas on stilts, and two- and three-bedroom villas with full kitchens; all rooms have ocean views. The hotel was built in 1964, renovated in 1990, and expanded in 1993. It sustained superficial hurricane damage this fall.

Reader Report

"A very nice resort, with excellent food and service, and a great beach. A very good resort for getting away from it all."
TERRY MARION, WEST MILFORD, NEW JERSEY

"Very pleasant resort with excellent food and an accommodating staff. Make sure you really want to be away from it all—there's so little to do that for the first time I actually looked forward to returning to civilization."
NAME WITHHELD, TOLEDO, OHIO

Address. Box 433, Road Town, Tortola, B.V.I., tel. 809/495– 4252 or Island Destinations, 800/729–9599, fax 914/833–3318.
Rooms. 62 rooms, 20 villas. All have showers only. All have air-conditioning, minibars, and small refrigerators. All villas have full kitchens.
Facilities. 2 restaurants, 3 bars/lounges, 2 lighted tennis courts, unlighted tennis court, freshwater pool, exercise room with weights and aerobic machines, aerobics classes, massages, sauna, salon, conference center with business services, outdooor activities desk.
TV and VCR. TVs in all beachfront rooms, cabanas, and villas , with 12 channels including CNN. VCRs in cabanas and villas.
No-smoking rooms. None.
Credit cards. AE, D, MC, V.
Wheelchair accessibility. No accessible rooms.??
Prices. Jan. 2–Apr 7: doubles $210–$325 EP; villas $450–$650 EP. Apr. 8–May 31 and Nov. 1–Dec. 20: doubles $150–$225EP; villas $320–$225 EP. June 1–Oct. 31: doubles $120–$195 EP; villas $260–$390 EP. Add $40 per adult, $25 per child under 12 for MAP.

NANNY CAY RESORT & MARINA

				TOTAL
58.3%	25%	50.0%	58.3%	47.9%

This 25-acre low-rise resort with its own marina was built in 1987 in Colonial Caribbean style. It's on Tortola's south coast, three miles from Road Town and had some hurricane damage this fall.

Reader Report

"A perfect location with a strange mix of people from all parts of the world—from rum-swilling pirate look-alikes to bejeweled heirs and heiresses on ten-million-dollar vacation vessels."

MICHAEL STANLEY, RADNOR, PENNSYLVANIA

"The marina facilities are good and well-organized, but the marina restaurant is well below par, and marina shops are not very friendly. Sleeping rooms are average. The satellite immigration office was convenient and the officers friendly and accommodating."

NAME WITHHELD, WAKARUSA, KANSAS

"The beaches were clean and quiet. Most attractive was the service: Everyone was so gracious and willing to help—waiters, bellboys, maids, and managers alike."

INA JEAN ENGEDAL, LONG BEACH, CALIFORNIA

Address. Box 281, Road Town, Tortola, B.V.I., tel. 809/494–2512 or 800/74CHARMS, fax 809/494–0555.
Rooms. 42 rooms. All have air-conditioning and ceiling fans.
Facilities. 2 restaurants, 2 bars/lounges, coffee shop, lighted tennis court, saltwater pool, freshwater pool, dry-cleaning, laundromat, on-site diving, sailing, waindsurfing, fishing, mountain biking.
TV and VCR. TVs in all rooms, with 20 channels. No VCRs.
No-smoking rooms. 20 rooms.
Credit cards. AE, MC, V.
Wheelchair accessibility. No accessible rooms.
Prices. Dec 20–Apr 13: doubles $165–205 EP. Low season: doubles $90–$145 EP.

PETER ISLAND RESORT & YACHT HARBOUR

				TOTAL
61.9%	47.6%	57.1%	90.5%	64.3%

Occupying an 1,800-acre private island south of Tortola, (accessible from there by launch), this low-rise resort has Scandinavian cedar-and-stone architecture, five beaches, and its own marina. The hotel was built in 1971 and renovated after Hurricane Hugo in 1989. The hotel sustained some serious damage during this fall's hurricanes and its opening was delayed; reservations can be placed after December 1.

Reader Report

"A fabulous resort. Rooms, pool, and beach are great; the food, although not outstanding, is fine for the week. The island tour is impressive for its views of the surrounding islands. There's a good scuba diving operation, though diving in the British Virgin Islands is only average."

NAME WITHHELD, PHILADELPHIA, PENNSYLVANIA

"The superb beach rooms have little gardens that you look at as you bathe. From the living room you see endless sandy beaches. The resort is the only thing on the island, so you can explore for days and never intrude on another soul. Honeymoon Beach is yours alone, if you get there first."

JUDY WADE, VAN NUYS, CALIFORNIA

Address. Peter Island (mailing address: Box 211, Road Town, Tortola. B.V.I.), tel. 809/494–2000 or 800/346–4451, fax 809/494–2500.

Affiliation. Sterling Hotels and Resorts.

Rooms. 50 rooms, 3 villas. All have minibars, air-conditioning, and ceiling fans.

Facilities. 2 restaurants, 2 bars/lounges, 2 lighted tennis courts, 2 unlighted, freshwater pool, exercise room with weights and aerobic machines, massages, dive center, sailboats.

TV and VCR. TV in public area only, with 15 channels including CNN and cable movie channels. VCR in public area.

No-smoking rooms. None.

Credit cards. AE, MC, V.

Restrictions. Min. 7 nights Jan 1–Mar 31 in beachfront rooms.

Wheelchair accessibility. No accessible rooms.

Prices. Dec 23–Mar 31: doubles $395–$565 EP; villas $695–$3,270 EP. Apr. 1–Apr. 30 and Oct. 1–Dec. 21: doubles: $275–$385 EP; villas $525–$3,270 EP. Low season: doubles $195–$325 EP; villas $475–$1,230 EP. Add $65 per person for MAP; $85 per person for AP.

CAYMAN ISLANDS

| 68.2% | 55.2% | 60.8% | 61.1% | **TOTAL** 64.5% |

Reader Report

"If you absolutely love to scuba dive, this [Grand Cayman] is the island to be on. The island is spotlessly clean and islanders are friendly and genuinely helpful. The larger hotels are high-priced and laid out building behind building, Vegas style."

MARY THOMPSON DENEWELLIS, JOLIET, ILLINOIS

"Diving and snorkeling were the best ever. We found the Caymans too Americanized—we prefer a more laid-back atmosphere, like Antigua's."

JERRY AND PAULA ANDERSON, YORK, PENNSYLVANIA

"Most importantly [Grand Cayman] is safe, with very little crime, and the people are very courteous. A little more expensive but well worth it."

TERRY MARION, WEST MILFORD, NEW JERSEY

"A lot of people say the shopping is good in Grand Cayman, but unless you are buying coral jewelry (which is not very environmentally correct), we did not find much to buy. On the other hand, swimming with the stingrays in Stingray City is totally awesome."

JEFF AND LAUREL CHANDLER, CINCINNATI, OHIO

Islands. The Cayman Islands, which include Grand Cayman, Cayman Brac and Little Cayman, are a 100-square-mile territory controlled by the United Kingdom, with a population of about 31,000.

Language. The official language is English.

Visitor Information

In the U.S. Contact the **Cayman Islands Department of Tourism** (6100 Waterford Bldg., 6100 Blue Lagoon Dr., Suite 150, Miami, FL 33126-2085, tel. 305/266–2300, fax 305/267–2932; 2 Memorial City Plaza, 820 Gessner Rd., Suite 170, Houston, TX 77204, tel. 713/461–1317, fax 713/461–7409; 420 Lexington Ave., Suite 2733, New York, NY 10170, tel. 212/682–5582, fax 212/986–5123; 9525 W. Bryn Mawr Ave., Suite 160, Rosemont, IL 60018, tel. 708/678–6446, fax 708/678–6675; 3440 Wilshire Blvd., Suite 1202, Los Angeles, CA 90010, tel. 213/738–1968, fax 213/738–1829).

In Canada. Contact the **Cayman Islands Department of Tourism** (Eglington Ave. E, Suite 306, Toronto, Ont. M4P 1K5, tel. 416/485–1550, fax 416/485–7578)

In the U.K. Contact the **Cayman Islands Department of Tourism** (Trevor House, 100 Brompton Rd., Knightsbridge, London SW3 1EX, tel. 071/581–9960, fax 071/584–4463).

LITTLE CAYMAN / CAYMAN BRAC

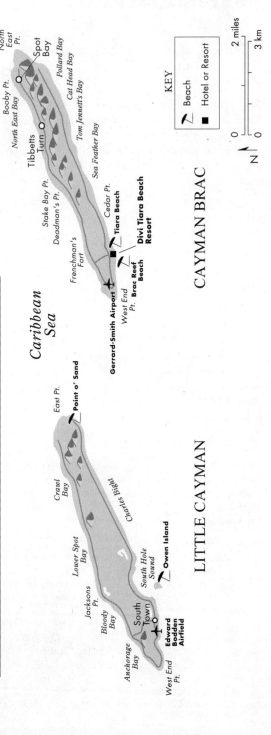

Caribbean Sea

LITTLE CAYMAN

West End Pt.
Anchorage Bay
Bloody Bay
Jacksons Pt.
Lower Spot Bay
Crawl Bay
East Pt.
Point o' Sand
South Town
Owen Island
South Hole Sound
Charles Bight
Edward Bodden Airfield

CAYMAN BRAC

North East Pt.
Spot Bay
Booby Pt.
Pollard Bay
North East Bay
Cat Head Bay
Tibbetts Turn
Tom Jennett's Bay
Stake Bay Pt.
Deadman's Pt.
Sea Feather Bay
Cedar Pt.
Tiara Beach
Frenchman's Fort
Divi Tiara Beach Resort
Gerrard-Smith Airport
West End Pt.
Brac Reef Beach

KEY

⅄ Beach
■ Hotel or Resort

0 ——— 2 miles
0 ——— 3 km

N

In the Cayman Islands. Contact the **Cayman Islands Department of Tourism** (Box 67, George Town, Grand Cayman, B.W.I., tel. 809/949–7999, fax 809/949–0623).

DIVI TIARA BEACH RESORT

				TOTAL
60.0%	40.0%	53.3%	66.7%	55.0%

This resort's contemporary-style, low-rise buildings sit on 12½ acres near the west end of 12-mile-long Cayman Brac island, a few miles east of the airport. Built in 1980, the hotel was expanded in 1984 and 1987.

Reader Report

"Definitely a scuba diver's mecca, but shaded beach hammocks beckon."

ELIZABETH J. REED, SOUTH GLASTONBURY, CONNECTICUT

"Excellent dive facilities and underwater photo/video shop. Very much oriented to the scuba diver. Go for the beachfront rooms over the standard ones. There's not much else on the island, so take the meal plan to save money."

JOHN HUBBARD, HUNTSVILLE, ALABAMA

"Pretty quiet and relaxing, though it's very close to the airport—planes would roar overhead at 11 PM and 7 AM. Room decor was nothing special; the food, always served buffet style, was mediocre. If you don't dive, the pool will usually be all yours; everyone pretty much clears out by 8 AM to go diving. If you expect a crystal-clear sea for swimming, be forewarned—the water the resort faces is a protected marine reserve, and plant life and coral begin at water's edge. The advantage (to us) was sighting a spotted ray gliding along only a couple of feet from shore."

KATHRYN SPEARY-DONAHUE, WEEDSPORT, NEW YORK

"The room was large with a firm mattress and a magnificent view of the water. During a sunrise walk, a nice gentleman from the kitchen offered me a cup of coffee and refused any tip—now that's service."

GERALDINE MCALISTER, MIAMI, FLORIDA

Address. Box 238, Stake Bay, Cayman Brac, B.W.I., tel. 809/948–7553 or 800/367–3484, fax 809/948–7316.
Affiliation. Divi Resorts.
Rooms. 59 rooms. All have air-conditioning and ceiling fans. 7 rooms have Jacuzzis. 34 rooms have showers only. Time-share condominiums are also available.
Facilities. Restaurant, bar/lounge, lighted tennis court, freshwater pool, conference center, dive center.
TV and VCR. TVs in some rooms, with 5 channels including CNN and cable movie channels. No VCRs.
No-smoking rooms. 10 rooms.

GRAND CAYMAN

Caribbean Sea

TO CAYMAN BRAC
85 miles

TO LITTLE CAYMAN
80 miles

Old Stores
Mount Pleasant
Hell
North West Pt.
West Bay
Batabano
Head of Barkers
Sting Ray City
Upper Land
Welsh Pt.
North Sound
Barkers

Rum Point
Cayman Kai
Water Cay
Little Sound
Booby Cay

North Side
Hutland
Malportas Pond
Old Man Bay

Colliers Pt.
Colliers
Tortuga
East End
Sand Bluff
Gun Bay
Blakes
East End

Frank Sound
IRONSHORE

Breakers
Pease Bay
Bodden Bay

Hyatt Regency Grand Cayman Resort & Villas
Owen Roberts Airport
Radisson Resort Grand Cayman
Seven Mile Beach

North Sound Estates
Newlands
Lower Valley
Omega Gardens
Bodden Town
Savannah

Red Bay
South Sound
IRONSHORE
Prospect

George Town
Smith Cove
South West Pt.

KEY

∠ Beach
■ Hotel or Resort

0   4 miles

Credit cards. AE, D, MC, V.
Restrictions. Min 5 nights Dec 23–Jan 1. Stays Dec 18–Jan 7 must be paid for 21 days in advance.
Wheelchair accessibility. 6 rooms.
Prices. Dec 23–Apr 7: $125–$255 EP. Low season: $95–$180 EP. Add $82 for AP; $41 for MAP.

HYATT REGENCY GRAND CAYMAN RESORT & VILLAS

👔	🛏	🍴	🌅	**TOTAL**
84.9%	**77.6%**	**76.3%**	**84.2%**	**80.8%**

At this blue-and-white property, built in 1986 across the road from Grand Cayman's Seven-Mile Beach, British colonial-style buildings surround a landscaped pool courtyard. It's part of the 90-acre Britannia Resort.

Reader Report

"Wonderful rooms, a full line of water sports, and excellent food, including great sandwiches and drinks on the beach. It's expensive, but worth the money."

DOUGLAS JOHNSON, HADDONFIELD, NEW JERSEY

"A first-class resort. It has a beautiful pool, and it's only a short walk to the beach. The rooms are great. The hotel really takes care of its guests."

NAME WITHHELD, PHILADELPHIA, PENNSYLVANIA

Address. Seven-Mile Beach, Grand Cayman, B.W.I., tel. 809/949–1234 or 800/233–1234, fax 809/949–8528.
Affiliation. Hyatt Hotels & Resorts.
Rooms. 236 rooms, 10 suites, 35 villas. All have air-conditioning, hair dryers, irons, coffee makers, and ceiling fans. All rooms and suites have minibars.
Facilities. 3 restaurants, 4 bars/lounges, 4 lighted tennis courts, 9-hole golf course, 4 freshwater pools, exercise room with weights and aerobic machines, sauna, salon, 24-hr room service, dry-cleaning, conference center with business services, supervised children's program, dive center, sailboats.
TV and VCR. TVs in all rooms, with 18 channels including CNN and cable movie channels. No VCRs.
No-smoking rooms. 101 rooms.
Credit cards. AE, CB, DC, D, MC, V.
Restrictions. Min. 5 nights Dec 20–Dec 30.
Wheelchair accessibility. 1 room.
Prices. Dec 22–Apr 21: doubles $300–$505 EP; suites $600–$1,750 EP; villas $500–$1,050 EP. Low season: doubles $185–$375 EP; suites $380–$1,350 EP; villas $315–$680 EP. Add $84 per person for AP, $64 for MAP, $19 for breakfast.

RADISSON RESORT GRAND CAYMAN

| 52.4% | 48.8% | 45.2% | 76.2% | **TOTAL** 55.7% |

A red-roofed, Mediterranean-style hotel building, five stories high, is the centerpiece of this five-acre property on Seven-Mile Beach, a half-mile north of George Town on Grand Cayman. The hotel was built in 1990.

Reader Report

"The ocean-front rooms were excellent, and the service was great. Excellent diving, too."

NAME WITHHELD, BRANT BEACH, NEW JERSEY

"A good but not great hotel. Terrific snorkeling, and the beach was magnificent."

NAME WITHHELD, WESTLAKE, OHIO

"We were very impressed; the rooms were spacious and clean and the employees helpful even with the smallest details. The only drawback was the amount of coral in the water; there was no sandy bottom, and you couldn't wade out."

NAME WITHHELD, ALAMO, CALIFORNIA

Address. Seven-Mile Beach, West Bay Rd., Grand Cayman, B.W.I., tel. 809/949–0088 or 800/333–3333, fax 809/949–0288.
Affiliation. Radisson Hotels International.
Rooms. 315 rooms, 4 suites. All have air-conditioning.
Facilities. 3 restaurants, 2 bars/lounges, exercise room with weights and aerobic machines, massages, salon, conference center with business services, dry-cleaning, dive center, sailboats.
TV and VCR. TVs in all rooms, with 10 channels including CNN and cable movie channels. No VCR.
No-smoking rooms. 50 rooms.
Credit cards. AE, CB, D, MC, V.
Wheelchair accessibility. No accessible rooms.
Prices. Dec 16–Jan 1: $275–$390 EP. Low season: $140–$340 EP.

CURAÇAO

				TOTAL
51.1%	**30.5%**	**33.6%**	**45.2%**	**38.7%**

Reader Report

"For an extended quiet stay away from winter, Curaçao is the place to be. The shopping is wonderful and the waters as inviting as Aruba's, without the hustling tourist activity."

DEE DEE BRIESE, CAROL STREAM, ILLINOIS

"Rich culture and history. The people are friendly and you don't feel as if you're in the U.S. as you do on the more populated islands."

NAME WITHHELD, PITTSTOWN, NEW JERSEY

"Even the Dutch culture cannot save this island. The beautiful buildings are overshadowed by the lack of activities."

KEVIN MAGUIRE, AUSTIN, TEXAS

"The island and its people are as sweet as the oranges used to make the drink named after it. Even the casino is light-hearted compared to most of the others in this area."

PAUL FRANCO, ROSEMEAD, CALIFORNIA

Islands. Curaçao is a 180-square-mile, independent protectorate of the Netherlands, with a population of about 200,000.
Language. The official is Dutch, though English and Spanish are widely spoken.

Visitor Information

In the U.S. Contact the **Curaçao Tourist Board** (475 Park Ave., New York, NY 10016, tel. 212/683–7660 or 800/270–3350, fax 212/683–9337; 330 Biscayne Blvd., Suite 330, Miami, FL 33132, tel. 305/374–5811, fax 305/374–6741).
In Canada. There is no tourist office in Canada.
In the U.K. There is no tourist office in the U.K.
In Curaçao. Contact the **Curaçao Tourist Development Bureau** (Pietermaai 19, Box 3266, Willemstad, Curaçao, Netherlands Antilles, tel. 599/961–6000, fax 599/961–2305).

AVILA BEACH HOTEL

				TOTAL
70.0%	**60.0%**	**70.0%**	**80.0%**	**70.0%**

Originally constructed in 1780 as the country residence of Curaçao's governor, this elegant, four-story, Dutch-colonial, plantation mansion with two private beaches has Moorish arches, Dutch red-gable roofs, and lighted walkways. A five-minute drive from downtown Willemstad, the hotel was renovated in

1990 and expanded in 1992; rooms have ocean and/or garden views.

Reader Report

"Watching the sunset from the bar on the pier was wonderful...I spent a lot of time on the patio off our rooms reading and relaxing; it looked out over the ocean.... [The resort's] not too big, just the right size, not impersonal like the big chain hotels."

BUDDY CLARK, DALLAS, TEXAS

"The staff was particularly excellent—very attentive. The rooms were spacious and well-kept."

BARBARA ABBOTT, MALIBU,CALIFORNIA

Address. Box 791, Penstraat 130, Willemstad, Curaçao, tel. 599/9–614377 or 800/448–8355, fax 599/9–611493.
Rooms. 80 rooms, 8 suites. All have air-conditioning. 40 rooms have showers only. 15 rooms have minibars.
Facilities. 2 restaurants, 2 bars/lounges, coffee shop, lighted tennis court, massages, conference center with business services.
TV and VCR. TV in all rooms, with 8 channels including CNN.
No-smoking rooms. None.
Credit cards. AE, DC, MC, V.
Wheelchair accessibility. No accessible rooms.
Prices. Dec. 16–Apr. 15: doubles $126–$211 AP, $217–$302 MAP, $105–$190 EP; suites $271–$441 AP, $362–$476 MAP, $250–$420 EP. Low season: doubles $121–$188 AP, $212–$277 MAP, $100–$165; suites $251–$366 AP, $342–$457 MAP, $230–$345 AP.

CURAÇAO CARIBBEAN HOTEL & CASINO

				TOTAL
36.8	31.6	21.1	52.6	35.5

This five-story, contemporary hotel, built in 1969 and renovated in 1990, is on Piscadera Bay, a 10-minute drive west of the center of Willemstad. It has its own casino.

Reader Report

"A delightful resort on a wonderful island—it is my favorite. The beach is on a secluded cove and most inviting."

ELIZABETH J. DRIVER, SEAFORD, NEW YORK

"A very comfortable place to stay. The rooms were extremely nice and service was wonderful. The food facilities were open air, with a great deal of variety, and a good bar. Beach was small but very nice. They draw an international crowd, and we found the guests to be a pretty congenial group."

NORMAN FOUNTAIN, RIDGEFIELD, CONNECTICUT

Address. J.F. Kennedy Blvd. z/n, Piscadera Bay, Curaçao, Netherlands Antilles, tel. 599/9–625000, fax 599/9–625846.

Rooms. 181 rooms, 15 suites. All have air-conditioning.

Facilities. 4 restaurants, 3 bars, lounges, coffee shop, 2 lighted tennis courts, freshwater pool, casino, laundry service, executive floor with business services, dive center.

TV and VCR. TVs in all rooms, with 12 channels including CNN and cable movie channels. VCRs in some rooms.

No-smoking rooms. None.

Credit cards. AE, DC, MC, V.

Wheelchair accessibility. 5 rooms.

Prices. Dec 21–Apr 16: doubles $140–$180 EP; suites $275–$850 EP. Low season: doubles $110–$150 EP; suites $275–$850 EP. Add $10.50 per person for full American breakfast; $5 per person for Continental breakfast.

PRINCESS BEACH RESORT & CASINO

👤	🛏	✗	☀	TOTAL
62.1	55.2	44.8	62.1	56.0

This low-rise, contemporary-style Crowne Plaza Resort hotel is adjacent to the Curaçao Underwater Marine Park, east of Willemstad. Built in 1967, and expanded and renovated in 1993. this full-service resort has a casino.

Reader Report

"A deluxe, well-managed resort with a customer-oriented staff,a good happy hour, and one of the best beaches on the island."

A. KENT SHAMBLIN, AFTON, MINNESOTA

"Very enjoyable place, with a very nice beach. Service was good and the staff very helpful, though the food wasn't great."

NAME WITHHELD, HAVEN, CONNECTICUT

Address. Dr. Martin Luther King Blvd. #8, Curaçao, Netherlands Antilles, tel. 599/9–367888 or 800/2-CROWNE and 800/327–3286 (reservations), fax 599/9–614131.

Affiliation. Holiday Inn Worldwide.

Rooms. 332 rooms, 9 suites. All have minibars and air-conditioning. 138 rooms have ceiling fans. 1 room and 1 suite have Jacuzzis.

Facilities. 3 restaurants, 4 bars/lounges, 2 lighted tennis courts, exercise room with weights and aerobic machines, salon, dry-cleaning, conference room with business services, supervised children's program, dive center.

TV and VCR. TVs in all rooms, with 10 channels including CNN and cable movie channels. VCRs in rooms on request.

No-smoking rooms. 34 rooms.

Credit cards. AE, DC, MC, V.

Restrictions. Min. 7 nights during the Christmas holidays.

Wheelchair accessibility. 4 rooms.

Prices. Dec 16–Apr 15: doubles $175–$265EP; suites $275–$575EP. Low season: doubles $115–$195 EP; suites $205–$500 EP. Add $65 per day for AP, $50 per person for MAP, $12 per person for American buffet breakfast.

SONESTA BEACH HOTEL & CASINO

👔	🛏	🍴	🌊	**TOTAL**
63.2%	**73.7%**	**60.5%**	**71.1%**	**67.1%**

This three-story, ochre-hued resort complex, built in 1992 in Dutch Colonial style, is on Curaçao's longest beach, on Piscadera Bay just west of Willemstad. It has a casino.

Reader Report

"Sparkling clean and very intimate, with a great variety of restaurants and easy access to public transportation. The beach was almost deserted, with great snorkeling."

MARLENE RAIN, RANCHOS PALOS VERDES, CALIFORNIA

"Excellent. The rooms were clean, the staff tremendous, the gourmet restaurant excellent. What was especially good was that you could feed a family for a reasonable price at the different restaurants at the resort. The water-sports program is extremely well run. It is so far above the rest of the hotels on Curaçao that the others don't even compare."

DANIEL N. SARISKY, PARLIN, NEW JERSEY

Address. Piscadera Bay, Curaçao, Netherlands Antilles, tel. 5999/368–800 or 800/SONESTA, fax 5999/627–502. (Sales office: 9300 S. Dadeland Blvd., Suite 302, Miami, FL 33156, tel. 305/662–2862, fax 305/662–4988.)
Affiliation. Sonesta International.
Rooms. 214 rooms, 34 suites. All have minibars and air-conditioning. 8 suites have Jacuzzis.
Facilities. 3 restaurants, 2 bars/lounges, 2 unlighted tennis courts, 2 outdoor hot tubs, casino, exercise room with weights and aerobic machines, aerobics classes, massages, sauna, salon, conference center with business services, supervised children's program, dive center, watersports.
TV and VCR. TVs in all rooms, with 12 channels including CNN. VCRs in rooms on request.
No-smoking rooms. 20 rooms.
Credit cards. AE, DC, MC, V.
Restrictions. Min. 5 nights Dec 22–Jan. 2.
Wheelchair accessibility. 6 rooms.
Prices. Dec 22–Apr 13: doubles $240–$315 EP; suites $350–$920 EP. Low season: doubles $170–$235 EP; suites $260–$680 EP. Rates around Christmas holiday are higher.

DOMINICAN REPUBLIC

				TOTAL
49.8%	40.4%	37.4%	45.3%	42.6%

Reader Report

"The palm trees, white sand, and beautiful sunrises made for some of the most memorable early-morning walks I've ever had."

CHARLIE EUBANKS, ST. LOUIS, MISSOURI

"Very beautiful. Most facilities are at resorts, for safety, [so] you feel confined. Beautiful beaches, mediocre food."

MARIANNE REDER, AKRON, OHIO

Islands. The 18,704-square-mile Dominican Republic is an independent nation. It is located on the island of Hispaniola, bordering Haiti, and has a population of about 7,069,000. **Language.** The official language is Spanish.

Visitor Information

In the U.S. Contact the **Dominican Tourist and Information Board** (1501 Broadway, Suite 410, New York, NY 10036, tel. 212/768–2480, fax 212/768–2677; 2355 Salzedo St., Suite 307, Coral Gables, FL 33134, tel. 305/444–4592, fax 305/444–4845).

In Canada. Dominican Republic Department of Tourism (2080 Crescent St., Montréal, Québec H3G 2B8, tel. 514/499–1918, fax 514/499–1393).

In the U.K. There is no tourist office in the U.K.

In the Dominican Republic. Contact the **Secretaria de Estado de Tourismo** (Av. Mexico Esq., 30 de Marzo, Santa Domingo, Dominican Repulbic, tel. 809/221–4660, fax 809/682–3806).

BAVARO BEACH RESORT HOTELS, GOLF & CASINO

				TOTAL
66.7%	50.0%	33.3%	83.3%	58.3%

This 100-acre resort complex at the eastern tip of the island consists of five four-story buildings. Most rooms front the over-20-mile-long Punta Cana beach. The hotel was built in 1985, expanded in 1993, and restored in 1994.

Reader Report

"The setting was beautiful—with lots of well-kept tropical landscaping, great beach, and a nice-looking golf course. The rooms are nice, too—and they're set in clusters that have

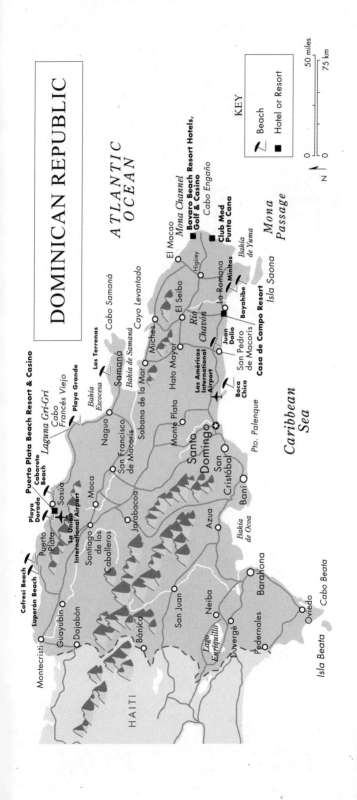

DOMINICAN REPUBLIC

ATLANTIC OCEAN

Caribbean Sea

Mona Passage

HAITI

KEY

Beach

Hotel or Resort

50 miles

75 km

N

Puerto Plata Beach Resort & Casino

Cofresi Beach
Luperón Beach
Puerto Plata
Playa Dorada
La Unión International Airport
Sosúa
Cabarete Beach
Laguna Grí-Grí
Cabo Francés Viejo
Playa Grande
Las Terrenas

Montecristi
Guayubin
Dajabón
Santiago de los Caballeros
Moca
Jarabacoa
Bánica
San Juan
Neiba
Lago Enriquillo
Duvergé
Pedernales
Barahona
Oviedo

Cabo Beata
Isla Beata

Bahía de Ocoa
Azua
Bani
San Cristóbal
Santo Domingo
Pto. Palenque

Cabo Samaná
Samaná
Bahía de Samaná
Cayo Levantado
Bahía Escocesa
Nagua
San Francisco de Macorís
Sabana de la Mar
Miches
Monte Plata
Hato Mayor
El Seibo
El Macao
Higüey

Mona Channel
Bavaro Beach Resort Hotels, Golf & Casino
Cabo Engaño
Club Med Punta Cana
Bahía de Yuma

La Romana
Minitas
Bayahibe
Casa de Campo Resort
Isla Saona
Río Chavón
Juan Dolio
San Pedro de Macorís
Las Américas International Airport
Boca Chica

access to the beach and several dining areas. The employees are very courteous and give you lots of smiles."

BARBARA NEWSOM, INDIANAPOLIS, INDIANA

"We loved it. It was quite economical at the time, though I understand prices have gone up. The beach is magnificent, clean with white sand and plenty of trees. There was entertainment every night. The food was very good."

ROLAND DELGADO, CHERRY HILL, NEW JERSEY

Address. Box #3177 Santo Domingo, Dominican Republic, tel. 809/686–5797, fax 809/686–5859.
Affiliation. Barceló Hotels.
Rooms. 1,297 rooms, 64 junior suites. All have minibars and air-conditioning.
Facilities. 9 restaurants, 15 bars/lounges, 4 coffee shops, 4 lighted tennis courts, 2 unlighted, 18-hole golf course, 4 fresh-water pools, casino, horseback riding, aerobics classes, massages, salon, conference center with business services, supervised children's program, dive center, windsurfing, waterskiing, and sailing schools, medical center, fitness center.
TV and VCR. TVs in all rooms, with 20 channels including CNN and cable movie channels. No VCRs.
No-smoking rooms. None.
Credit cards. AE, MC, V.
Restrictions. Min. 7 nights around Christmas, New Year's, and Easter.
Wheelchair accessibility. No accessible rooms.
Prices. Dec 20–Apr 30: doubles $180–$240 MAP; suites $200–$300 MAP. Low season: doubles $70–$180 MAP; suites $90–$200 MAP.

CASA DE CAMPO RESORT

| 68.9% | 66.0% | 68.0% | 76.7% | TOTAL 69.9% |

This 7,000-acre resort in La Romana, on the island's southeastern corner, features single-story casitas and villas. It's a mile from the beach, but there's continuous shuttle service. The hotel was built in 1971 and has been renovated regularly since then.

Reader Report

"A true sportsman's paradise with incredible golf, tennis (the ball boys are famous), and water sports, plus polo and shooting. Altos de Chavón, a re-created 16th-century village on the grounds, is a sight to behold and experience."

JOEL M. CHUSID, IRVING, TEXAS

"A beautiful resort with lovely facilities and views. A place to go when you need to relax—there's not much action or

nightlife. One thing is kind of scary, though: armed guards are posted discreetly around the compound."

MARY JANE KOVALCIK, CLINTON TOWNSHIP, MICHIGAN

"You need a golf cart to get around—it's very spread-out, with the beach far away—and nothing else is close by except a small specialty shopping center. I felt confined."

E. TISH BRISSETTE, WILMINGTON, NORTH CAROLINA

Address. Box 140, La Romana, Dominican Republic, tel. 809/523–3333 or 800/877–3643, fax 809/523–8548 or 305/858–4677.

Affiliation. Premier Resorts & Hotels.

Rooms. 300 rooms, 150 villas. All have air-conditioning. All rooms have minibars. 150 rooms have ceiling fans. Many villas have private pools or Jacuzzis.

Facilities. 9 restaurants, 7 bars/lounges, 2 coffee shops, 10 lighted tennis courts, 3 unlighted, 2 18-hole golf courses, 14 freshwater pools, horseback riding, exercise room with weights aerobic machines, aerobics classes, massages, sauna, salon, dry-cleaning, conference center with business services, supervised children's program, sailboats, polo and shooting center, Altos de Chavon artist's village.

TV and VCR. TVs in all rooms, with 27 channels including CNN. VCRs in rooms on request.

No-smoking rooms. None.

Credit cards. AE, MC, V.

Wheelchair accessibility. 3 rooms.

Prices. Jan 4–Apr 7: doubles $200 per person EP; villas $445–$1015 EP; inclusive packages offered. Low season: doubles $145 per person EP; villas $260–$678 EP; inclusive packages offered.

CLUB MED PUNTA CANA

63.2%	36.8%	57.9%	78.9%	**TOTAL** 59.2%

This all-inclusive resort consists of three-story garden bungalows on 60 acres along Punta Cana Beach, at the island's eastern end. The hotel was built in 1981.

Reader Report

"A camp-for-all-ages with a nice pool and a beautiful palm-lined beach. Accommodations were very spartan, the mess-hall-style food was decent—but with excellent breads and cheeses. Overall, a place for an upbeat fun time."

JESSICA BETHONEY, LEXINGTON, MASSACHUSETTS

"Rooms were modest, yet comfortable, but what you come for is not inside your room. The atmosphere, the congeniality,

and the beautiful surroundings made this a great vacation spot for our family."

CHARLE EUBANKS, ST. LOUIS, MISSOURI

Address. Punta Cana, Provincia La Altagracia, Apartado Postal 106, Dominican Republic, tel. 809/686–5500 or 800/258–2633, fax 809/686–5287.
Affiliation. Club Med.
Rooms. 319 rooms. All have air-conditioning, but showers only.
Facilities. 3 restaurants, 3 bars/lounges, 5 lighted tennis courts, 5 unlighted, freshwater pool, nightclub, theater, exercise room with weights and aerobic machines, aerobics classes, trapeze classes, supervised children's program, sailboats, waterskiing, windsurfing, snorkeling, kayaking.
TV and VCR. TV in public area only, with 22 channels including CNN, cable movie channels, and pay movies. No VCRs.
No-smoking rooms. None.
Credit cards. AE, MC, V.
Restrictions. Min. 7 nights during major holidays. Mini Club available for children 2–5 years old.
Wheelchair accessibility. No accessible rooms.
Prices. Dec 17–Apr 15: $120–$230. Low season: $100–$110. Prices are all-inclusive and per person.

CLUB ON THE GREEN

| 50.0% | 50.0% | 40.0% | 50.0% | **TOTAL** **47.5%** |

The former Playa Dorada Princess, built in 1986, is a Victorian-style resort with clusters of two-story casitas. It's near Puerto Plata, on the north coast.

Reader Report
"Beautiful beaches for water sports, games, or just relaxing in the sun. A good variety of restaurants, and even [nearby] gambling for those who dare."

DONNA ZINGO, STRATFORD, CONNECTICUT

Address. Playa Dorada, Puerto Plata, Dominican Republic, tel. 809/320–1111, fax 809/320–5386.
Affiliation. Allegro Resorts.
Rooms. 188 rooms, 144 junior suites. All have air-conditioning and ceiling fans.
Facilities. 3 restaurants, 2 bars/lounges, 2 lighted tennis courts, 4 unlighted, 18-hole golf course, freshwater pool, horseback riding, casino nearby, exercise room with weights and aerobic machines, aerobics classes, sauna, salon, conference center with business services, supervised children's program, sailboats.
TV and VCR. TVs in all rooms, with about 20 channels including CNN. No VCRs.

No-smoking rooms. None.
Credit cards. AE, CB, MC, V.
Restrictions. Min. 3 nights year-round.
Wheelchair accessibility. No accessible rooms.
Prices. Year-round: doubles $80; junior suites $135. Rates are all-inclusive and per person.

PUERTO PLATA BEACH RESORT & CASINO

				TOTAL
44.4%	36.1%	36.1%	36.1%	38.2%

Cobblestone paths connect the two- and three-story Victorian-style buildings at this seven-acre resort "village," which was built in 1985 and renovated in 1994. It's just outside Puerto Plata (not in Playa Dorado), across the street from the beach.

Reader Report

"The location was absolutely beautiful. The staff was very accommodating; they couldn't do enough for you. The grounds are very safe, so guests can feel very secure."

NAME WITHHELD, NORTH BERGEN, NEW JERSEY

"Large rooms, good quality beaches, good meals."

JEFFREY ROSENKER, ST. LOUIS PARK, MINNESOTA

Address. Ave. Malecón, Puerto Plata, Dominican Republic, tel. 809/586–4243 or 800/348–5395, fax 809/586–4377.
Affiliation. Amhsa Hotels.
Rooms. 216 rooms, 192 suites. All have air-conditioning, and all have minibars on request.
Facilities. 3 restaurants, 2 bars/lounges, 2 lighted tennis courts, freshwater pool, horseback riding, casino, aerobics classes, massages, supervised children's program.
TV and VCR. TVs in all rooms, with 10 channels including CNN and cable movie channels. No VCRs.
No-smoking rooms. None.
Credit cards. AE, MC, V.
Wheelchair accessibility. No accessible rooms.
Prices. Dec 21–Apr 16: doubles $180 MAP; suites $210 per person MAP. Low season: doubles $160 MAP; suites $190 MAP.

GRENADA

| 70.1% | 30.7% | 32.1% | 55.1% | TOTAL 47.4% |

Reader Report

"A quaint, brightly colored harbor town bustles with local flavor. This 'spice island' has underpopulated beaches and a rain forest. Our #1 choice for anchoring in the Caribbean."

JANELLE MCDONALD AND ROBERT REID, CAMPBELL, CALIFORNIA

"St. George's harbor is picturesque from a distance, but be prepared for the onslaught of locals peddling their spices and crafts, or doggedly trailing in hopes of acting as your personal tour guide—it can be intimidating."

SUSAN CHAMBERS, ROCKVILLE, MARYLAND

"A marvelous place to relax and enjoy some of the most beautiful beaches in the Caribbean. But relaxation should be your main objective, because other island activities are limited, at best."

KEVIN MAGUIRE, AUSTIN, TEXAS

"A picturesque Caribbean delight! Everyone we met—vendors, police, waitress, sales clerks—was very outgoing, pleasant, and genuine."

DONNA BANACH, BUFFALO, NEW YORK

Islands. Grenada is a 133-square-mile independent nation with a population of about 95,000.
Language. English is the official language.

Visitor Information
In the U.S. Contact the **Grenada Tourist Office** (820 2nd Ave., Suite 900D, New York, NY 10017, tel. 212/687–9554 or 800/927–9554, fax 212/573–9731).
In Canada. Contact the **Grenada Tourist Office** (Suite 820, 439 University Ave., Toronto, Ont. M5G 1Y8, tel. 416/595–1339, fax 416/595–8278 or 416/595–8278).
In the U.K. Contact the **Grenada Tourist Office** (1 Collingham Gardens, Earl's Ct., London SW5 0HW, tel. 0171/370–5164 or 0171/370–5165, fax 0171/244–0177).
In Grenada. Contact the **Grenada Board of Tourism** (Box 293, St. George's, Grenada, W.I., tel. 809/440–2001, fax 809/440–6637).

TO
CARRIACOU

*Isle la
Ronde*

*Caille
Island*

GRENADA

*The
Sisters*

*ATLANTIC
OCEAN*

*London Bridge
Island*

**Levera National Park
and Bird Sanctuary**

*Green
Island*

*David
Pt.*

*Sauteurs
Bay*

Sauteurs ○

Morne Fendre

*Grenada
Bay*

*David
Bay*

Tivoli ○

*St. Mark
Bay*

Victoria ○

Mt. St. Catherine

*Great
River
Bay*

*Caribbean
Sea*

Gouyave ○

*Mt.
Granby*

Grenville ○

*Telescope
Pt.*

*Gouyave
Bay*

*Mt.
Qua Qua*

*Grenville
Bay*

Marquis ○

*Black Bay
Pt.*

Mt. Lebanon

Pomme
Rose ○

*Grand
Bacolet
Bay*

*Halifax
Harbor*

Constantine ○

St. David's

*Molinière
Pt.*

Mt. Sinai

Bacolet

Westerhall

*Grand Mal
Bay*

St. George's

*Westerhall
Bay*

*St. George's
Harbour*

Woburn

Grand Anse Beach

**Grenada
Renaissance
Resort**

**St. George's U.
2nd Campus**

**Morne
Rouge
Beach**

■ **Secret Harbour**

Morne Rouge Bay

**Spice
Island Inn**

L'Anse aux
Epines

**Pt. Salines
Int'l. Airport**

*Prickly
Bay*

Pt. Salines

LaSource

Calabash Hotel

KEY

🌴 Beach

⛴ Cruise Ship Dock

■ Hotel or Resort

N

| 0 | | 4 miles |
| 0 | | 6 km |

CALABASH HOTEL

 76.9%	 61.5%	 61.5%	 76.9%	TOTAL 69.2%

This all-suite resort has one- and two-story, cottage-style accommodations on eight acres, on Prickly Bay, just east of the airport on the island's southern tip. Built in 1962, the hotel was renovated and expanded in 1994.

Reader Report

"Staying here is like going back to the old British Empire. Some find it rather stuffy, but I love it. Everything is very correct, right down to high tea at 4 o'clock. Some think this is going a bit too far, but I love the atmosphere."

ALDEN A. DARNELL, FAIRFIELD BAY, ARKANSAS

"The guests tended to be older British people. There was a timeless quality to the place. It was very private, and the service was very unobtrusive: They even carried your beach chair down to the water's edge. The beach was fabulous."

CORINNE KOPEC, MENDON, VERMONT

Address. Box 382, St. George's, Grenada, W.I., tel. 809/444–4334 or 800/528–5835, fax 809/444–5050.
Rooms. 30 rooms. All with air-conditioning and ceiling fans. 22 have Jacuzzis. 8 have private plunge pools.
Facilities. 2 restaurants, 2 bars/lounges, lighted tennis court, freshwater pool, exercise room with weights and aerobic machines, dry-cleaning, sailboats.
TV and VCR. TV in public area only, with 10 channels including CNN and cable movie channels. No VCRs.
No-smoking rooms. None.
Credit cards. AE, MC, V.
Restrictions. Min. 7 nights around Christmas and in February. No children under 12 between mid-Jan and mid-Mar.
Wheelchair accessibility. 2 rooms.
Prices. Dec 23–Apr 5: $360–$460 BP. Low season: $220–$310 BP. $30 supplement per person for dinner.

GRENADA RENAISSANCE RESORT

 42.1%	 36.8%	 42.1%	 68.4%	TOTAL 47.4

The island's largest resort, this property is on 20 acres directly on Grand Anse beach and across from the Grand Anse shopping center, just south of St. George's. It was built in 1972 and expanded and renovated in 1985.

Reader Report

"Overall, the atmosphere was very nice, good ambience. The staff was courteous, and the facilities and food both good."

ROBERT ADAMSON, FOUNTAIN HILLS, ARIZONA

"It was the best available accommodations, with a beach, on Grenada. We were happy there."

CLARA CORDWELL, JACOBSTOWN, NEW JERSEY

Address. Box 441, St. George's, Grenada, W.I., tel. 809/444-4371 or 800/228-9898, fax 809/444-4800.
Affiliation. Renaissance Hotels.
Rooms. 186 rooms, 2 suites. All have air-conditioning.
Facilities. Restaurant, 2 bars/lounges, 2 lighted tennis courts, 9-hole golf course nearby, horseback riding, exercise room with weights and aerobic machines, massages, dry-cleaning.
TV and VCR. TVs in all rooms, with 5 channels including CNN and cable movie channels. No VCRs.
No-smoking rooms. None.
Credit cards. AE, DC, D, MC, V.
Restrictions. Min. 7 nights Dec 14–Jan 2.
Wheelchair accessibility. 2 rooms.
Prices. Dec 14–Apr 15: doubles $253–$313 MAP, $204–$264 with breakfast, $180–$240 EP; suites $433–$673 MAP, $360–$600 EP. Low season: doubles $193–$243 MAP, $144–$194 with breakfast, $120–$170 EP; suites $373–$573 MAP, $300–$500 EP.

LA SOURCE

				TOTAL
85.7%	100%	85.7%	85.7%	89.3%

The sister of St. Lucia's Le Sport, this serene, all-inclusive resort is on the southern tip of Grenada. Its rooms, which have balconies, are in four-story, red-tile-roof buildings that are on or above the main beach. The resort was built in late 1993, and its rates include meals, tipping, spa treatments, and an impressive sports program.

Reader Report

"A rejuvenating experience...they served healthy food (we had special vegetarian requirements), and they were pretty well able to accommodate us.... Rooms are set up on hills, so steep walks to the rooms are a possibility, but the views are fantastic."

NANCY BECKER, MIQUON, PENNSYLVANIA

"A sybaritic experience. I felt pampered and restored. The decor is better than average for a Caribbean resort, especially the antiques—which I wanted to bring home!"

NAME WITHHELD, NEW YORK, NEW YORK

Address. Box 852, Pink Gin Beach, St. George's, Grenada, W.I., tel. 809/444–2556 or 800/544–2883, fax 809/444–2561.

Affiliation. SunSwept Resorts.

Rooms. 100 rooms, 9 suites. All have air-conditioning, ceiling fans, and minifridges.

Facilities. 2 restaurants, 2 bars/lounges, freshwater pool, 2 lighted tennis courts, exercise room with weights and aerobic machines, aerobics classes, massages, salon, sauna, dive center, sailboats..

TV and VCR. No TV or VCR.

No-smoking rooms. None.

Credit cards. AE, D, DC, MC, V.

Wheelchair accessibility. 20 accessible rooms.

Prices. Dec. 1–March 31: doubles and suites $240–$290 AP per person. Low season: doubles and suites $210–$260 AP per person.

SECRET HARBOUR

| 63.6% | 72.7% | 54.5% | 68.4% | **TOTAL** 47.4% |

The Mediterranean-style villas at this 6½-acre resort near the island southern tip are on a bluff overlooking Mount Hartman Bay. The hotel was built in 1963 and has its own marina.

Reader Report

"Very romantic—we loved it. Each room has its own very private porch and one wall that's entirely windows. There are also four-poster beds and beautiful tiled tubs. We didn't even go anywhere else to eat. But they did have boats you could charter for a day to go off on your own with a picnic lunch."

NANCY MURRAY, NEW LONDON, CONNECTICUT

"The landscaping was incredibly colorful, and there were spectacular views from absolutely everywhere—the restaurant, lodge, pool, and our room all overlooked the harbor. It's unbelievable. And all dining was in the open air."

MAUREEN LARROUX, INDIAN ROCKS BEACH, FLORIDA

Address. Box 11, St. George's, Grenada, W.I., tel. 809/444–4439 or 800/334–2435, fax 809/444–4819.

Affiliation. The Moorings.

Rooms. 20 rooms. All have minibars, air-conditioning, safes, direct-dial telephones and ceiling fans. Each room has a balcony.

Facilities. 2 restaurants, bar/lounge, unlighted tennis court, freshwater pool, sailboats, watersports center, boutique.

TV and VCR. No TV.

No-smoking rooms. None.

Credit cards. AE, D, MC, V.

Restrictions. No children under 12.

Wheelchair accessibility. No accessible rooms.

Prices. Dec 20–Apr 14: $225 EP. Low season: $135 EP. $49 per person supplement for MAP.

SPICE ISLAND INN

 76.9%	 69.2%	 69.2%	 96.2%	TOTAL 77.9%

At this eight-acre resort on Grand Anse Beach, just south of St. George's, guests stay in one-story bungalows, while public areas are in an open-air Caribbean-style building. The property was built in 1961 and renovated in 1992.

Reader Report

"Grenada is my favorite Caribbean island and the Spice Island Inn is on its best white sand beach. It's low-key, with friendly service in a pretty setting. An ideal romantic spot—also a great buy."

PHYLLIS WEINBERG, NEW YORK, NEW YORK

Address. Box 6, Grand Anse Beach, St. George's, Grenada, W.I., tel. 809/444–4258, fax 809/444–4807.

Rooms. 56 rooms. All with minibars, air-conditioning, patios or balconies, coffee makers, safes, direct-dial telephones, and ceiling fans. 17 have plunge pools and double whirlpool baths; 39 have double whirlpool baths only.

Facilities. Restaurant, bar/lounge, lighted tennis court, 9-hole golf course nearby, exercise room with weights and aerobic machines, dry-cleaning, conference center with business services, dive center nearby, sailboats.

TV and VCR. TV in public area only, with 22 channels including CNN and cable movie channels. No VCRs.

No-smoking rooms. None.

Credit cards. AE, DC, D, MC, V.

Restrictions. Min. 7 nights Dec 20–Jan 10 and all of February. No children under 5 during high season.

Wheelchair accessibility. No accessible rooms.

Prices. Dec 15–Apr 15: $320–$575 MAP. Low season: $250–$420 MAP. Add $55 per person for all-inclusive.

GUADELOUPE

				TOTAL
61.5%	31.5%	34.3%	35.7%	42.7%

Reader Report

"A volcano, a rain forest, mountains, and spectacular unspoiled beaches with white or black sand. Its many fine restaurants serve everything from fine French cuisine to good local fare. Drawbacks: intolerance for people who don't speak French, fairly high prices for lodging and food."

NANCY KOGER, BIG SPRING, TEXAS

"An interesting and beautiful island—relaxed. Try getting a native to show you around."

NAME WITHHELD, HOLLYWOOD, FLORIDA

"Guadeloupe is difficult until you get your own transportation—then it became the best of the 12 or 15 Caribbean islands I've visited."

ED DEBRECHT, WEBSTER GROVES, MISSOURI

Islands. Guadeloupe, with 530 square miles, is arégion of France, with a population of about 387,000.

Language. The official language is French, though a French-Creole patois is widely spoken by the islanders.

Visitor Information

In the U.S. Contact the **French West Indies Tourism Board** (tel. 900/990–0040, fax 212/838–7855) or the **French Government Tourist Office** (9454 Wilshire Blvd., Beverly Hills, CA 90212, tel. 310/271–6665, fax 310/276–2835; 676 N. Michigan Ave., Chicago, IL 60611, tel. 312/751–7800, fax 312/337–6339).

In Canada. Contact the **French Government Tourist Office** (1981 McGill College Ave., Suite 490, Montreal, Que. H3A 2W9, tel. 514/288–4264 or 514/845–4868; 30 St. Patrick St., Suite 700, Toronto, Ont. M5T 3A3, tel. 416/593–6427, fax 416/979–7587).

In the U.K. Contact the **French Government Tourist Office** (178 Picadilly, London WIV 0AL, tel. 071/499–6911, no fax).

In Guadeloupe. Contact the **Office Departmental du Tourisme de Guadeloupe** (5 Square de la Banque, Pointe-à-Pitre, 97110 Guadeloupe, F.W.I., tel. 590/82–09–30, fax 590/83–89–22).

AUBERGE DE LA VIEILLE TOUR

				TOTAL
42.9%	28.6%	57.1%	57.1%	46.4%

This four-acre resort sits on a hill just south of Point-à-Pitre and the airport, near an old sugar mill. Guests stay in a three-story hotel unit and newer town houses; stairs go down to a beach. The hotel was built in 1982 and renovated in 1992.

Reader Report

"I was disappointed—the rooms were very small. There are many, many steps leading down to the beach, so it's very difficult to get back up to the rooms."

EVA JAMNER, BROOKLYN, NEW YORK

"We really loved it. It was secluded, away from the hustle and bustle. Very little English was spoken, but it wasn't a problem. We are considering going back again."

CAROL PARKER, CLIO, MICHIGAN

Address. Montauban, 97190 Gosier, Guadeloupe, F.W.I., tel. 590/84–23–23 or 800/763-4835, fax 590/84–33–43.
Affiliation. Sofitel.
Rooms. 104 rooms including 32 suites. All have minibars and air-conditioning.
Facilities. 3 restaurants, 2 bars/lounges, 2 coffee shops, 2 lighted tennis courts, tennis lessons, casino nearby, freshwater pool,room service, horseback riding, exercise room with weights and aerobic machines, sauna, conference center with business services, supervised children's program.
TV and VCR. TVs in all rooms, with 8 channels including CNN and cable movie channels. No VCRs.
No-smoking rooms. None.
Credit cards. AE, DC, MC, V.
Wheelchair accessibility. No accessible rooms.
Prices. Dec 21–Mar 31: doubles $231–$407 AP; duplexes $410 AP; suites $490 AP. Low season: doubles $137–$216 AP; duplexes $410 AP; suites $476 AP.

CLUB MED LA CARAVELLE

👔	🛏	🍴	🌅	**TOTAL**
52.8%	**25.0%**	**63.9%**	**77.8%**	**54.9%**

This 50-acre all-inclusive resort on Caravelle Beach, on the south coast of Grande-Terre, has three hotel units and a latticed open-air central building.

Reader Report

"A civilized shangri-la where palm trees emerge from a magnificent beach and their leaves dance above the gentle surf."

CHRISTINA BRAUN, OCEANSIDE, NEW YORK

"Great location, good beaches, lots of sports opportunities. There is an interesting mix of different nationalities: not too American, not too European. The resort is somewhat isolated

La Pointe de la Grande Vigie

La Désirade

Porte
d'Enfer

Grande-Anse

D122

Campêche

N8 Gros-Cap
Anse de la
Savane Brûlée

Les Mangles

N6 D120

ATLANTIC
OCEAN

Baie du
Nord Ouest

N5 Morne-à-l'Eau
N5 N7 Le Moule

Jabrun
du Nord

GRANDE-TERRE

ud

Anse á la
Baie

Anse de la
Gourde

St-François Hamak

N4 Anse
Kahouanne Tarare
Pte. des
Châteaux

Raisin-
Clairs

Gosier

Le Méridien
Guadeloupe TO
LA DÉSIRADE

Ste-Anne

Caravelle
Beach

Club Med
La Caravelle

de la
ur

Ilet du Gosier

Iles de la
Petite Terre

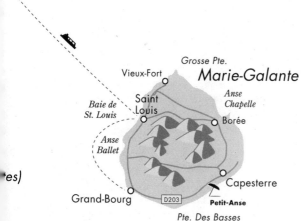

Grosse Pte.
Marie-Galante

Vieux-Fort

Anse
Chapelle

Saint
Louis

Baie de
St. Louis

Borée

Anse
Ballet

es)

Capesterre

Grand-Bourg D203

Petit-Anse

Pte. Des Basses

from the rest of the island, so nightlife opportunities are limited."

JAN KROMSCHROEDER, NEW YORK, NEW YORK

Address. 97180 Ste. Anne, Guadeloupe, F.W.I., tel. 590/88–21–00 or 800/258–2633, fax 590/88–06–06.
Affiliation. Club Med.
Rooms. 311 rooms. All have air-conditioning, but showers only.
Facilities. 2 restaurants, 2 bars/lounges, nightclub, theater, 6 lighted tennis courts, 6 unlighted, exercise room with weights and aerobic machines, aerobics classes, sailboats, circus workshops, kayaking, snorkeling, archery, volleyball, basketball.
TV and VCR. TV in public area only, with about 12 channels including CNN and cable movie channels. No VCRs.
No-smoking rooms. None.
Credit cards. AE, MC, V.
Restrictions. Mini Club available to children 6 to 11 during holiday weeks.
Wheelchair accessibility. No accessible rooms.
Prices. Dec 10–Apr 30: $170–$260. Low season: $112. Prices are all-inclusive and per person.

HAMAK

👔	🛏	✕	🌅	**TOTAL**
83.3%	**33.3%**	**50.04%**	**83.3%**	**62.5%**

In an attractive tropical park, this 6-acre resort on a private, white-sand beach has bungalow suites—each with a living room, a small bedroom, and a private patio. Built in 1978 and renovated in 1993, the hotel sits right beween a 600-acre lagoon and an 18-hole golf course designed by R. Trent-Jones.

Reader Report

"Of all the places I've been in the Caribbean [Hamak is] extremely peaceful, refined, and relaxing. It attracts a high caliber of clientele with low pretension.... The superb staff is unusually friendly towards non-French speaking people."

ROBERT HALL, CHICAGO, ILLINOIS

"The service is superb and waiters and waitresses go out of their way to do special things for you—they took the lobster out of the shell for my husband when he asked.... Each bungalow has its own hammock; I sit there every night and read."

KRISTEN COLBY, FREDERICK, MARYLAND

Address. St-Francois 97118, Guadeloupe, F.W.I., tel. 590/88–59–99, fax 590/88–41–92.
Rooms. 56 suites in bungalows. All have air-conditioning and minibars.
Facilities. 2 restaurants, bar/lounge, 6 lighted tennis courts nearby, 18-hole golf course nearby, hot tub, casino nearby, an

exercise room with weights and aerobic machines, dry-cleaning, 18-hour room service, sailboats

TV and VCR. TVs in rooms on request, with only French channels. No VCRs.

No-smoking rooms. None.

Credit cards. AE, MC, V.

Restrictions. Min. 11 nights Dec. 20–Jan. 3

Wheelchair accessibility. 56 suites.

Prices. Dec. 21–Mar. 15: suites $345–$440 AP. Low season: suites $265–$320 AP.

LE MERIDIEN GUADELOUPE

🕴️⛵	🛏️	✕	☀️🌊	**TOTAL**
55.6%	**66.7%**	**77.8%**	**77.8%**	**69.4%**

Guests at this 150-acre resort stay in a four-story hotel building located just south of St-François, near Grande-Terre's eastern tip, on the Raisin-Clairs beach. The hotel was built in 1973 and renovated in 1989.

Reader Report

"The food was wonderful, the staff very helpful. What a beautiful location!"

JAMES S. REYNOLDS, PROVIDENCE, RHODE ISLAND

"It's a great place, a delightful, historically enlightening cab ride from the main town, with the best beach on the island. The staff is outstanding, the food excellent. I highly recommend it."

JOHN C. O'MALLEY, MASSACHUSETTS

"The setting is magnificent, near a fishing village and a beautiful golf course."

EVA JAMNER, BROOKLYN, NEW YORK

Address. Box 37–97118 St–François, Guadeloupe, F.W.I., tel. 590/88–51–00, fax 590/88–40–71.

Affiliation. Meridien Hotels.

Rooms. 265 rooms including 11 suites. All have air-conditioning.

Facilities. 2 restaurants, bar/lounge, coffee shop, 2 lighted tennis courts, 18-hole golf course nearby, freshwater pool, casino nearby, massages.

TV and VCR. TV in all rooms, with 4 channels including CNN. No VCRs.

No-smoking rooms. None.

Credit cards. AE, CB, DC, MC, V.

Restrictions. Min 5 nights Dec 17–Mar 31.

Wheelchair accessibility. No accessible rooms.

Prices. Dec 18–Mar 1: doubles $272–$464; suites $420–$780. Low season: doubles $196; suites $357–$535. All rates include Continental breakfast.

JAMAICA

    TOTAL

68.7% | **53.2%** | **55.7%** | **39.9%** | **55.5%**

Reader Report

"Beautiful beaches and the spectacular Blue Mountains—with a great variety of scenery and excellent cuisine. If you drive, allow plenty of time—roads are primitive and 30 miles may take two hours."

BETTY M. VAN IERSEL, BRISTOL, RHODE ISLAND

"Visit the Dunn's River falls, and stay out of every town and in the resort (or on your ship). The locals will hound you; if you must go into town, shave your head to avoid the braiding vendors and wear a cleric's collar to discourage the people trying to sell you marijuana."

P. J. FAGLEY, WEXFORD, PENNSYLVANIA

"We have found that staying at one of the many all-inclusive resorts shelters a visitor from the unfortunate negative aspects of this otherwise happy and relaxed destination."

NAME WITHHELD, STERLING HEIGHTS, MICHIGAN

"Outside of Kingston and Montego Bay proper, it is a wonderful vacation experience—friendly people, light breezes, azure waters, virgin vegetation, and great Blue Mountain coffee."

GARY W. VAUGHN, ARLINGTON, TEXAS

Islands. Jamaica is an independent nation, with 4,244 square miles and a population of about 2,470,000.

Language. The official language is English, though a Jamaican patois is widely spoken by the islanders.

Visitor Information

In the U.S. Contact the **Jamaica Tourist Board** (801 2nd Ave., 20th floor, New York, NY 10017, tel. 212/856–9727 or 800/233-4JTB, fax 212/856–9730; 500 N. Michigan Ave., Suite 1030, Chicago, IL 60611, tel. 312/527–1296, fax 312/527–1472; 1320 S. Dixie Hwy., Coral Gables, FL 33146, tel. 305/665–0557, fax 305/666–7239; 3440 Wilshire Blvd., Suite 1207, Los Angeles, CA 90010, tel. 213/384–1123, fax 213/384–1123).

In Canada. Contact the **Jamaica Tourist Board** (1 Eglinton Ave. E, Suite 616, Toronto, Ont. M4P 3A1, tel. 416/482–7850, fax 416/482–1730).

In the U.K. Contact the **Jamaica Tourist Board** (1-2 Prince Consort Rd., London, SW7 2BZ, tel. 071/224–0505, fax 071/224–0551).

In Jamaica. Contact the **Jamaica Tourist Board** (2 St. Lucia Ave., Box 360 Kingston 5, Jamaica, W.I., tel. 809/929–9200, fax 809/929–9375). Other branches include Cornwall Beach,

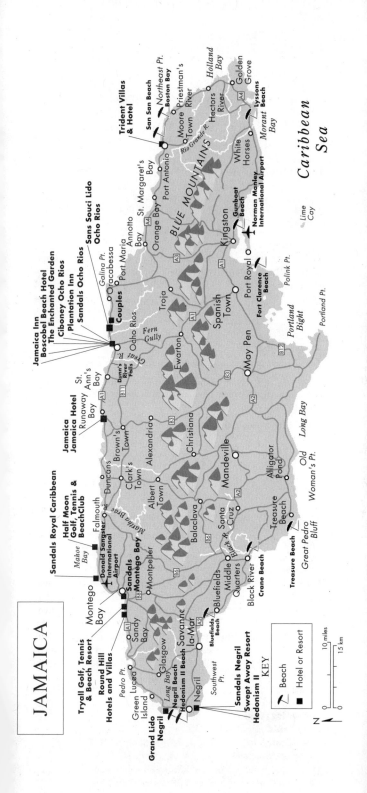

Box 67, Montego Bay, Jamaica, W.I., tel. 809/952–4425, fax 809/952–3587; Adrija Plaza, Negril P.O., Jamaica, W.I., tel. 809/957–4243, fax 809/957–4489; Ocean Village Shopping Centre, Box 240, Ocho Rios, Jamaica, W.I., tel. 809/974–2582, fax 809/974–2559; City Centre Plaza, Box 151, Port Antonio, Jamaica, W.I., tel. 809/993–3051, fax 809/993–2117; and Hendriks Bldg., 2 High St., Black River P.O., St. Elizabeth, Jamaica, W.I., tel. 809/965–2074, fax 809/965–2076.

BOBSCOBEL BEACH HOTEL

				TOTAL
60.3%	53.3%	70.0%	80.0	70.0%

This all-inclusive 14-acre resort on the beach welcomes families and has exemplary day care centers. Built in 1957, the three-story hotel sits in a tiered landscape with lush tropical gardens; it was renovated in 1987 and additional rooms were added in 1991.

Reader Report

"A great family vacation...we played tennis as a family; my wife and I played as a couple; my son got lost in the computer camp for children. The chef was outstanding. [There were] a lot of authentic Jamaican dishes—breadfruit with run-down sauce—and some Caribbean buffets."

DR. BRUCE HANDELSMAN, UPPER NYACK, NEW YORK

"They have an orientation the first night that offered a terrific bike trip—Blue Mountain Bike Tour—and we biked 18 miles downhill.... It gives you a good idea of the island."

PATRICIA YEATON, HAMPTON, NEW HAMPSHIRE

Address. Box 63, Ocho Rios, St. Ann, Jamaica, W.I., tel. 809/975–7330 or 800/859–7873, fax 809/975–7370.
Affiliation. Superclubs Super-Inclusive Hotels.
Rooms. 196 rooms, 11 suites. All have air-conditioning and ceiling fans.
Facilities. 3 restaurants, 5 bars/lounges, 4 lighted tennis courts, 18-hole golf course, 9-hole golf course, 2 freshwater pools, 2 hot tubs, slot machines, exercise room with weights and aerobic machines, aerobic classes, massages, salon, dry-cleaning, conference center with business services, supervised children's program, dive center, sailboats.
TV and VCR. TVs in all rooms, with 11 channels including CNN and cable movie channels. VCRs in public area.
No-smoking rooms. None.
Credit cards. AE, MC, V.
Restrictions. Min. 7 nights Dec. 24–31, Feb. 17–24, Apr. 6–13.
Wheelchair accessibility. No accessible rooms.
Prices. Dec 16–Apr 12: doubles $235–$255 MAP; suites $305–$375 MAP. Low season: $165–$185 MAP; suites $235–$305 MAP.

CIBONEY OCHO RIOS

👤	🛏	🍴	☀	**TOTAL**
75.9%	**81.5%**	**74.1%**	**70.4%**	**75.5%**

This 45-acre, all-inclusive resort has a four-story plantation-style great house, scattered villas, and its own spa. The hotel was built in 1990 and renovated in 1993.

Reader Report

"A nice resort with a unique concept—your own villa where meals can be served. The beach is small and the grounds a little too spread-out for my taste. Unlimited massages were a plus—book early in your stay."

TED SMARZ, BERKELEY HEIGHTS, NEW JERSEY

"What luxury! The food and service is the most outstanding we've experience in the islands. The restaurant choice made this like a landlocked cruise—only better!"

RICHARD L. HUGGINS, ALTAMONTE SPRINGS, FLORIDA

Address. Box 728, Main St., Ocho Rios, St. Ann, Jamaica, W.I., tel. 809/974–1036 or 800/333–3333, fax 809/974–5838 or 809/974–7148.
Affiliation. Radisson Hotels International.
Rooms. 38 rooms and 80 villas with 251 suites. All have air-conditioning and ceiling fans. All villas have minibars. 14 villas have Jacuzzis.
Facilities. 4 restaurants, 2 cafés, 8 bars/lounges, 6 lighted tennis courts, 2 freshwater pools plus 90 freshwater pools (each is private and shared by several villas), exercise room with weights and aerobic machines, aerobics classes, massages, sauna, salon, dry-cleaning, conference center with business services, dive center, sailboats.
TV and VCR. TV in all rooms, with 14 channels including CNN and cable movie channels. VCRs upon request.
No-smoking rooms. None.
Credit cards. AE, CB, DC, D, MC, V.
Restrictions. No children under 16.
Wheelchair accessibility. No accessible rooms.
Prices. Yearly rates: doubles $400–$420; suites $460– $700. $100 additional Dec 23–31; $50 additional Feb 3–Mar 31. Rates are all-inclusive.

COUPLES

👤	🛏	🍴	☀	**TOTAL**
67.5%	**60.0%**	**65.0%**	**75.0%**	**66.9%**

This all-inclusive beachfront resort for couples consists of a five-story, contemporary-style hotel building set on 19 acres near Ocho Rios. It was built in 1954 and renovated in 1995.

Reader Report

"Rooms are quite nice, with lovely views of either the sparkling water or the fabulous Blue Mountains. Service was outstanding. The food and drink were excellent and plentiful. The private island is delightful."

PHIL AND DEBBIE NOBLE, TEMPLE, TEXAS

"Any sport you could want is available, and the staff was beyond compare—you are treated like royalty. Extremely romantic."

NAME WITHHELD, POTOMAC, MARYLAND

"I loved the fact that Couples freed me from carrying wads of cash or signing vouchers for drinks and food throughout the resort. Once you get there, your money worries are nonexistent. There's never a dull moment, with all the daily activities, but you never feel rushed to do anything. I enjoyed having only couples—no kids and no groups of spring-breakers. It made the vacation very romantic."

ANDRIS ZVERS, GREENDALE, WISCONSIN

Address. Tower Isle, St. Mary, Jamaica, W.I., tel. 809/975–4271 or 800/859–7873, fax 809/975–4439.

Affiliation. None.

Rooms. 164 rooms, 8 suites. All have air-conditioning. All suites have Jacuzzis.

Facilities. 4 restaurants, 4 bars/lounges, 3 lighted tennis courts, 2 unlighted, freshwater pool, horseback riding, exercise room with weights and aerobic machines, aerobics classes, massages, salon, dive center, sailboats, games room with slot machines.

TV and VCR. TVs in all rooms, with 24 channels including CNN and cable movie channels. No VCRs.

No-smoking rooms. None.

Credit cards. AE, MC, V.

Restrictions. Min. 3 nights. Couples 18 and older only; no gay couples.

Wheelchair accessibility. No accessible rooms.

Prices. Dec 22–Mar 28: doubles $2,920–$3,220 weekly: suites $1,985 per person weekly. Low season: doubles $2,260–$2,920 weekly; suites $1,805 per person weekly. Rates are all-inclusive.

THE ENCHANTED GARDEN

				TOTAL
57.1%	71.4%	50.0%	85.7%	66.1%

Built in 1991, this two-story resort has 20 acres of lush botanical gardens with 14 waterfalls and exotic tropical plants and flowers. Guests also enjoy an aviary and seaquarium. The beach is 10 minutes away by shuttle.

Reader Report

"Service was delightful—the employees were wonderful, from the wine steward to the groundskeeper. The only thing I didn't like was that it wasn't on the beach. The gardens were magnificent...we felt like we were in a tropical paradise—set on the hillside, waterfalls cascaded down.... You could arrange your own private meal near the falls in the garden."

MARY HAEGELE, WAUWATOSA, WISCONSIN

"A very enjoyable, very lush, very tropical setting.... There were hammocks placed throughout the property."

NAME WITHHELD, NORTH MIAMI BEACH, FLORIDA

Address. Box 284, Ocho Rios, St. Ann, Jamaica, W.I., tel. 809/974–1400 or 800/554–2008, fax 809/974–5823.
Affiliation. DHC Resorts.
Rooms. 58 rooms and 55 suites. All have air-conditioning. All suites have minibars. 40 suites have ceiling fans and plunge pools.
Facilities. 5 restaurants, 4 bars/lounges, 2 lighted tennis courts, 2 freshwater pools, an exercise room with weights and aerobic machines, aerobic classes, spa, salon, sauna, dry-cleaning.
TV and VCR. TVs in all rooms, with 8 channels including CNN and movie channels. TV and VCR in public area.
No-smoking rooms. None.
Credit cards. AE, DC, MC, V.
Restrictions. Min. 7 nights Dec. 26-Jan. 2. No children under 16.
Wheelchair accessibility. No accessible rooms.
Prices. Dec. 23–Apr. 19: doubles $160–$235 AP; suites $215–$225 AP. Low season: doubles $135–$210 AP; suites $195–$205 AP.

GRAND LIDO NEGRIL

👔	🛏	🍴	🌅	**TOTAL**
85.0%	**80.0%**	**80.0%**	**90.0%**	**83.8%**

This all-inclusive 24-acre resort for adults combines Mexican, European, and Caribbean architecture in its two-story beach-front hotel units. It's near Negril, on the western tip of the island. The hotel was built in 1989.

Reader Report

"Fantastic. A beautiful nude beach, and a great pool and bar; my room was excellent. The staff was very helpful, and the food was superb. A wonderful all-inclusive holiday—one week was not enough."

BEVERLEY HODDINOTT, TAMPA, FLORIDA

"Champagne at the Jacuzzi around midnight, lamb chops whenever you want, and service that is outstanding—I've

been there four times and will keep going back. It has to be the best all-inclusive resort around."

TED SMARZ, BERKELEY HEIGHTS, NEW JERSEY

Address. Box 88, Norman Manley Blvd., Negril, Jamaica, W.I., tel. 809/957–4010 or 800/859–7873, fax 809/957–4158.
Affiliation. Super Clubs Resorts.
Rooms. 182 junior suites, 18 1–bedroom suites. All have air-conditioning and ceiling fans.
Facilities. 3 restaurants, 9 bars/lounges, 2 lighted tennis courts, 2 unlighted, wind-surfing, sailing, scuba-diving, 2 freshwater pools, exercise room with weights and aerobic machines, massages, sauna, salon, 24-hr room service, dry-cleaning, conference center with business services, sailboats.
TV and VCR. TV in all rooms, with 13 channels including CNN and cable movie channels. VCR in public area.
No-smoking rooms. None.
Credit cards. AE, MC, V.
Restrictions. No children under 16. Min. 3 nights.
Wheelchair accessibility. No accessible rooms.
Prices. Dec 24–Apr 7: $2,070–$2,250 for 3 nights. Low season: $1,760–$1,940 for 3 nights. Rates are all-inclusive and per person.

HALF MOON GOLF, TENNIS & BEACH CLUB

				TOTAL
75.7%	75.7%	65.7%	78.6%	73.9%

This two-story, colonial-style resort complex, with some cottages on the beach, was built in 1953 and last renovated in 1995. It's on 400 acres on the north coast, seven miles east of Montego Bay.

Reader Report

"A one-of-a-kind resort experience ideal for a laid-back Jamaica holiday. There's plenty to do—golf, tennis, snorkeling, scuba diving, windsurfing, sailing, fishing—but there is no pressure to do it. The food is superb, the help friendly, the overall ambience relaxing."

WILL GODDARD, ST. PAUL, CALIFORNIA

"Service and quality from the moment we arrived. It was never a problem to order drinks from poolside or the beach. Meals were excellent, service polite. We felt like we were guests in someone's home."

PHILIP H. FEATHER, ANNVILLE, PENNSYLVANIA

Address. Box 80, Rose Hall, Montego Bay, Jamaica, W.I., tel. 809/953–2211 or 800/626–0592, fax 809/953–2731.
Rooms. 220 rooms, 165 suites, 20 villas. All rooms have mini-bars and air-conditioning.
Facilities. 6 restaurants, 5 bars/lounges, 7 lighted tennis courts,

6 unlighted, 18-hole golf course, 2 freshwater pools plus 35 private pools for individual villas, horseback riding, exercise room with weights and aerobic machines, aerobics classes, massages, sauna, salon, conference center with business services, supervised children's program, dive center, sailboats, croquet court.

TV and VCR. TV in public area and in all rooms, with 7 channels including CNN and cable movie channels. VCRs in rooms on request.

No-smoking rooms. None.

Credit cards. AE, CB, DC, C, V.

Restrictions. Min. 14 nights during Christmas and New Year's.

Wheelchair accessibility. 40 rooms.

Prices. Dec 15–Apr 15: doubles $560–$740 AP, $430–$610 MAP, $300—$480 EP; suites $790–$920 AP, $660–$790 MAP, $530–$660 EP; villas $560 AP, $430 MAP, $300 EP. Low season: doubles $450–$530 AP, $320–$400 MAP, $190–$270 EP; suites $560–$660 AP, $430–$530 MAP, $300—$400 EP; villas $450 AP, $320 MAP, $190 EP.

HEDONISM II

| 74.5% | 36.4% | 58.2% | 80.0% | **TOTAL** 62.3% |

Set on 22 acres of landscaped gardens along Negril's 7-mile beach on Jamaica's western shore, this two-story resort is designed for singles and couples who enjoy high-energy activity as well as relaxation. The hotel was built in 1975 and restored in 1986.

Reader Report

"[Having a good time] depends a lot on who you meet; the people make it...the rooms are OK for the time you spend in there. When you're out all night, it doesn't really matter."

JOHN KANNON, PLYMOUTH, MINNESOTA

"A noisy place.... It attracts a large crowd of people that enjoy that partying lifestyle."

NAME WITHHELD, FAIR HAVEN, NEW JERSEY

Address. Box 25, Negril, Jamaica, W.I., tel. 809/957–4200 or 800/859–7873, fax 809/957–4289.

Affiliation. Superclubs Super-Inclusive Hotels.

Rooms. 280 rooms. All have air-conditioning.

Facilities. 2 restaurants, 5 bars/lounges, 6 lighted tennis courts, 2 squash courts, freshwater pool, 2 hot tubs, horseback riding, exercise room with weights and aerobic machines, aerobic classes, trapeze and trampoline clinics, massages, dive center, sailboats.

TV and VCR. TV with 5 sports channels in disco area.

No-smoking rooms. None.

Credit cards. AE, MC, V.

Restrictions. Min. age 18 years.
Wheelchair accessibility. No accessible rooms.
Prices. Dec 23–Apr 12: doubles $675–$1,470 AP. Low season: doubles $535–$1,260 AP.

JAMAICA INN

🍸	🛏	✕	☀	TOTAL
76.0%	80.0%	76.0%	72.0	76.0%

On the north coast of the island, this vintage, two-story, colonial-style retreat on 7 acres has a private beach, and each room has its own balcony or large veranda. The quiet hotel was built in 1950 and expanded in 1969; renovation is on-going

Reader Report

"The owner was there the whole time, and he made sure that each guest enjoyed his/her stay.... The worst part is getting to and from the airport.... I recommend the American plan, breakfast and dinner included; the food is good, and the wine choices are excellent. You can dine on the terrace; they have a live Jamaican band, and you can dance under the stars on the veranda—a definite high point of our trip."

NAME WITHHELD, BAYSIDE , NEW YORK.

"This was the closest place to heaven I've ever been, with an Old World charm. It's very laid-back.... There was a lot to do if you like to shop, but if you don't know how to relax, you'll probably get bored."

CAROL GILES, FORT WORTH, TEXAS

Address. Box 1, Main St., Ocho Rios, Jamaica, W.I., tel. 809/974–2514 or 800/837–4608, fax 809/974–2449.
Rooms. 42 rooms, 3 suites. All have air-conditioning and ceiling fans.
Facilities. Restaurant, 2 bars/lounges, freshwater pool, 2 lighted tennis courts nearby, croquet, exercise room with weights and aerobic machines, massages, dry-cleaning, sailboats, kayaks, snorkel equipment.
TV and VCR. No TV or VCR.
No-smoking rooms. None.
Credit cards. AE, D, DC, MC, V.
Restrictions. Min. 7 nights Dec. 20–Jan. 2. No children under 14.
Wheelchair accessibility. No accessible rooms.
Prices. Dec. 16–Apr. 15: doubles $385–$475 AP; suites $490–$800 AP. Low season: doubles $220–$275 MAP; suites $290–$475 MAP.

JAMAICA JAMAICA HOTEL

				TOTAL
78.4%	40.5%	59.5%	78.4%	64.2%

Built in the mid-1960s and renovated in 1993, this all-inclusive adults-only resort has a two-story hotel building and 22 acres in Runaway Bay, in the middle of the island's north coast.

Reader Report

"Geared for active, fun people. The food is good and very Jamaican. The staff makes you feel at home. I travel alone and was very comfortable there, with a fun-filled week of games, climbing a waterfall, dancing, swimming, jogging on the beach, and swinging in a hammock in the moonlight."

NAN MCMAHAN, PACIFIC GROVE, CALIFORNIA

"We both enjoyed it very much. The food was local Jamaican fare, which we liked. There was entertainment every night, similar to a cruise ship. Everyone sat around the piano in the evening, singing and enjoying their cocktails. It was very laid back, very relaxed."

JOHN AND CAROLYN SHEEHAN, SOUTH PLAINFIELD, NEW JERSEY

Address. Box 58, Runaway Bay, St. Ann, Jamaica, W.I., tel. 809/973–2436 or 800/859–7873, fax 809/973-2352.
Affiliation. Super Clubs Resorts.
Rooms. 238 rooms, 4 suites. All have air-conditioning. All suites and 4 rooms have minibars.
Facilities. 2 restaurants, 4 bars/lounges, 4 lighted tennis courts, 18-hole golf course, 2 freshwater pools, horseback riding, exercise room with weights and aerobic machines, aerobics classes, dive center, sailboats.
TV and VCR. TVs in public area and in all rooms, with over 10 channels including CNN and cable movie channels. VCRs in all suites.
No-smoking rooms. None.
Credit cards. AE, MC, V.
Restrictions. No children under 16. Min. 3 nights.
Wheelchair accessibility. 4 rooms.
Prices. Jan 6–Apr 12: doubles $745 for 3 nights; suites $788 for 3 nights. Low season: doubles $640 for 3 nights; suites $683 for 3 nights. Rates are all-inclusive and per person.

PLANTATION INN

				TOTAL
80.8%	61.5%	65.4%	76.9%	71.2%

This hotel just east of Ocho Rios occupies a three-story colonial-style plantation house, with a colonnaded portico. It was built in 1957 and renovated in 1993.

Reader Report

"Loved the resort—it was restful and lush. I would go back."

NAME AND ADDRESS WITHHELD

"I've stayed there twice, and enjoyed it thoroughly both times. Off-season, you have the place to yourselves. It's not the best choice if you want a lot of action—it's a quiet little resort, good if you want to play on the beach, read, and relax."

ELISA SCHWARTZ, SANTA MARIA, CALIFORNIA

"Charming, with a delightful location on the beach. This is certainly a deluxe resort, offering all the amenities one would hope to find. I give it five stars for ambience."

ROBERT P. SCHRON, NEW YORK, NEW YORK

"Very peaceful and quiet. The food is exceptional, even by good resort standards. They have a spa program where you receive massages in what seems to be a stone castle turret, overlooking the ocean."

DONNELLE OXLEY, LINDEN, VIRGINIA

Address. Box 2, Ocho Rios, Jamaica, W.I., tel. 809/974–5601 or 800/752–6824, fax 809/974–5912.

Affiliation. Friends International Resorts.

Rooms. 80 rooms including 13 junior suites, 2 penthouse suites, 2 villas. All have air-conditioning, private balconies, an ocean view and ceiling fans. 16 rooms and all suites have minibars.

Facilities. Restaurant, 2 bars/lounges, lighted tennis court, 1 unlighted, freshwater pool, private freshwater pools for both villas, exercise room with weights and aerobic machines, aerobics classes, massages, sauna, salon, gift shop, tour desk, conference center with business services, supervised children's program, sailboats, windsurfing, snorkeling, kayaking, glass bottom boat ride, billiards, croquet.

TV and VCR. TVs in all rooms, with 17 channels including CNN and cable movie channels. VCR in public area.

No-smoking rooms. None.

Credit cards. AE, DC, MC, V.

Restrictions. 7 night minimum stay during holidays.

Wheelchair accessibility. No accessible rooms.

Prices. Dec 19–Mar 14: doubles $195–$270 EP; suites $345–$715 EP; villas $4,375–$5,110 EP. Low season: doubles $135–$155 EP; suites $180–$310 EP; villas $2,205–$3,080 EP. Add $50 per person for MAP.

ROUND HILL HOTEL AND VILLAS

| 90.6% | 81.3% | 78.1% | 87.5% | **TOTAL** 84.4% |

This 98-acre all-inclusive resort, eight miles west of Montego Bay, has a two-story seaside main building and scattered privately owned villas, all in tropical colonial architecture. The hotel was built in 1953, and renovation has been ongoing.

Reader Report

"We've been there twice. The setting, on a hill, is spectacular and the staff treats us like a king and queen. The only thing my husband missed was exercise equipment—and that's been put in since our visit."

BARBARA SPENCER, GREENWICH, CONNECTICUT

"A beautiful place, well laid-out—no need to go too far to find interesting flora and fauna."

STUART FLEISHMAN, MYRTLE BEACH, SOUTH CAROLINA

"Romantic and enchanting. The service was good; one of the waiters brought us a bouquet of flowers while we were having drinks in the lounge. He said 'You two look like you're in love.' Staff people always stopped to answer a question and never frowned."

CHRIS BACHMAN, ROLLING HILLS ESTATES, CALIFORNIA

Address. Box 64, Montego Bay, Jamaica, W.I., tel. 809/952–5150 or 800/972–2159, fax 809/952–2505.
Rooms. 36 rooms in main building and 74 suites in 27 villas. All have air-conditioning and ceiling fans.
Facilities. Restaurant, 3 bars/lounges, 2 lighted tennis courts, 3 unlighted, 18-hole golf course nearby, freshwater pool, plus 17 villas with private pools, exercise room with weights and aerobic machines, aerobics classes, massages, salon, gift shop, art gallery, dry-cleaning, dive center, sailboats.
TV and VCR. The hotel gets no channels, but you can rent VCRs and TV monitors.
No-smoking rooms. None.
Credit cards. AE, DC, MC, V.
Restrictions. Min. 14 nights during Christmas and New Year's.
Wheelchair accessibility. No accessible rooms.
Prices. Dec 15–Apr 16: doubles $470–$550 FAP, $430–$510 MAP, $300–$380 EP; suites $640–$860 FAP, $600–$820 MAP, $470–$690 EP; entire villas $5,000–$9,000 weekly with breakfast. Low season: doubles $350–$390 FAP, $310–$350 MAP, $190–$230 EP; suites $420–$520 FAP, $380–$480 MAP, $260–$360 EP; entire villas $2,500–$4,500 weekly with breakfast.

SANDALS MONTEGO BAY

| 62.3% | 43.4% | 49.1% | 52.8% | **TOTAL** 51.9% |

This all-inclusive resort for couples, located on a 26-acre coastal strip right next to the airport in Montego Bay, has a three-story main hotel, villas, and a 1,700-foot beach. The hotel was built in 1951, renovated in 1981, and expanded in 1990.

Reader Report

"Food, service, accommodations, and activities are all very good. The beach is one-half-mile long, sandy, and beautiful. It's five minutes away from the airport, and you can hear the planes landing and taking off, but we would return in a second—we plan to do so for our next vacation."

DONNA AND MARK BUDKA, ROTTERDAM, NEW YORK

"Tons of fun, superb service, excellent barefoot elegance—you can do as much or as little as you wish."

NAME WITHHELD, ROSLINDALE, MASSACHUSETTS

Address. Box 100, Kent Ave., Montego Bay, Jamaica, W.I., tel. 809/952–5510 or 800/726–3257, fax 809/952–0816.
Affiliation. Sandals Resorts International.
Rooms. 215 rooms, 28 suites. All have air-conditioning. All suites have minibars and ceiling fans.
Facilities. 4 restaurants, 4 bars/lounges, 4 lighted tennis courts, 2 freshwater pools, exercise room with weights and aerobic machines, massages, sauna, salon, sailboats.
TV and VCR. TVs in all rooms, with 11 channels including cable movie channels. No VCRs.
No-smoking rooms. None.
Credit cards. MC, V.
Restrictions. Min. 3 nights year-round. No children under 18, gay couples, or singles.
Wheelchair accessibility. No accessible rooms.
Prices. Dec 22–Mar 29: doubles $1,350–$1,610 for 3 nights; suites $1,740–$3,030 for 3 nights. Low season: doubles $1310–$1,560 for 3 nights; suites $1690–$2940 for 3 nights. All rates are all-inclusive.

SANDALS NEGRIL

👤	🛏	🍴	☀	TOTAL
82.9%	73.2%	78.0%	87.8%	80.5%

Two 1970s-era resorts were combined and reopened in 1989 as this 21-acre, all-inclusive, couples-only resort just east of Negril. Guests stay in three-story rustic- and tropical-style accommodations. The hotel was renovated in 1988, and rooms were added in 1994.

Reader Report

"The beach is great and located on seven miles of white sand. The resort is clean and well kept, the staff among the friendliest you can find. Activities and entertainment are good and the food is excellent. Not to be left out are the fantastic sunsets."

GARY A. GREENQUIST, FRANKSVILLE, WISCONSIN

"The best beach and the best sunsets."

NAME WITHHELD, ROSLINDALE, MASSACHUSETTS

Address. Box 12, Negril, Westmoreland, Jamaica, W.I., tel. 809/957–4216 or 800/726–3257, fax 809/957–4338.
Affiliation. Sandals Resorts International.
Rooms. 187 rooms, 28 suites. All have air-conditioning and ceiling fans. All suites have minibars.
Facilities. 4 restaurants, 3 bars/lounges, 4 lighted tennis courts, 2 freshwater pools, horseback riding, exercise room with weights and aerobic machines, aerobics classes, sauna, salon, conference center with business services.
TV and VCR. TVs in all rooms, with 12 channels including CNN and cable movie channels. VCR in public area.
No-smoking rooms. None.
Credit cards. MC, V.
Restrictions. Min. 3 nights year-round. No children under 18, gay couples, or singles.
Wheelchair accessibility. 4 rooms.
Prices. Dec 22–Mar 29: doubles $1,610–$1,960 for 3 nights; suites $2,170–$2,390 for 3 nights. Low season: doubles $1,550–$1,880 for 3 nights; suites $2,080–$2,290 for 3 nights. All rates are all-inclusive.

SANDALS OCHO RIOS

👤 75.6%	🛏 60.0%	🍴 66.7%	☀ 66.7%	**TOTAL** 67.2%

This 12-acre all-inclusive resort built in 1989, for couples only, is a mile west of Ocho Rios. Guests stay in a high-rise main building or garden cottages.

Reader Report

"Sandals is a great place for couples and honeymoons–it's a great time."

Tony Knickerbocker, Ballwin, Missouri

"Food, service, accommodations, and activities are very good—the desserts are very good. The beach is very small and manmade—you have to fight for a lounge chair—and the sea floor is rocky."

Donna and Mark Budka, Rotterdam, New York

Address. Box 771, Ocho Rios, Jamaica, W.I., tel. 809/974–5691 or 800/726–3257, fax 809/974–5700.
Affiliation. Sandals Resorts International.
Rooms. 237 rooms, all with air-conditioning and ceiling fans.
Facilities. 4 restaurants, 4 bars/lounges, 2 lighted tennis courts, 18-hole golf course, 3 freshwater pools, slot machines, dive center, sailboats.
TV and VCR. TVs in all rooms, with 11 channels including CNN and cable movie channels. No VCRs.
No-smoking rooms. None.
Credit cards. MC, V.
Restrictions. Min. 3 nights year-round. No children under 18, gay couples, or singles.

Wheelchair accessibility. No accessible rooms.
Prices. Dec 22–Mar 29: doubles $1,450–$1,780 for 3 nights.
Low season: doubles $1,390–$1,720 for 3 nights. Rates are
all-inclusive.

SANDALS ROYAL JAMAICAN

				TOTAL
89.3%	67.9%	78.6%	75.0%	77.7%

This 17-acre all-inclusive resort, for couples only, sits on the
north coast, east of Montego Bay. Guests stay in 11 two- and
three-story British colonial–style units, first built in 1957. The
hotel was renovated in 1986 and expanded in 1990.

Reader Report

*"The resort has a friendly, helpful staff giving impeccable
service. Be sure to request a song in the piano bar."*

SHIRLEY FIHN, DETROIT LAKES, MINNESOTA

*"My personal favorite among the Jamaican all-inclusive
properties."*

NAME WITHHELD, STERLING HEIGHTS, MICHIGAN

Address. Box 167, Kent Ave., Montego Bay, Jamaica, W.I., tel.
809/953–2231 or 800/726–3257, fax 809/953–2788.
Affiliation. Sandals Resorts International.
Rooms. 176 rooms, 14 suites. All have air-conditioning and
ceiling fans. All suites and 37 rooms have minibars.
Facilities. 4 restaurants, 4 bars/lounges, 2 lighted tennis courts, 1
unlighted, 18-hole golf course, 3 freshwater pools, exercise room
with weights, aerobics classes, massages, sauna, salon, dry-cleaning, conference center with business services, dive center, sailboats.
TV and VCR. TVs in all rooms, with 10 channels including CNN
and cable movie channels. No VCRs.
No-smoking rooms. None.
Credit cards. AE, MC, V.
Restrictions. Min. 3 nights year-round. No children under 18,
gay couples, or singles.
Wheelchair accessibility. 24 rooms.
Prices. Dec 22–Mar 29: doubles $1,400–$1,750 for 3 nights;
suites $1,970 for 3 nights. Low season: doubles
$1,350–$1,680 for 3 nights; suites $1,890 for 3 nights. All
rates are all-inclusive.

SANS SOUCI LIDO OCHO RIOS

				TOTAL
80.0%	73.3%	80.0%	70.0%	75.8%

This 12-acre spa resort, with its own mineral spring, houses
guests in three-story, pink terraced buildings set into a steep

hillside above a bay. Located a few miles east of Ocho Rios, the hotel was built in 1969, expanded in 1990, and renovated in 1993.

Reader Report

"Our first visit was for our honeymoon (a perfect spot). We loved it so much we returned for our first anniversary. The service, food, and atmosphere are wonderful! The beach is small but the water is fantastic, due to natural springs emptying directly into the sea."

JEANNE HALKOWICH, WILLIAMSBURG, VIRGINIA

"We had a glorious week in an oceanview penthouse. Loved the pristine beach cove and the hotel's glass-bottom boat. Sans Souci means relaxation, and that's just what you'll do in the mineral spring."

MARGEE DREWS, CORONA DEL MAR, CALIFORNIA

"A lovely oasis in the middle of terrible poverty, which is probably why we haven't gone back. Rooms aren't fancy, but are more than adequate, with lovely views. Service and food are both excellent."

JENEANE PEARLMAN, DALLAS, TEXAS

Address. Box 103, Ocho Rios, Jamaica, W.I., tel. 809/974–2353 or 800/203–7456, fax 809/974-2544.
Affiliation. Super Clubs Resorts.
Rooms. 8 rooms, 103 suites. All have air-conditioning and ceiling fans. 64 suites have Jacuzzis.
Facilities. 3 restaurants, 3 bars/lounges, 2 lighted tennis courts, 1 unlighted, 2 freshwater pools, exercise room with weights and aerobic machines, aerobics classes, massages, sauna, salon, 24-hr room service, dry-cleaning, conference center with business services, dive center, sailboats.
TV and VCR. TV in all rooms, with 11 channels including CNN and cable movie channels. No VCRs.
No-smoking rooms. None.
Credit cards. AE, DC, MC, V.
Restrictions. Min. 3 nights. No children under 16.
Wheelchair accessibility. No accessible rooms.
Prices. Dec 14–Apr 15: doubles $1,100 for 3 nights; suites $1,200–$1,700 for 3 nights. Low season: doubles $850 for 3 nights; suites $900–$1,250 for 3 nights.

SWEPT AWAY RESORT

👔	🛏	🍴	☀	**TOTAL**
89.5%	**84.2%**	**84.2%**	**84.2%**	**85.5%**

Built in 1990, this 20-acre, all-inclusive resort for couples-only, has two-story beachfront bungalows on Long Bay, just north of Negril. Across the road is a 10-acre sports complex.

Reader Report

*"On a seven-mile-long beach, this is a lovely all-inclusive
resort with large rooms built among tropical plants and trees.
It has two excellent restaurants and a large exercise center
with an Olympic-size pool and jogging track."*

BRUCE WEISS, CLINTON, CONNECTICUT

*"Everything was really nice. The service was wonderful, the
food great, the beach absolutely gorgeous. Good for sports-
minded people—the dive instruction was excellent."*

JUDY LINSTROM, ACTON, MASSACHUSETTS

Address. Box 77, Negril, Jamaica, W.I., tel. 809/957–4061 or
800/545–7937, fax 809/957–4060.

Rooms. 134 rooms, all with air-conditioning and ceiling fans, all
with showers only.

Facilities. 2 restaurants, 5 bars/lounges, 10 lighted tennis
courts, freshwater pool, exercise room with weights and aerobic
machines, aerobics classes, jogging track, spa services and
massages at an additional cost, sauna, conference center with
business services, dive center, sailboats.

TV and VCR. 2 TVs in public areas only, with 22 channels
including CNN and cable movie channels. VCR in public area.

No-smoking rooms. None.

Credit cards. AE, DC, MC, V.

Restrictions. Min. 3 nights Dec 24–Jan 3.

Wheelchair accessibility. No accessible rooms.

Prices. Dec 24–Apr. 1: $450–$570 AP. Low season:
$416–$520 AP.

TRIDENT VILLAS & HOTEL

👨‍💼	🛏️	🍴	☀️	TOTAL
66.7%	57.1%	52.4%	61.9%	59.5%

This 16-acre resort in Port Antonio, on the island's northeast
coast, features old Jamaica plantation-style architecture; guests
stay in villas or in suites in the hotel. The hotel was built in
1968 and renovated in 1983.

Reader Report

*"One of the most idyllic locations in the Caribbean—quiet,
with manicured lawns trimmed with lush vegetation and
coral. The only noise you hear all day is the pounding surf.
Terrific privacy, and white-glove dining."*

BRUCE WEISS, CLINTON, CONNECTICUT

*"The gardens are incredibly well-kept, and peacocks roam the
lawn. It gets a rather unique clientele of wealthy, offbeat
types...professors, publishers, and the like. The location near
Port Antonio, overlooking the sea and the town, is a big draw."*

ALDEN A. DARNELL, FAIRFIELD BAY, ARKANSAS

Address. Box 119, Port Antonio, Jamaica, W.I., tel. 809/993–2602 or 800/237–3237, fax 809/993–2590.
Affiliation. The Elegant Resorts of Jamaica.
Rooms. 8 rooms, 14 villas. All have minibars, air-conditioning, and ceiling fans.
Facilities. 2 restaurants, 2 bars/lounges, 2 unlighted tennis courts, freshwater pool, horseback riding, massages, conference center with business services, sailboats.
TV and VCR. TV in public area only, with 24 channels including CNN and cable movie channels. VCR in public area.
No-smoking rooms. None.
Credit cards. AE, MC, V.
Restrictions. Min. 7 nights Dec 25–Jan 1.
Wheelchair accessibility. No accessible rooms.
Prices. Dec 15–Apr 14: doubles $480 MAP, $350 EP; villas $670–$930 MAP, $550–$800 EP. Low season: doubles $340 MAP, $220 EP; villas $440–$570 MAP, $320–$450 EP.

TRYALL GOLF, TENNIS & BEACH RESORT

👷	🛏	🍴	🌅	**TOTAL**
84.6%	**76.9%**	**65.4%**	**76.9%**	**76.0%**

This converted 19th-century sugar plantation sits on a hilltop on 2,200-acres 12 miles west of Montego Bay. There's a renovated great house with hotel wings and scattered private villas. All the rooms in the hotel were renovated between 1992 and 1994.

Reader Report

"Gorgeous setting, excellent service and food, and a beautiful and challenging golf course."

NAME WITHHELD, STAMFORD, CONNECTICUT

"We take golf vacations every year, and Tryall offers the best. It's relatively exclusive, the golf course is uncrowded, and caddies are available."

KENNETH BRAUDE, HIGHLAND PARK, ILLINOIS

"A lovely place with great accommodations and household staff. But it's a little remote. Also, the armed guards on the property were a little unnerving, and the beach was barely adequate for us—we're very beach-oriented."

E. K. ROGERS, LEAWOOD, KANSAS

Address. Box 1206, Jamaica, W.I., tel. 809/956–5660 or 800/336–4571, fax 809/956–5673.
Rooms. 27 rooms, 20 junior suites, 47 villas. All have ceiling fans. All rooms and suites and 14 villas have air-conditioning. 20 villas have minibars. 2 villas have Jacuzzis.
Facilities. 2 restaurants, 5 lighted tennis courts, 4 unlighted, 18-hole golf course, freshwater pool, horseback riding, massages, salon, dry-cleaning, dive center, sailboats.
TV and VCR. TVs in public area, with over 20 channels including CNN and cable movie channels. All rooms and junior suites and

most villas have satellite TV. VCRs for rent.
No-smoking rooms. None.
Credit cards. AE, MC, V.
Restrictions. Min. 7 nights Dec 18–Jan 1.
Wheelchair accessibility. No accessible rooms.
Prices. Dec 15–Apr 10: doubles $295–$395 EP per night; junior suites $460–$490 EP per night; villas $3,550–$11,150 EP per week. Low season: doubles $185–$215 EP per night; junior suites $235–$260 EP per night; villas $2,250–$4,550 EP per week. Add $66 per person MAP (not available in villas).

MARTINIQUE

				TOTAL
59.6%	30.9%	33.1%	28.3%	38.4%

Reader Report

"More heavily developed than neighboring Guadeloupe, but the natives are friendlier, more tolerant of non-Francophones, and more ready to share their attractions and customs. Food and lodging are expensive, especially in city and resort areas."

NANCY KOGER, BIG SPRING, TEXAS

"Not my favorite place. But I enjoyed the flower gardens and the rain forest; everything was really green. St. Pierre and the old volcano ruins are beautiful. And although taxi drivers are difficult to deal with, the tour guides are nice."

KAREN KING, EDGAR, WISCONSIN

"Simply the snobbiest group of individuals I have ever met; I felt as if my money wasn't good enough for them in the shops. Vive la France. Couldn't wait to get back to the ship."

NAME WITHHELD, MARSHFIELD, MASSACHUSETTS

"I enjoyed the open-air markets but resented the price gouging of the merchants and therefore refused to buy. But I did like the Mardi Gras and touring the island."

MARY-LOUISE JOHNSON, CAMP HILL, PENNSYLVANIA

Islands. Martinique is a 425-square-mile région of France, with a population of about 360,000.
Language. The official language is French, though a French-Creole patois is widely spoken by the islanders.

Visitor Information

In the U.S. Contact the **Martinique Promotion Bureau** (tel. 800/391–4909, fax 212/838–7855) or the **French Government Tourist Office** (9454 Wilshire Blvd., Beverly Hills, CA 90212, tel 310/271–6665, fax 310/276–2835; 676 N. Michigan Ave., Chicago, IL 60611, tel. 312/751–7800, fax 312/337–6339).
In Canada. Contact the **French Government Tourist Office** (La Maison de France, 1981 McGill College Ave., Suite 490, Montreal, Que. H3A 2W9, tel. 514/288–4264 or 514/845–4868; 30 St. Patrick St., Suite 700, Toronto, Ont. M5T 3A3, tel. 416/593–6427, fax 416/979–7587).
In the U.K. Contact the **French Government Tourist Office** (178 Picadilly, London WIV 0AL, tel. 071/499–6911, no fax).
In Martinique. Contact the **Office Departmental du Tourisme de la Martinique** (B.P. 520, Blvd. Alsassa, Bord de la Mer, Fort de France, Martinique, F.W.I., tel. 596/63–79–60, fax 596/73–66–93).

MARTINIQUE

Martinique Passage

Grand-Rivière   Macouba   Basse-Pointe

Anse-Ceron

Mont Pelée   Ajoupa-Bouillon

D21   N1

Le Lorrain

Marigot

Morne Jakob

Le Prêcheur

N3

Le Morne Rouge

N2

Rade de St-Pierre   St-Pierre

Le Carbet

N3

St-Joseph

Pitons du Carbet

N2

Bellefontaine

Case-Pilote

N1

Fort-de-France

Schoelcher

Baie des Flamands

Pointe du Bout

Baie de Fort-de-France

Anse-Mitan

Hotel

Caribbean Sea   Anse-à-l'Ane   Hote

Les Trois-Ilets

Mt. Bigot

D7

Le Diamant

Anses-d'Arlets

D37

Diamant

Diamond Rock

KEY

- Beach
- Ferry Route
- Hotel or Resort

0 _____ 10 miles
0 _____ 15 km

N

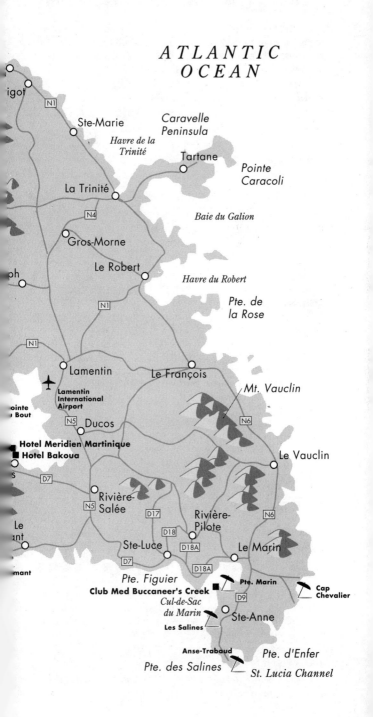

ATLANTIC OCEAN

igot

N1

Ste-Marie

Caravelle Peninsula

Havre de la Trinité

Tartane

Pointe Caracoli

La Trinité

N4

Baie du Galion

Gros-Morne

Le Robert

Havre du Robert

oh

Pte. de la Rose

N1

N1

Lamentin

Le François

Mt. Vauclin

Lamentin International Airport

ointe Bout

N5

Ducos

N6

Hotel Meridien Martinique
Hotel Bakoua

Le Vauclin

s

D7

Rivière-Salée

N5

D17

Rivière-Pilote

N6

Le
nt

D18

Ste-Luce

D18A

Le Marin

mant

D7

D18A

Pte. Figuier

Pte. Marin

Cap Chevalier

Club Med Buccaneer's Creek

D9

Cul-de-Sac du Marin

Les Salines

Ste-Anne

Anse-Trabaud

Pte. d'Enfer

Pte. des Salines

St. Lucia Channel

HOTEL BAKOUA

| 70.0% | 50.0% | 60.0% | 70.0% | TOTAL 62.5% |

Three buildings of this hotel are set in a hilltop garden above Pointe du Bout overlooking the Bay of Fort-de-France; a fourth low-rise structure is down on the hotel's man-made beach. The property was built in 1966 and renovated in 1990.

Reader Report

"A really nice place. In fact, we went there again just to visit for the day a few years later while on a cruise. The rooms were not plush, but were nice and we were comfortable. If we go back to Martinique, that is where we'd stay."

NAME WITHHELD, GREENSBORO, NORTH CAROLINA

"The location right across the bay from Fort-de-France, was good. So were the food and service. Rooms were typically European—rather small. The beach was nice enough."

NAME WITHHELD, VESTAL, NEW YORK

Address. Pointe du Bout, 97229 Trois-Ilets, Martinique, F.W.I., tel. 596/66–02–02 or 800/471–9090, fax 596/66–00–41.
Affiliation. Sofitel.
Rooms. 134 rooms, 5 suites. All have minibars and air-conditioning.
Facilities. 2 restaurants, 2 bars/lounges, coffee shop, 2 lighted tennis courts, 18-hole golf course nearby, freshwater pool, horseback riding nearby, dry-cleaning, dive center, sailboat.
TV and VCR. TV in all rooms, with 5 channels. No VCRs.
No-smoking rooms. None.
Credit cards. AE, DC, MC, V.
Wheelchair accessibility. No accessible rooms.
Prices. Nov. 1–Apr. 24: doubles $153–$506 EP. Low season: doubles $120–$265 EP. Add $33 per person for MAP, $62 for AP.

CLUB MED BUCCANEER'S CREEK

| 57.7% | 13.5% | 57.7% | 78.8% | TOTAL 51.9% |

This 48-acre all-inclusive resort village has pastel Créole-style cottages and its own marina. It's near the island's southern tip, on the Caribbean side. The hotel was built in 1969, and renovation has been ongoing.

Reader Report

"Beautiful beaches (one of them nude), but no pool. Excellent food, many great day trips. The staffers do their best to keep

*you busy well into the wee hours. If all you want to do is lie
on a beach, pick a quieter resort."*

MARY THOMPSON DENEWELLIS, JOLIET, ILLINOIS

*"Lots of fun for every age and nationality. Rooms are only
adequate, but you're not in them very much anyway, since
there's so much else to do."*

LAUREL GLICKMAN, CHICAGO, ILLINOIS

*"A great water sports club and great views. You have the
feeling of being on a secluded island, yet you can walk along
the beach to the nearest town, St. Anne."*

CHRISTINA BRAUN, OCEANSIDE, NEW YORK

Address. Pointe du Marin, 97227 Ste. Anne, Martinique, F.W.I.,
tel. 596/76–72–72 or 800/258–2633, fax 596/76–72–02.
Affiliation. Club Med.
Rooms. 256 rooms, all with air-conditioning, and all with show-
ers only.
Facilities. 2 restaurants, 2 bars/lounges, nightclub, theater, 6
lighted tennis courts, 1 unlighted, aerobics classes, conference
center with business services, snorkeling, waterskiing, volley-
ball, basketball, windsurfing, scuba diving, sailboats.
TV and VCR. TV in public area only, with about 7 channels. VCR
in public area.
No-smoking rooms. None.
Credit cards. AE, MC, V.
Restrictions. No children under 12.
Wheelchair accessibility. No accessible rooms.
Prices. Dec 10—Apr 30: $135–240. Low season: $105. Prices
are per person. Rates are all-inclusive and per person.

HOTEL MERIDIEN MARTINIQUE

| 64.7% | 58.8% | 55.9% | 61.8% | **TOTAL** 60.3% |

This seven-story hotel has its own marina, casino, and private
beach. It's set on the southern coast of the Bay of
Fort-de-France on Pointe du Bout, a resort-lined peninsula. The
hotel was built in 1972 and renovated in 1990.

Reader Report

*"Typically European style, with less of the fawning service
than Americans might be used to. Absolutely beautiful
panoramic views. Rooms were on the small side."*

KEVIN ZIMMERMAN, SCOTTSDALE, ARIZONA

"Run down—needs work."

NAME WITHHELD, NEW HAVEN, CONNECTICUT

Address. Box 894, 97245 Fort-de-France, Martinique, F.W.I.,
tel. 596/66–00–00 or 800/543–4300, fax 596/66–00–74.

Affiliation. Meridien Hotels.

Rooms. 293 rooms, 2 suites. All have air-conditioning. Both suites and 60 rooms have minibars.

Facilities. Restaurant, 2 bars/lounges, 2 lighted tennis courts, 2 unlighted tennis courts, 18-hole golf course nearby, freshwater pool, horseback riding, casino, aerobics classes, 24-hr room service, dry-cleaning, dive center, sailboats.

TV and VCR. TVs in all rooms, with 4 channels including CNN. No VCRs.

No-smoking rooms. None.

Credit cards. AE, DC, MC, V.

Restrictions. None.

Wheelchair accessibility. No accessible rooms.

Prices. Dec 10–Mar 1: doubles $355; suites $560. Low season: doubles $243; suites $560. All rates include Continental breakfast.

MONTSERRAT

			👤	**TOTAL**
64.2%	**35.8%**	**24.5%**	**62.3%**	**42.6%**

Reader Report

"The greenest place in the Caribbean! Not much nightlife, but for sheer relaxation, it can't be topped."

JOSEPH GRANT, BERNARDSVILLE, NEW JERSEY

"Natives are friendly and open—just don't expect anyone to hurry. There are few tourist lodgings, and not too many choices for dining, but it's reasonably priced and interesting. Activities center around laid-back local celebrations. A charming spot for lazy sun-seekers."

NANCY KOGER, BIG SPRING, TEXAS

"Very quiet, great for relaxing. Not much shopping or nightlife, and difficult to get to."

BERNARD FENSTERWALD, RESTON, VIRGINIA

"Beaches are limited, and the best (Rendezvous Bay) is reachable only by boat. But, I have never felt more secure on any island, even walking the streets at night. Best seen living in a villa."

RUSSELL L. DUNFEE, JR., SMITHVILLE, NEW JERSEY

Islands. Montserrat is a 40-square-mile territory of the United Kingdom, with a population of about 12,000.

Language. The official language is English, though a French-Creole patois is widely spoken by the islanders.

Visitor Information

In the U.S. Contact the **Caribbean Tourism Organization** (20 E. 46th St., New York, NY 10017, tel. 212/682–0435, fax 212/697–4258).

In Canada. Contact the **Caribbean Tourism Organization** (3300 Bloor St. W, Suite 3120, Center Tower, Toronto, Ont. MHX 2X3, tel. 416/233–7879, fax 416/233–9367).

In the U.K. Contact the **Caribbean Tourist Organization** (2 Cinnamon Row, Plantation Wharf, York Pl., London SW11 3TW, tel. 071/978–5262, fax 071/924–3171).

In Montserrat. Contact the **Montserrat Tourist Board** (Box 7, Marine Dr., Plymouth, Montserrat, B.W.I., tel. 809/491–2230, fax 809/491–7430).

MONTSERRAT SPRINGS HOTEL

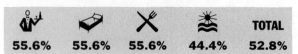

👔	🛏	✕	☀	TOTAL
55.6%	55.6%	55.6%	44.4%	52.8%

Built in 1962 and slated to complete renovation in Dec 1995, this 16-acre spa resort in the capital, Plymouth, has a two-story hilltop main building and bungalows on a steep hillside that runs down to the beach.

Address. Box 259, Plymouth, Montserrat, B.W.I., tel. 809/491–2481 or 800/253–2134, fax 809/491–4070.

Rooms. 40 rooms, 6 suites. All have air-conditioning and ceiling fans.

Facilities. Restaurant, 2 bars/lounges, coffee shop, lighted tennis court, 1 unlighted , freshwater pool, natural mineral water hot spring, freshwater spa, excercise facilities, massages, conference room.

TV and VCR. TVs in all rooms, with 20 channels including CNN. VCR in public area.

No-smoking rooms. None.

Credit cards. AE, D, MC, V.

Wheelchair accessibility. No accessible rooms.

Prices. Dec 16–Apr 15: doubles $225–$245 MAP, $145–$165 EP; suites $285–$295 MAP, $205–$215 EP. Low season: doubles $195–$210 MAP, $115–$130 EP; suites $230–$240 MAP, $150–$160 EP.

PUERTO RICO

| 58.4% | 53.9% | 49.3% | 42.8% | **TOTAL** 50.4% |

Reader Report

"An island full of treasures—beaches, nightlife, restaurants, old city walls, mountains, caves, and even a rain forest. Delights the senses, down to the sound of the little coquí. . . "

DONNA ZINGO, STRATFORD, CONNECTICUT

"People go out of their way to be helpful. It's like a foreign country, but with efficient U.S. mail service and telephones. Everyone is bilingual, so you can speak Spanish or English. Great weather, too."

ANGELA MCEWAN, WHITTIER, CALIFORNIA

"San Juan is so much like Europe—a little Spain in the Caribbean. I enjoyed the forts . . . and the Bacardi Rum tour."

WANEECE F. PAYTON, SAN JOSE, CALIFORNIA

"We stayed in paradors around the island for two weeks. These inns were all clean and well-kept with very friendly people. Driving around was a pleasure. You do need to watch your valuables on the beaches in San Juan."

MARY CRICHLOW, DARIEN, ILLINOIS

Islands. Puerto Rico is a 3,515-square-mile territory of the United States, with a population of about 3.6 million.
Language. Puerto Rico has two official languages, Spanish and English.

Visitor Information

In the U.S. Contact the **Puerto Rican Tourism Company** (tel. 800/223–6530; 575 5th Ave., 23rd Floor, New York, NY 10017, tel. 212/599-6262, fax 212/818–1866; 3575 W. Cahuenga Blvd., Suite 560, Los Angeles, CA 90068, tel. 213/874–5991, fax 213/874–7257; 901 Ponce De Leon Blvd., Suite 604, Coral Gables, FL 33134, tel. 305/445–9112 or 800/815–7391, fax 305/445–9450).
In Canada. Contact the **Puerto Rican Tourism Company** (41–43 Colbourne St., Suite 301, Toronto, Ont. M5E 1E3, tel. 416/368–2680, fax 416/368–5350).
In the U.K. There is no tourist office in the U.K.
In Puerto Rico. Contact the **Puerto Rican Tourism Company** (Paseo La Princesa, Old San Juan, P.R. 00902, tel. 809/721–2400, fax 809/725–4417).

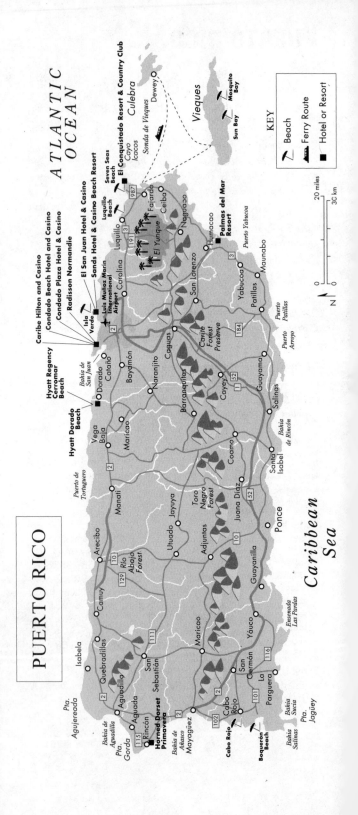

PUERTO RICO

ATLANTIC OCEAN

El Conquistador Resort & Country Club

Culebra

Dewey

Mosquito Bay

Sun Bay

Vieques

Sonda de Vieques

Sonda de Vieques

KEY

⚐ Beach

⛴ Ferry Route

■ Hotel or Resort

0   20 miles
0   30 km

Caribe Hilton and Casino
Condado Beach Hotel and Casino
Condado Plaza Hotel & Casino
Radisson Normandie
El San Juan Hotel & Casino
Sands Hotel & Casino Beach Resort

Seven Seas Beach
Cayo Icacos
Luquillo Beach

987
Fajardo
Ceiba

Hyatt Regency Cerromar Beach

Hyatt Dorado Beach

Luis Muñoz Marín International Airport

Isla Verde

Carolina

191
3
El Yunque

San Lorenzo

Palmas del Mar Resort

Humacao

Puerto Yabucoa

Maunabo

Bahía de San Juan

Dorado

Cataño

Bayamón

Naranjito

Caguas

Carite Forest Preserve

Yabucoa

3

Patillas

Puerto Patillas

Vega Baja

Manati

Maricao

Barranquitas

Comerío

Cayey

52
1

Guayama

Puerto Arroyo

184

Puerto de Tortuguero

2

Jayuya

Toro Negro Forest

Coamo

Solinas

Santa Isabel

Bahía de Rincón

Arecibo

Camuy

10

129

Río Abajo Forest

Utuado

Adjuntas

Juana Díaz

10

52

Ponce

Guayanilla

Caribbean Sea

Isabela

Quebradillas

2

Aguadilla

Aguada

Rincón

111

San Sebastián

Maricao

Yauco

Ensenada Las Pardas

115
Pta. Gorda
Bahía de Aguadilla
Pta. Jiguero

Horned Dorset Primavera

Bahía de Añasco
Mayagüez

101
102

San Germán

La Parguera

Cabo Rojo

116

Cabo Rojo

Boquerón Beach

Bahía Sucia
Pta. Jaguey
Bahía Salinas

N

CARIBE HILTON AND CASINO

				TOTAL
62.3%	52.9%	52.0%	67.3%	58.6%

This 20-story, contemporary, high-rise hotel—built in 1949 and renovated in 1994—sits on 17 acres in San Juan's Puerta de Tierra. A casino and a 16th-century fort are on the grounds.

Reader Report

"A great experience in an urban setting. The rooms were very nice, with great views of the ocean or the city. Great food and attentive service. The beach club is not crowded. It's like a Hilton of the '50s or '60s."

EUGENE HEAP, HOUSTON, TEXAS

"Festive, with music and dancing in the afternoon and at night."

ANDREW KLATSKIN, CHERRY HILLS VILLAGE, COLORADO

"An older hotel that's been kept up-to-date—very professional and very exciting. There's a lot going on without being · distracting. The location in San Juan is great."

ROBERT WAHLERT, DUBUQUE, IOWA

Address. Box 1872, San Juan, P.R. 00902, tel. 809/721–0303 or 800/468–8585, fax 809/724–6992.
Affiliation. Hilton International.
Rooms. 672 rooms, 49 suites. All have minibars and air-conditioning. 138 rooms and 7 suites have ceiling fans.
Facilities. 5 restaurants, 3 bars/lounges, coffee shop, 6 lighted tennis courts, 6 unlighted tennis courts, 2 freshwater pools, casino, exercise room with weights and aerobic machines, aerobics classes, massages, sauna, salon, dry-cleaning, conference center with business services, supervised children's program.
TV and VCR. TV in all rooms, with 20 channels including CNN and pay movies. No VCRs.
No-smoking rooms. 118 rooms.
Credit cards. AE, DC, D, MC, V.
Restrictions. None.
Wheelchair accessibility. 13 rooms.
Prices. Dec. 24–Apr. 30: doubles $330 EP; suites $515–$1,248 EP. Low season: doubles $239 EP; suites $495–$1,200 EP.

CONDADO BEACH HOTEL AND CASINO

				TOTAL
53.1%	49.6%	50.4%	61.1%	53.5%

Cornelius Vanderbilt built this nine-story Spanish colonial–style hotel in 1919, and it was renovated in 1993. It is in San

Juan's Condado district, and is part of the Condado Beach Trio, along with La Concha Hotel and El Centro convention center.

Reader Report

"Next to the convention center, convenient for businesspeople. Very nice beach, pleasant restaurant. The hotel has a kind of old-world Spanish atmosphere."

ADELAIDE AND ROBERT BOWLER, EAST MEADOW, NEW YORK

"It's right in the middle of the Condado, which is great, even though it doesn't have a great beach."

KEVIN ZIMMERMAN, SCOTTSDALE, ARIZONA

"The beach, a public beach, was very disappointing; but the one at the hotel's sister property, 20 minutes away via a shuttle bus, was great."

DONNA OLIVA, BROOKLYN, NEW YORK

Address. 1061 Ashford Ave., Condado, P.R. 00907, tel. 809/721–6090 or 800/468–2822, fax 809/724–7222.
Affiliation. Carnival Hotels and Casinos.
Rooms. 245 rooms, 22 suites. All have air-conditioning.
Facilities. 2 restaurants, 3 bars/lounges, coffee shop, freshwater pool, horseback riding, casino, massages, salon, 24-hr room service, dry-cleaning, conference center with business services, dive center, sailboats.
TV and VCR. TVs in all rooms, with 33 channels, including CNN, cable movie channels, and pay movies. VCRs in some rooms.
No-smoking rooms. None.
Credit cards. AE, DC, D, MC, V.
Restrictions. Min. 2 nights during major U.S. holidays.
Wheelchair accessibility. 4 rooms.
Prices. Dec 24–Apr 16: doubles $150–$170 EP; suites $335–$340 EP. Low season: doubles $140–$160 EP; suites $185–$215 EP.

CONDADO PLAZA HOTEL & CASINO

🧑‍💼	🛏	✕	≋	**TOTAL**
56.9%	**61.3%**	**51.8%**	**56.9%**	**56.8%**

This two-building, 10-story casino hotel, in San Juan's Condado district, sits on an isthmus between the Atlantic and Condado Lagoon. Guests have exchange privileges with El San Juan Hotel. The hotel was built in 1919, expanded in 1952, and renovated in 1993.

Reader Report

"We faced the lagoon and it was a pleasant view. The pool/bar and beach area was especially nice. Expect a small, average room and great amenities throughout the facility."

DAVE AND CARROLL SHROYER, DIXON, CALIFORNIA

142 *"The oceanview rooms afford a spectacular view of the surf*

pounding a rocky beach. The service was very good, but take a taxi—the parking in the garage would challenge an experienced parking-lot jockey."

JAMES LOCKER, DANVILLE, CALIFORNIA

"The lack of a private beach is a shortcoming. The rooms are tastefully appointed and comfortable, and the entire facility is clean and friendly."

TIMOTHY BAKER, WOODSTOWN, NEW JERSEY

Address. 999 Ashford Ave., San Juan, P.R. 00902, tel. 809/721–1000 or 800/468–8588, fax 809/721–4613.

Affiliation. Preferred Hotels & Resorts Worldwide.

Rooms. 569 rooms, 62 suites. All have minibars, refrigerators, coffee makers, dual-line telephones, balconies, ironing boards, and air-conditioning. 300 rooms have ceiling fans. 11 suites have Jacuzzis.

Facilities. 5 restaurants, 4 bars/lounges, 3 coffee shops, 2 lighted tennis courts, 3 freshwater pools, 2 jacuzzis, saltwater pool, casino, fitness center with spa, sauna, salon, 24-hr room service, dry-cleaning, tour and travel desk, boutiques, art gallery, conference center with business services, supervised children's program, complimentary transportation to Old San Juan, car rental.

TV and VCR. TVs in all rooms, with 48 channels including CNN, cable movie channels, and pay movies. VCRs in all rooms.

No-smoking rooms. 240 rooms, 30 suites.

Credit cards. AE, CB, DC, D, MC, V.

Restrictions. No children under 18.

Wheelchair accessibility. 2 rooms. 6 rooms equipped for partially disabled.

Prices. Nov 23–Apr 30: doubles $310–$420 EP; suites $390–$1,160 EP. Low season: $220–$360 EP; suites $330–$750 EP.

EL CONQUISTADOR RESORT & COUNTRY CLUB

				TOTAL
70.0%	82.0%	68.0%	78.0%	74.5%

Set on a 300-foot cliff 31 miles east of San Juan, this 500-acre resort consists of one main hotel, three "villages" with Spanish, Mediterranean, and Caribbean themes, as well as a casino and a marina. The hotel was built in 1962 and renovated in 1993.

Reader Report

"Rooms were nicely decorated and spacious with beautiful views. The beach is a boat ride away, but well worth the trip. Our children enjoyed the pool area very much. A most accommodating and friendly staff."

SHARON OLBRYCH, ALBANY, NEW YORK

"The renovation was a magnificent undertaking, but this fabulous resort has been reborn and is back on top as a shining star of the Caribbean."

CARMEN DELLA BELLA, ALBANY, NEW YORK

Address. 1000 Conquistador Ave. Fajardo, P.R. 00738–7001), tel. 809/863–1000 or 800/468–8365, fax 809/863–6500.

Affiliation. Williams Hospitality Group.

Rooms. 918 rooms, 184 suites, 90 villas. All have minibars, air-conditioning, and ceiling fans. All suites and 90 rooms have Jacuzzis.

Facilities. 9 restaurants, 7 bars/lounges, coffee shop, 4 lighted tennis courts, 3 unlighted, 18-hole golf course, 6 freshwater pools, horseback riding, casino, exercise room with weights and aerobic machines, aerobics classes, massages, salon, 24-hr room service, 11 retail outlets, dry-cleaning, conference center with business services, supervised children's program, dive center, sailboats.

TV and VCR. TVs in all rooms, with 26 channels including CNN and pay movies. VCRs in all rooms.

No-smoking rooms. 230 rooms.

Credit cards. AE, CB, DC, D, MC, V.

Wheelchair accessibility. 27 rooms.

Prices. Dec 20–Apr 15: doubles $345–$565 EP; suites $970–$1,950 EP; villas $970–$2,290 EP. Low season: doubles $245–$465 EP; suites $855–$1,950 EP; villas $500–$1,565 EP.

EL SAN JUAN HOTEL & CASINO

👔	🛏	✗	🌅	**TOTAL**
67.0%	**63.4%**	**65.2%**	**63.4%**	**64.8%**

Dating from 1958, this 10-story, contemporary-style high-rise with additional garden bungalows and a casino is on 15 acres on the beach of San Juan's Isla Verde. The hotel was built in 1958 and renovated in 1985.

Reader Report

"It's the best hotel in San Juan, with the best beach, an excellent restaurant, and good security. The elevators are noisy—get a room at the end of the corridor."

RICHARD ATCHISON, SOLANA BEACH, CALIFORNIA

"Beautifully remodeled. Our room was spectacular and the pool area is large enough that it doesn't feel overcrowded even in high season."

LYNN AND RAY BRINKER, OXNARD, CALIFORNIA

"The ultimate classy vacation. If you do nothing but sit in the elegant lobby, you will be drenched in luxury and Old World

*charm. Treat yourself to a swim in the free-form pool and a
meal in any of the hotel's restaurants."*

CERIE SEGAL, PLANO, TEXAS

Address. Box 2872, San Juan, P.R. 00902, tel. 809/791–1000
or 800/468–6659, fax 809/791–0390.
Affiliation. Williams Hospitality Group.
Rooms. 392 rooms, 28 suites, 13 casitas (large private rooms in
a separate building). All accommodations have minibars, air-
conditioning, and ceiling fans. 22 rooms, 4 suites, and 12
casitas have Jacuzzis.
Facilities. 6 restaurants, 6 bars/lounges, coffee shop, 3 lighted
tennis courts, 2 freshwater pools, health club with weights and
aerobic machines, aerobics classes, massages, sauna, salon,
24-hr room service, dry-cleaning, conference center with business services, supervised children's program, dive center.
TV and VCR. TVs in all rooms, with 40 channels including CNN
and pay movies. VCRs in all rooms.
No-smoking rooms. 105 rooms, 4 suites, 10 casitas.
Credit cards. AE, CB, DC, D, MC, V.
Restrictions. Min. 7 nights during Christmas. Children under 18
must be accompanied by an adult. Guests must be 23 to enter
the disco, 18 to enter the casino.
Wheelchair accessibility. 8 rooms.
Prices. Nov 23–Apr 30: doubles $320–$465 EP; suites $535–$1360
EP. Low season: doubles $250–$395 EP; suites $760–$1,585.
Meal plans available.

HORNED DORSET PRIMAVERA

| 88.9% | 81.5% | 85.2% | 85.2% | **TOTAL** 85.2% |

A hacienda-like great house anchors this 4½ acre Spanish
Mediterranean—style resort, built in 1988, on the west coast,
north of Mayagüez. Accommodations are in low-rise suite units
stepped up a hillside.

Reader Report
*"There was a five course gourmet meal each evening: 'You
don't like tonight's soup? What can we make for you?'
Accommodations are roomy, the resort elegant. A quiet place
to get away from it all."*

ROBERT J. HASH, CINCINNATI, OHIO

*"Enveloped in lush tropical flora. Wonderfully quiet with a
superb kitchen."*

HOWARD M. DEUTCH, FAYETTEVILLE, NEW YORK

Address. Box 1132, Carr. 429, Km 3, Rincón, P.R. 00677, tel.
809/823–4030 or 800/633–1857, fax 809/823–5580.
Affiliation. Relais & Châteaux.
Rooms. 30 rooms. All have air-conditioning and ceiling fans. 4

with plunge pools, 2 with sun decks, 2 with balconys
Facilities. Restaurant, bar/lounge, freshwater pool, massages, conference facilities, lighted tennis court nearby, and casino nearby.
TV and VCR. No TV.
No-smoking rooms. None.
Credit cards. AE, MC, V.
Restrictions. Min. 4 nights Dec. 15–Apr 15. No children under 12.
Wheelchair accessibility. No accessible rooms.
Prices. Dec 15–Apr 15: $451.50–$471.50 MAP, $325–345 EP. Low season: $316.50–$336.50 MAP, $190–$210 EP.

HYATT DORADO BEACH

				TOTAL
73.6%	66.0%	60.4%	77.1%	69.3%

Low-rise Spanish plantation–style units, built in 1958 and recently renovated, house guests at this 1,000-acre resort west of San Juan in Dorado. The Hyatt Regency Cerromar Beach shares the site.

Reader Report

"Our rooms opened out to the sand and ocean—nicely decorated and large enough to share with the kids! Quiet, with shuttle service to the other Hyatt, which has great pools and a water slide."

NAME WITHHELD, CHATSWORTH, CALIFORNIA

"The food has been consistently good over the 25 years we've been going there. The beach is most unusual—there's a big breakwater in the ocean that creates a giant saltwater swimming pool."

BARBARA TUCKER, BLOOMFIELD HILLS, MICHIGAN

"Fine atmosphere and food et cetera. We found no fault with our accommodations."

JUNE SHILKA, FORT MYERS, FLORIDA

Address. Rte. 693, Dorado, P.R. 00646, tel. 809/796–1234 or 800/233–1234, fax 809/796–2022.
Affiliation. Hyatt Hotels and Resorts.
Rooms. 280 rooms, 17 casitas (extra large rooms), 1 suite. All have minibars, air-conditioning, and ceiling fans. All casitas and suites have showers only.
Facilities. 4 restaurants, 3 bars/lounges, coffee shop, 2 lighted tennis courts, 5 unlighted, 2 18-hole golf courses, 2 freshwater pools, casino, fitness center, aerobics classes, massages, sauna, salon, 24-hr room service, dry-cleaning, conference center with business services, supervised children's program at the Hyatt Regency Cerromar Beach, watersports.
TV and VCR. TVs in all rooms, with 16 channels including CNN and pay movies. VCRs in rooms on request (at additional cost).
No-smoking rooms. 146 rooms.

Credit cards. AE, DC, D, MC, V.

Restrictions. Min. 8 nights Dec 22–30. No arrivals on Dec 23.

Wheelchair accessibility. 2 rooms.

Prices. Dec 20–Apr 14: doubles $493–$643 MAP; suites $769–$1,913 MAP. Low season: doubles $170–$240 EP; suites $368–$870 EP. MAP is standard in high season; add $64 per person for MAP in low season.

HYATT REGENCY CERROMAR BEACH

👨‍💼	🛏️	🍴	☀️	**TOTAL**
63.1%	**56.6%**	**54.1%**	**82.0%**	**63.9%**

This contemporary seven-story resort shares a 1,000-acre site with the Hyatt Dorado Beach, with which it has exchange privileges. It has the world's longest freshwater river-pool and a casino. The hotel was built in 1970.

Reader Report

"The beaches, rooms, and especially the golf courses were great."

BEVERLY A. KING, MARCELLUS, NEW YORK

"Friendly and well-run, though not intimate. It's great for kids—Camp Hyatt runs both during the day and in the evening, so parents can go out to dinner (and the kids prefer the food at the camp!). Food is only fair."

MARK IGER, NEW YORK, NEW YORK

Address. Rte. 693, Km 12.9, Dorado, P.R. 00646, tel. 809/796–1234 or 800/233–1234, fax 809/796–4647.

Affiliation. Hyatt Hotels and Resorts.

Rooms. 485 rooms, 19 suites. All have minibars and air-conditioning.

Facilities. 4 restaurants, 4 bars/lounges, 2 lighted tennis courts, 12 unlighted tennis courts, 2 18-hole golf courses, 2 freshwater pools, casino, fitness center, aerobics classes, massages, sauna, salon, 24-hr room service, dry-cleaning, conference center with business services, supervised children's program, dive center nearby and watersports.

TV and VCR. TVs in all rooms, with about 25 channels including CNN and cable movie channels. VCRs in rooms on request.

No-smoking rooms. About 100.

Credit cards. AE, DC, MC, V.

Restrictions. Min. 8 nights Dec 22–30. No arrivals on Dec 23.

Wheelchair accessibility. 6 rooms.

Prices. Dec 20–Apr 20: doubles $310–$445 EP; suites $745–$1,085 EP. Low season: doubles $175–$210 EP; suites $435–$690 EP. Add $64 per person for MAP.

PALMAS DEL MAR RESORT

🍸	🛏	🍴	🌅	TOTAL
60.6%	65.2%	57.6%	78.8%	65.5%

This 2,750-acre, Mediterranean-style resort complex occupies a former coconut plantation on the island's southeast coast. It consists of two hotels, private homes, condo villas, a marina, and a casino. The hotel was built in 1972 and renovated and expanded in 1992.

Reader Report

"Nice location, with lots of private houses right around the hotel. The beach was lovely, with thatched umbrellas and little huts. The restaurant was excellent."

ADELAIDE AND ROBERT BOWLER, EAST MEADOW, NEW YORK

"Excellent beaches and accommodations, good golf, good food, great location."

JEFFREY ROSENKER, ST. LOUIS PARK, MINNESOTA

Address. Box 2020, Humacao, P.R. 00792, tel. 809/852–6000 or 800/PALMAS–3, fax 809/852–6320.
Affiliation. None.
Rooms. 102 rooms, 23 junior suites, 120 villas. All have air-conditioning. All suites have minibars. Some villas have jacuzzis.
Facilities. 13 restaurants, 3 bars/lounges, 2 coffee shops, 8 lighted tennis courts, 14 unlighted tennis courts, 18-hole golf course, 7 freshwater pools, horseback riding, casino, exercise room with weights and aerobic machines, aerobics classes, massages, salon, dry-cleaning, conference center with business services, supervised children's program, dive center, sailboats.
TV and VCR. TVs in all rooms, with 15 channels including CNN, cable movie channels, and pay movies. VCRs in some rooms.
No-smoking rooms. 7 rooms.
Credit cards. AE, CB, DC, D, MC, V.
Restrictions. Min. 7 nights Dec 22–Jan 1.
Wheelchair accessibility. 3 rooms.
Prices. Dec 21–Apr 16: doubles $216 EP; suites $328 EP; villas $320–$740 EP. Low season: doubles $123 EP; suites $195 EP; villas $192–$426 EP.

RADISSON NORMANDIE

🍸	🛏	🍴	🌅	TOTAL
47.5%	37.5%	35.0%	40.0%	40.0%

Built in 1939 and renovated in 1988, this eight-story Art Deco landmark modeled after the ocean liner *Normandie* is on the beach in San Juan's Puerta de Tierra neighborhood.

Reader Report

"A nice, small hotel. The rooms were very large and clean. There were not enough choices for dining."

NORMA FRENCH, DALLAS, TEXAS

"A valiant attempt by Radisson to re-open a vintage Art Deco beachfront building near old San Juan—but a failure, with absolutely no soundproofing (one can hear neighbors turning on light switches!). The front desk staff is slow, inept, and by and large indifferent."

CHRISTOPHER SMITH, BALTIMORE, MARYLAND

Address. Box 50059, San Juan, P.R. 00902, tel. 809/729–2929 or 800/333–3333, fax 809/729–3083.
Affiliation. Radisson Hotels International.
Rooms. 177 rooms, 3 suites.
Facilities. Restaurant, bar/lounge, freshwater pool, salon, dry-cleaning, conference center with business services.
TV and VCR. TV in all rooms, with 35 channels including CNN and pay movies. No VCRs.
No-smoking rooms. 68 rooms.
Credit cards. AE, CB, DC, D, MC, V.
Restrictions. No children under 18.
Wheelchair accessibility. 2 accessible rooms.
Prices. Dec 1–Apr 12: doubles $250–$280 MAP, $200–$230 EP; suites $515 MAP, $465 EP. Low season: doubles $215–$260 MAP, $165–$210 EP; suites $480 MAP, $430 EP.

SANDS HOTEL & CASINO BEACH RESORT

55.9%	47.5%	42.4%	52.5%	**TOTAL** 49.6%

Located on 4.8 acres on San Juan's Isla Verde beach, this hotel is an 18-story tower dating from the mid-1960s and renovated in 1990. It has a casino and large free-form swimming pool.

Reader Report

"Our room was nicer than we expected—a bedroom with an adjoining sitting room. There was a beautiful outside pool area and ready access to ocean beaches."

ROBERT E. GLASSFORD, JR., EFFINGHAM, NEW HAMPSHIRE

"Ultramodern, with a great casino and beautifully landscaped grounds."

ANNAMARIA GERASIMOU, JAMAICA HILLS, NEW YORK

Address. Box 6676, San Juan, P.R. 00914–6676, tel. 809/791–6100 or 800/544–3008, fax 809/791–7540.
Affiliation. Pratt Corporation.
Rooms. 412 rooms, 7 suites. All have air-conditioning and mini-bars on request. 1 suite has a Jacuzzi.

Facilities. 4 restaurants, 2 bars/lounges, freshwater pool, casino, exercise room with weights and aerobic machines, massages, salon, dry-cleaning, 24-hr room service in winter, conference center with business services.

TV and VCR. TVs in all rooms, with 33 channels including CNN, cable movie channels, and pay movies. VCRs in some rooms.

No-smoking rooms. 65 rooms.

Credit cards. AE, CB, DC, C, MC, V.

Restrictions. Min. 3 nights during many U.S. holidays.

Wheelchair accessibility. 5 rooms.

Prices. Dec 22–Apr 30: doubles $325–$370; suites $390–$800. Low season: doubles: $240–$265; suites $300–$800. Rates for concierge level accommodations (30 rooms and 6 suites) include breakfast; all other rates are EP.

SABA

 | | | TOTAL
87.2 | 38.3 | 34.0 | 74.5 | 49.4

Reader Report

"Unique and laid-back, with gorgeous scenery. Basically it is a single steep mountain—and not easy to reach by ship. Bring your books and take it easy."

HOWARD T. LUDLOW, ORANGE BEACH, ALABAMA

"My favorite island, Saba looks hostile from a distance but is actually lush and unique. Its mountainous top is usually shrouded in fog. Definitely off the beaten path."

KATHY COAKLEY, WEST PALM BEACH, FLORIDA

"It's like being in the Alps. We especially liked the architecture, and the neatness and orderliness of it all!"

MARY ANNE WINSCHEL-SPANN, NAPLES, FLORIDA

"A private paradise with very friendly people, good hiking, and great diving. It's nice to sit on the wall by Big Rock Market and pick up gossip. A great place."

HOWARD BRAYER, WASHINGTON, DC

Islands. Five-square-mile Saba is an independent protectorate of the Netherlands, with a population of about 1,000.
Language. Saba's official language is Dutch, though English is widely spoken.

Visitor Information

In the U.S. Contact the **Caribbean Tourism Organization** (20 E. 46th St., New York, NY 10017, tel. 212/682–0435, fax 212/697–4258).
In Canada. Contact the **Caribbean Tourism Organization** (512 Duplex St. Toronto, Ont. M4R 2E3, tel. 416/485–8724, fax 416/485–8256).
In the U.K. Contact the **Caribbean Tourist Organization** (120 Wilton Rd., Victoria, London SW1 V16Z, tel. 71/233–8382, fax 71/873–8551).
In Saba. Contact the **Saba Tourist Office** (Windwardside, Saba, Netherlands Antilles, tel. 599/46–2231, fax 599/46–2350).

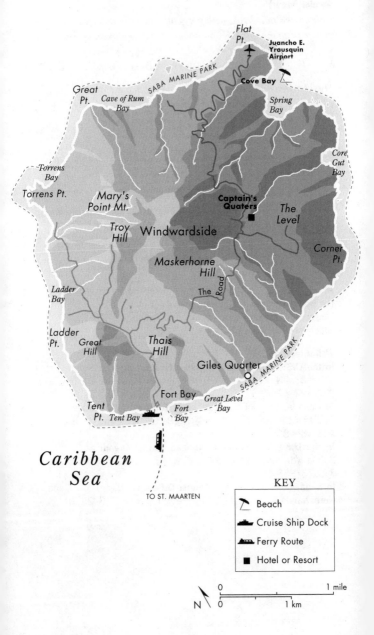

SABA

ATLANTIC OCEAN

Flat Pt.

Juancho E. Yrausquin Airport

SABA MARINE PARK

Cove Bay

Great Pt.

Cave of Rum Bay

Spring Bay

Core Gut Bay

Torrens Bay

Torrens Pt.

Mary's Point Mt.

Captain's Quaters

The Level

Troy Hill

Windwardside

Corner Pt.

Maskerhorne Hill

The Road

Ladder Bay

Ladder Pt.

Great Hill

Thais Hill

Giles Quarter

SABA MARINE PARK

Fort Bay

Tent Pt.

Tent Bay

Fort Bay

Great Level Bay

Caribbean Sea

TO ST. MAARTEN

KEY

↗ Beach

⛴ Cruise Ship Dock

⛴ Ferry Route

■ Hotel or Resort

N

0   1 mile

0   1 km

CAPTAIN'S QUARTERS

75.0%	87.5%	62.5%	100.0%	TOTAL 81.3%

This 19th-century sea captain's house is up on the mountain in Windwardside. Guests stay there or in a long two-story bungalow-style unit built in 1963 and has been continuously renovated from 1993 to the present.

Reader Report

"The view of lush foliage falling steeply to the sea was awesome."

KATHY COAKLEY, WEST PALM BEACH, FLORIDA

"We got to stay in Queen Beatrix's room...the view is just captivating—you can see St. Martin in the distance. Sitting out on the porch at night was one of our favorite things. My other favorite thing was the full American breakfast!"

BEVERLY BERIDAN, SPRINGFIELD, VIRGINIA

Address. Windwardside, Saba, Netherlands Antilles, tel. 599/4–62201, fax 599/4–62377.

Rooms. 12 rooms, expanded to 16 by Dec 1995. All have showers, ceiling fans, minibars, 4-posted or canopy beds. 2 have air-conditioning. All have balconies and an ocean view.

Facilities. Restaurant, bar/lounge, freshwater pool, library, hiking, dive center, museum and shopping nearby.

TV and VCR. TV in all rooms, with 12 channels including CNN and cable movie channels. VCR in public area.

No-smoking rooms. Some.

Credit cards. AE, D, MC, V.

Wheelchair accessibility. 2 easy access rooms.

Prices. Dec 21–Apr 15: $125–$150 with breakfast. Low season: $125 with breakfast. Special dive package rates available.

ST. BARTHÉLEMY

				TOTAL
81.4%	**56.1%**	**47.2%**	**46.8%**	**61.4%**

Reader Report

"A totally charming, Gallic island with a host of pleasures, including deserted off-the-beaten-path white sand beaches and tiny villages accessible only by Jeep. Avoid the big-splurge hotel restaurants for dinner—they're not comparable to Paris or New York City dining rooms and cost almost as much."

DAVID E. BEDRI, MENLO PARK, CALIFORNIA

"There are so many restaurants on St. Barts that you never have to eat at the same place twice; the food here was good enough to bring us back."

K.C. AND ELLEN SPENGLER, EXETER, NEW HAMPSHIRE

"A beautiful, friendly island, but overcrowded when more than one cruise ship is in port. The people welcome everyone and are very proud of their small island."

ARTHUR F. HOBDAY, NEW BERN, NORTH CAROLINA

"Despite a lot of unfavorable publicity, St. Barts is still a beautiful way to experience France—and it's more like the Riviera than the Riviera these days. The best people-watching in the West Indies."

NAME WITHHELD, SARASOTA, FLORIDA

"My favorite island in the Caribbean. Excellent restaurants, somewhat expensive. Good shopping, if you don't mind the prices. Warm atmosphere. No mass tourism. St. Barts has been able to preserve its charm."

ROLF M. LUDWIG, YUCAIPA, CALIFORNIA

Islands. St. Barthélemy is an 8-square-mile sub-prefecture of Guadeloupe, with a population of about 5,000.

Language. French is the official language, though a Norman dialect is widely spoken by islanders.

Visitor Information

In the U.S. Contact the **French West Indies Tourism Bureau** (610 Fifth Ave., New York, NY 10020, fax 212/838–7855)or call France-On-Call (tel. 900/990–0040; .50 a minute). Also contact the **French Government Tourist Office** (444 Madison Ave., New York, NY 10022, tel. 212/838–7800, fax 212/838–7855; 9454 Wilshire Blvd., Beverly Hills, CA 90212, tel 310/ 271–6665, fax 213/276–2835; 676 N. Michigan Ave., Chicago, IL 60611, tel. 312/751–7800, fax 312/337–6339).

In Canada. Contact the **French Government Tourist Office** (Maison de la France, 1981 McGill College Ave., Suite 490, Montreal, Que. H3A 3W9, tel. 514/288–4264, fax

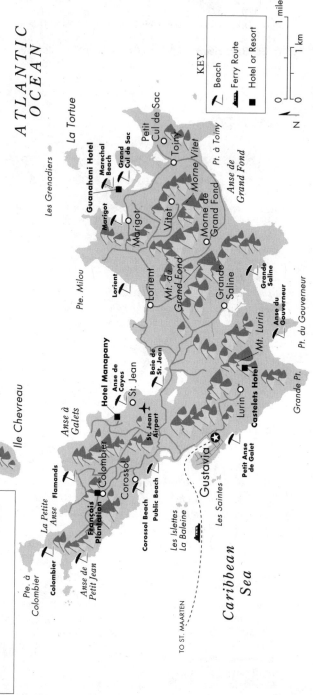

ST. BARTHÉLEMY

ATLANTIC OCEAN

Caribbean Sea

TO ST. MAARTEN

KEY

⌐ Beach
◄─ Ferry Route
■ Hotel or Resort

N

0   1 mile
0   1 km

Ile Chevreau

La Petite Anse
Flamands
Anse à Galets
Pte. à Colombier
Colombier
Anse de Petit Jean
Colombier
François Plantation
Corossol
Corossol Beach
Public Beach
Les Islettes
La Baleine
Les Saintes
Gustavia
Petit Anse de Galet
Lurin
Mt. Lurin
Castelets Hotel
Grande Pt.
Pt. du Gouverneur
Anse du Gouverneur
Grande Saline
Grande Saline
Mt. da Grand Fond
Morne de Grand Fond
Anse de Grand Fond
Pt. à Toiny
Toiny
Morne Vitet
Petit Cul de Sac
Grand Cul de Sac
Marechal Beach
Guanahani Hotel
Marigot
Marigot
Vitet
Orient
Lorient
Pte. Milou
Les Grenadiers
La Tortue
Hotel Manapany
Anse de Cayes
St. Jean
Baie de St. Jean
St. Jean Airport

514/845–4868; **French Tourist Office** 30 St. Patrick St., Suite 700, Toronto, Ont. M5T 3A3, tel. 416/593–4723, fax 416/979–7587).

In the U.K. Contact the **French Government Tourist Office** (178 Picadilly, London W1V 0AL, tel. 071/491–7622).

In St. Barthélemy. Contact l'**Office Municipal du Tourisme** (Quai de General de Gaulle, Gustavia 97133, St. Barthélemy, F.W.I., tel. 590/27–87–27, fax 590/27–74–47).

CASTELETS HOTEL

78.6%	71.4%	100.0%	78.6%	**TOTAL** 82.1%

Steep paths connect the main house and the terraced villas of this Provençal-style resort with views of Gustavia harbor. It's inland atop Morne Lurin. The nearest beach is about a mile away. The hotel was built in 1970.

Reader Report

"A small European-like inn in the Caribbean, serving delicious food on a patio near the water—quite picturesque."

JUDY ROBERSON, KENILWORTH, ILLINOIS

"Castelets is very isolated on a mountain peak—scary drive to get there but well worth the effort. Spectacular views and a bathtub-size dipping pool."

CLIFFORD HOCH, FORT LAUDERDALE, FLORIDA

"Everybody was polite and friendly—we became friends with the maître d', our waiter, and another couple who had dinner at the same time we did. Atmosphere was light and casual."

RICHARD FINDER, FORT LEE, NEW JERSEY

"Take one of the chalets for a real treat. Furnished in French Caribbean style, all have living rooms and balconies. A tiny pool refreshes, but head for St. Jean's beach down below for a good tan and plenty of company."

PATRICIA NEISSER, NEWPORT BEACH, CALIFORNIA

Address. Box 60, Lurin, 97133 St. Barthélemy, F.W.I., tel. 590/27–61–73 or 800/223–1108, fax 310/440–4220.
Rooms. 7 rooms, 1 suites, 1 villa. All have air-conditioning, refrigerators, and balconies/terraces.
Facilities. Restaurant, bar/lounge, small freshwater pool.
TV and VCR. No TV.
No-smoking rooms. None.
Credit cards. AE, MC, V.
Wheelchair accessibility. No accessible rooms.
Prices. Dec 18–Apr 19: doubles $170–$330; suite $500; villa $500–$650. Low season: doubles $115–$220; suite $320; villa $340–$440. Rates include Continental breakfast. Hotel is generally closed in September.

FRANÇOIS PLANTATION

				TOTAL
66.7%	66.7%	83.3%	75.0%	72.9%

This inland mountain resort with sea views consists of pastel West Indian—style bungalows in a hilltop garden. It's two miles northwest of Gustavia and a five-minute drive from Flamands beach. The hotel was built in 1987. Note that the resort sustained some serious damage during Hurricane Luis.

Reader Report

"The view of the ocean was not just from the room or the deck but from the bed itself. There were wonderful, colorful flowers everywhere you looked.

K. C. AND ELLEN SPENGLER, EXETER, NEW HAMPSHIRE

"The restaurant was very good. We ate there while our ship was in port, and it was the best meal we had on our cruise."

DENNIS SCHUMER, SILVER SPRING, MARYLAND

Address. Colombier, 97133 St. Barthélemy, F.W.I., tel. 590/27–78–82, fax 590/27–61–26.
Rooms. 12 rooms. All have minibars, air-conditioning, telephones, safes, and ceiling fans. All have shower only.
Facilities. Restaurant, freshwater pool.
TV and VCR. TVs in all rooms, with 4 channels including CNN, cable movie channels, and pay movies.
No-smoking rooms. None.
Credit cards. AE, D, MC, V.
Wheelchair accessibility. No accessible rooms.
Prices. Dec 20–Apr 15: $300–$450 AP. Low season: $240–$280 AP.

GUANAHANI HOTEL

				TOTAL
75.0%	70.0%	65.0%	75.0%	71.3%

Gingerbread woodwork fills the one-story Antilles-style bungalows of this beachfront resort set on seven sloping acres. The property adjoins the Rothschild estate at Grand Cul de Sac, on the island's east end. The hotel was built in 1986 and renovated and expanded in 1993. Note that the resort sustained some superficial damage during Hurricane Luis.

Reader Report

"Beautiful bayfront location, private beaches with sun and shade plus windsurfing. The open-air restaurant is beautiful and good. The rooms have a cabana-like feel."

BRIAN CRAIG, NEW YORK, NEW YORK

Address. Anse de Grand Cul de Sac, 97098 St. Barthélemy, F.W.I., tel. 590/27–66–60 or 800/223–6800, fax 590/27–70–70.

Affiliation. Leading Hotels of the World.

Rooms. 76 rooms including 21 suites. All have minibars, air-conditioning, ceiling fans, and terrace. 13 suites have private pools. 15 rooms and 5 suites have showers only.

Facilities. 2 restaurants, 3 bars/lounges, 2 lighted tennis courts, 2 freshwater pools, jacuzzi, fitness center, excercise classes, hairdresser, boutique, room service, car rental, conference room, watersports.

TV and VCR. TVs in all rooms, with 6 channels including CNN and cable movie channels. VCRs in rooms on request.

No-smoking rooms. None.

Credit cards. AE, DC, MC, V.

Restrictions. Min. 10 nights Dec 22–Jan 7, min. 5 nights in Feb.

Wheelchair accessibility. No accessible rooms.

Prices. Oct 28–Apr 21: doubles $385–$610; suites $720–$885. Low season: doubles $205–$275; suites $505–$590. All rates include Continental breakfast and airport transportation.

HOTEL MANAPANY

👔	🛏	🍴	🌅	**TOTAL**
52.4%	**52.4%**	**42.9%**	**71.4%**	**54.8%**

This red-roofed, cottage-style resort stairsteps up three levels from a beach, Anse de Cayes, in the curve of the island's north coast. The hotel was built in 1985 and renovated in 1992. Suites were added in 1990 and apartments were added in 1995. It sustained some superficial hurricane damage this fall.

Reader Report

"A beautiful place, lush, tropical—a self-contained paradise, where you receive the utmost privacy. It has the most beautiful pool that I've ever been in, and the food is good and so rich that it was difficult to find room for every meal. The cottages are lovely, and ours was right on the sand."

CAROL BURK, BREMERTON, WASHINGTON

"There are better beaches on St. Barts. Our cottage, up on a cliff, was designed for indoor-outdoor living and was lovely. The view of the water, which you could see from the bed right over the tops of your toes, was beautiful."

JERI WEINSTEIN BLUM, LONG BEACH, NEW YORK

Address. Box 114, 97133 St. Barthélemy, F.W.I., tel. 590/27–66–55, 212/719–5750 in NY, or 800/847–4249 outside NY, fax 212/719–5763.

Rooms. 14 rooms, 14 suites, 12 villas and 6 apartments. Rooms have balconies, all others have terraces. All have air-conditioning and ceiling fans. 2 villas have Jacuzzis. All suites have showers only.

Facilities. 2 restaurants, 2 bars/lounges, lighted tennis court, freshwater pool, exercise room with weights and aerobic machines, aerobic classes, bocce court. Massages, boat trips, deep-sea fishing, windsurfing and gymnastics available by appointment

TV and VCR. TVs in all rooms, with 5 channels. VCRs in public area and in rooms on request.

No-smoking rooms. None.

Credit cards. AE, DC, MC, V.

Restrictions. Min. 10 nights Dec 24–Jan 7.

Wheelchair accessibility. No accessible rooms.

Prices. Dec 24–Apr 7: doubles $390–$575; suites $465–$925; villas $855–$1,380; apartments $830–$1,035. Low season: doubles $150–$240; suites $290–$385; villas $385–$485; apartments: $410–$440. All rates include breakfast.

ST. EUSTATIUS (STATIA)

				TOTAL
N/A	N/A	N/A	N/A	N/A

Reader Reports

"A good place for history buffs, or for coming to a standstill. No digs worth shouting about—which is why I like it here."

RICHARD RUBINSTEIN, WEST HARTFORD, CONNECTICUT

"There's a great rain forest, where everything seems either very big or very small. Most visitors come for the day from St. Maarten to explore the historic sights and have a relaxed meal at the Old Gin House. Those who stay longer tend to be collectors of unspoiled islands."

NAME WITHHELD, WESTPORT, CONNECTICUT

Islands. St. Eustatius is an 8-square-mile, independent protectorate of the Netherlands, with a population of about 1,800.
Language. Statia's official language is Dutch, though English is widely spoken.

Visitor Information
In the U.S. Contact the **Caribbean Tourism Organization** (20 E. 46th St., New York, NY 10017, tel. 212/682–0435, fax 212/697–4258) or **Statia Tourist Information** (4 Daniels Farm Rd., Suite 125, Trumbull, CT 06611, tel. 203/261–8603, fax 203/261–8295).
In Canada. Contact the **Caribbean Tourism Organization** (512 Duplex St., Toronto Ont. M4R 2E3, tel. 416/485–8724, fax 416/485–8256).
In the U.K. Contact the **Caribbean Tourist Organization** (120 Wilton Rd. Victoria London SW1 V16Z, tel. 71/233–8382, fax 71/873–8551).
In St. Eustatius. Contact the **St. Eustatius Tourist Office** (Government Guest House, Oranjestad 3, St. Eustatius, Netherlands Antilles, tel. 599/38–24–33, fax same as telephone).

OLD GIN HOUSE

				TOTAL
66.7%	66.7%	77.8%	77.8%	72.2%

An 18th-century cotton mill and a ruined molasses warehouse in Lower Town, Oranjestad, are both part of this hostelry, a cluster of one- and two-story buildings fronting a beach. The hotel was built in 1972.

Reader Report

"The best possible honeymoon spot."

NAME WITHHELD, SAN FRANCISCO, CALIFORNIA

"The food and the service were unexceptional. The rooms were fine though rather small, but you spend so much time outside the room that it really isn't a concern."

HAROLD A. KNUTSON, BERKELEY, CALIFORNIA

Address. Box 172, St. Eustatius, Netherlands Antilles, tel. 599/38–23–19 or 800/223–9832, fax 599/38–25–55.

Rooms. 20 rooms. All have ceiling fans and showers only.

Facilities. 2 restaurants, 2 bars/lounges, freshwater pool, dive center nearby.

TV and VCR. No TV.

No-smoking rooms. None.

Credit cards. AE, CB, DC, D, MC, V.

Restrictions. No children under 10.

Wheelchair accessibility. No accessible rooms.

Prices. Dec 15–Apr 14: doubles $115–$150 EP. Low season: doubles $75–$100 EP.

ST. KITTS AND NEVIS

 79.3% | 55.2% | 49.3% | 66.0% | **TOTAL** 63.4%

Reader Report

"Both are very remote and undeveloped for tourism but have much to offer. We enjoyed the relaxed atmosphere and loved the beautiful scenery."

NAME WITHHELD, GARY, INDIANA

"For me, the best part about St. Kitts was that in addition to the island being so pretty, the people were really down-to-earth. The downtown area was charming and the batik factory fascinating."

KATHY COAKLEY, WEST PALM BEACH, FLORIDA

"[St. Kitts is] one of the last truly friendly islands. Taste the sugarcane, enjoy the people."

JOYCE AND CLIF HEIDEL, SOMERVILLE, NEW JERSEY

"[Nevis is] one of the best-kept secrets in the Caribbean, despite global advertising by the Four Seasons Resort! Plantation inns are where it's at—they offer a diversity of accommodations, food, and mood, but are all interesting. Not an island for those who need planned activities."

NAME WITHHELD, SARASOTA, FLORIDA

"Except at the better resorts, the service could be better. It's a good thing they add in their 10 percent, because I wouldn't have left a tip!"

LARRY KUHNER, BOSTON, MASSACHUSETTS

Islands. St. Kitts, 65 square miles, and Nevis, 36 square miles, form an independent nation with a population of about 45,000.
Language. English is the official language.

Visitor Information

In the U.S. Contact the **St. Kitts and Nevis Tourist Board** (414 E. 75th St., New York, NY 10021, tel. 212/535–1234 or 800/582–6208, fax 212/734–6511) or **Tim Benford Associates**, 1464 Whippoorwill Way, Mountainside, NJ 07092, tel. 908/232–6701, fax 908/233–0485).
In Canada. Contact the **St. Kitts and Nevis Tourist Board** (11 Yorkville Ave., Suite 508, Toronto, Ont. M4W 1L3, tel. 416/921–7717, fax 416/921–7997).
In the U.K. Contact the **St. Kitts and Nevis Tourist Office** (10 Kensington Ct., London W8 5DL, tel. 071/376–0881, fax 071/937–3611).
In St. Kitts and Nevis. Contact the **St. Kitts and Nevis Department of Tourism** (Box 132, Basseterre, St. Kitts, W.I., tel. 809/465–2620, fax 809/465–8794); **Nevis Island Administration** Main St., Charlestown, Nevis, W.I., tel. 809/1469–1042, fax 809/469–1066.

ST. KITTS

ATLANTIC OCEAN

Caribbean Sea

Turtle Bay

Mosquito Bluff

St. Anthonys Peak

Great Salt Pond

Cockleshell Bay

Banana Bay

Major's Bay

Nag's Head

White House Bay

South Friar's Bay

North Friar's Bay

North Frigate Bay

Frigate Bay

Conaree Bay

Muddy Pt.

Basseterre Bay

TO NEVIS

Basseterre

Golden Rock Airport

Monkey Hill

Hermitage Bay

Keys

Cayon

Nicola Town

Tabernacle

Sadlers

Sandy Bay

The Golden Lemon

Dieppe Bay

Willett's Bay

St. Paul's

Rawlins Plantation Inn

Newton Ground

Pump Bay

Sandy Point Town

Half Way Tree

Middle Island

Old Road Town

Challengers

Verchild's Peak

NORTH WEST RANGE

SOUTH EAST RANGE

Mt. Liamuiga

KEY

Beach

Ferry Route

Hotel or Resort

10 miles

15 km

N

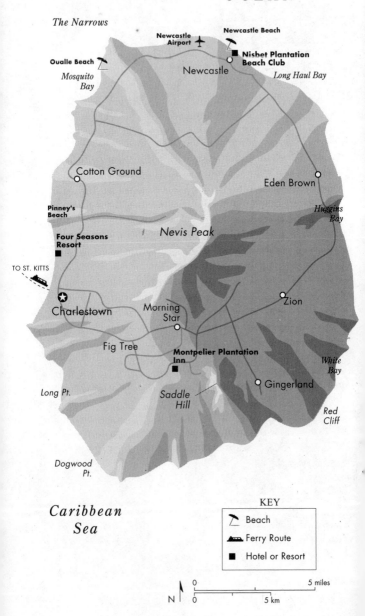

NEVIS

ATLANTIC OCEAN

The Narrows

Newcastle Airport

Newcastle Beach

Nisbet Plantation Beach Club

Oualie Beach

Mosquito Bay

Newcastle

Long Haul Bay

Cotton Ground

Eden Brown

Huggins Bay

Pinney's Beach

Four Seasons Resort

Nevis Peak

TO ST. KITTS

Zion

Charlestown

Morning Star

Fig Tree

Montpelier Plantation Inn

White Bay

Gingerland

Saddle Hill

Long Pt.

Red Cliff

Dogwood Pt.

Caribbean Sea

KEY

Beach

Ferry Route

Hotel or Resort

0   5 miles

N

0   5 km

FOUR SEASONS RESORT

| 86.4% | 94.9% | 86.4% | 89.8% | **TOTAL** 89.4% |

This 350-acre resort on Nevis, just north of Charlestown, was built in 1991 in plantation style. There's a main house and two-story cottages. A private launch transports guests from St. Kitts.

Reader Report

"Absolutely top-notch in all respects. It has a good beach with all the amenities and equipment for water sports, a very fine golf course right on the property, and absolutely the best food we have enjoyed anywhere—and we travel extensively. It's not inexpensive, but it's worth every penny."

FRANK W. JACKSON, LAGRANGE, GEORGIA

"Elegant, colonial chic. This magnificent resort has rooms with bathrooms to die for, a staff with a positive attitude that never wavers, and great food, golf, and tennis. Don't expect white sandy beaches—they're darker due to the volcanic nature of the island."

JOEL M. CHUSID, IRVING, TEXAS

"This resort is second to none when it comes to rooms, service, and recreational facilities. There's great food at both its restaurants."

NAME WITHHELD, BRIGANTINE, NEW JERSEY

"A bit too formal—and although the beach is lovely there's no snorkeling right off the beach. First-rate sports facilities."

JUDY F. OLIPHANT, LAFAYETTE, CALIFORNIA

Address. Box 565, Charlestown, Nevis, W.I., tel. 809/469–1111 or 800/332–3442, fax 809/469–1112.

Affiliation. Four Seasons Regent Hotels and Resorts.

Rooms. 196 rooms, 17 suites. All have minibars, air-conditioning, and ceiling fans.

Facilities. 3 restaurants, 2 bars/lounges, 3 lighted tennis courts, 7 unlighted, 18-hole golf course, 2 freshwater pools, horseback riding, exercise room with weights and aerobic machines, aerobics classes, massages, sauna, salon, 24-hr room service, dry-cleaning, conference center with business services, supervised children's program, sailboats.

TV and VCR. TVs in all rooms, with 24 channels including CNN and cable movie channels. VCRs in all rooms.

No-smoking rooms. 122 rooms, 10 suites.

Credit cards. AE, CB, DC, MC, V.

Restrictions. Min. 10 nights Dec 20–Jan 2.

Wheelchair accessibility. 2 rooms.

Prices. Jan 2–Apr 7: doubles $600–$660 EP; suites $1,000–$3,460 EP. Apr 8–May 31 and Nov 1–Dec 15: doubles $350–$400, suites $725–$3,060. Low season: doubles $250–$300 EP; suites $450–$2,850 EP.

THE GOLDEN LEMON

				TOTAL
73.3%	60.0%	66.7%	60.0%	65.0%

Located in Dieppe Bay, a fishing village on St. Kitts's northern point, this inn occupies a converted 17th-century sugar merchant's house and low-rise garden condos built in the 1980s.

Reader Report

"This is a very beautiful resort; service and cuisine are outstanding. Truly an enjoyable spot for a honeymoon."

NAME WITHHELD, PITTSTOWN, NEW JERSEY

"For a taste of the old Caribbean, ask for a room in the main house. The veranda provides a quiet vantage point on the ocean and palms while you savor one of the Lemon's terrific rum punches and read a good book."

ALLAN JONES, ALEXANDRIA, VIRGINIA

Address. Dieppe Bay, St. Kitts, W.I., tel. 809/465–7260 or 800/633–7411, fax 809/465–4019.
Rooms. 28 rooms in 15 villas. All have ceiling fans.
Facilities. Restaurant, unlighted tennis court, 1 freshwater pool, 14 private pools (in villas), horseback riding, massages.
TV and VCR. No TV.
No-smoking rooms. None.
Credit cards. AE, DC, D, MC, V.
Restrictions. Min. 7 nights Christmas and New Year's. No children under 18.
Wheelchair accessibility. No accessible rooms.
Prices. Dec 16–Apr 15: doubles $220; villas $435. Low season: doubles $216; villas $240. Full American breakfast included.

MONTPELIER PLANTATION INN

				TOTAL
66.7%	66.7%	100%	66.7%	75%

This quiet, 12-acre, hillside resort shelters most of its guests in simple, tropical-style cottages, but cocktails and dinner are served in the great house, an imposing fieldstone structure furnished with antiques. The large pool has a mountain view, and the inn provides a daily bus to a private beach about 20 minutes away. The hotel was built in 1965 and renovated between 1994 and 1995.

Reader Report

"It's a very unique spot, and much quieter than on other

islands. I was impressed by all of it, and the service is impeccable."

LEE BOWERS, FRESNO, CALIFORNIA

Address. Box 474, Nevis, W.I., tel. 809/469–3462, fax 809/469–2932.
Affiliation. Romantik Hotels International.
Rooms. 17 rooms, 1 suite, 1 villa. All have ceiling fans.
Facilities. Restaurant, 2 bars/lounges, unlighted tennis court, 18-hole golf course nearby, freshwater pool, horseback riding.
TV and VCR. No TV.
No-smoking rooms. None.
Credit cards. MC, V.
Restrictions. Min. 7 nights between Christmas and New Year's. Min. 3 nights for reservations. No children under 8 Dec.–Feb.
Wheelchair accessibility. No accessible rooms.
Prices. Dec. 15–Apr. 15: doubles $280; suite $330; villa $330–$500. Low season: doubles $180; suite $230; villa $230–$350. Full American breakfast included.

NISBET PLANTATION BEACH CLUB

| 76.2% | 71.4% | 71.4% | 66.7% | **TOTAL** 71.4% |

An avenue lined by coconut palms leads to a beach at this resort on 30 acres of an 18th-century plantation on Nevis's north coast. The great house has been renovated, and guests stay in colonial-style cottages. Also on the grounds: a ruined sugar mill. Restoration has been ongoing, and rooms were added to the hotel in 1989.

Reader Report
"Relaxed and comfortable. The layout of the grounds is very nice, and the beach is one of the nicest on the island, after that at the Four Seasons."

MARK FRANKEL, NEW YORK, NEW YORK

Address. St. James Parish, Nevis, W.I., tel. 809/469–9325 or 800/742–6008, fax 809/628–1732.
Rooms. 38 rooms. All have minibars and ceiling fans. 16 have showers only.
Facilities. 2 restaurants, 2 bars/lounges, unlighted tennis court, freshwater pool.
TV and VCR. TV in public areas only, with 27 channels including CNN and cable movie channels. VCR in public area.
No-smoking rooms. None.
Credit cards. AE, MC, V.
Restrictions. No children under 5 in certain rooms.
Wheelchair accessibility. No accessible rooms.
Prices. Dec. 21–Apr 14: $355–$455 MAP. Low season: $255–$325 MAP.

RAWLINS PLANTATION INN

👨	🛏	✕	☀	**TOTAL**
60.0%	**70.0%**	**80.0%**	**80.0%**	**72.5%**

This 12-acre resort on a hilltop on St. Kitts's northwest coast was built in 1974 on an old sugar plantation. It includes a reconstructed manor house and sugar mill and modern cottages.

Reader Report

"Once you get there, Rawlins is hard to leave. The old sugar plantation is situated high enough on the slopes of the island for impressive views and for catching the cooling trade winds. The innkeepers cater to your every need, upholding their British tradition to pamper to the utmost."

RICHARD REEDY, PORTLAND, OREGON

"Structurally varied cottages provide romantic and different views of the plantation, while the beautiful aroma of West Indian cuisine enriches the day. Service, atmosphere, and dining are totally relaxed and truly indicative of St. Kitts's cultural style."

WILLIAM TINSLEY, BANGOR, PENNSYLVANIA

"The accommodations are in individual cottages, each unique, from the windmill to the cistern to the chimney house. We lounged by the pool, read books on our private balcony, hiked the paths, and visited local places of interest. It's not bright lights and glitter, but a tranquil adult oasis."

JANICE CLINKENBEARD, TROPHY CLUB, TEXAS

Address. Box 340, St. Kitts, W.I., tel. 809/465–6221 or 800/346–5358, fax 809/465–4954.
Rooms. 10 rooms. All have ceiling fans.
Facilities. Restaurant, bar/lounge, unlighted tennis court, freshwater pool.
TV and VCR. No TV.
No-smoking rooms. None.
Credit cards. AM, MC, V
Restrictions. Min. 4 nights Dec. 15–Apr 15. No children under 13.
Wheelchair accessibility. No accessible rooms.
Prices. Dec 15–Apr 15: $390 MAP. Low season: $265 MAP.

ST. LUCIA

				TOTAL
82.9%	**57.1%**	**51.4%**	**58.9%**	**61.6%**

Reader Report

" *Here is simple Caribbean village life untouched by time. Hurry to see it before condos are scattered all over the hillsides.* "

MARY M. GODDARD, WATERFORD, MICHIGAN

"Small, relaxed, and friendly, with lovely scenery, an interesting volcano, good snorkeling—no bugs!"

SARA LAFRANCE, LAFAYETTE, CALIFORNIA

"One of the most beautiful spots I've ever seen, St. Lucia is like heaven on one end and hell on the other. The heaven part is lush green, very tropical. The hell part is the Piton mountains—with the smell of sulfur suffusing the steam coming up out of the volcanoes."

NAN MCMAHAN, PACIFIC GROVE, CALIFORNIA

"People were super friendly every place we went. We were disappointed in the shopping (it was very limited), but the Mardi Gras was terrific."

KAREN ROBICHAUD, GREENWICH, CONNECTICUT

Islands. St. Lucia is a 238-square-mile independent nation, with a population of about 148,000.
Language. Although French-Creole patois is widely spoken by the islanders, the official language is English.

Visitor Information

In the U.S. Contact the **St. Lucia Tourist Board** (820 2nd Ave., 9th floor, New York, NY 10017, tel. 212/867–2950 or 800/456–3984, fax 212/867–2795).
In Canada. Contact the **St. Lucia Tourist Board** (3 Robert Speck Pkwy., Suite 900, Mississague, Ont. L4Z 2G5, tel. 905/270–9892, fax 905/270–8086).
In the U.K. Contact the **St Lucia Tourist Board** (421A Finchley Rd., London NW3 6HJ, tel. 071/431–4045, no fax) or the **High Commission for Eastern Caribbean States** (10 Kensington Court, London W8 5DL, tel. 071/937–1969, fax 071/937–3611).
In St. Lucia. Contact the **St. Lucia Tourist Board** (Box 221, Castries, St. Lucia, W.I., tel. 809/452–4094, fax 809/453–1121).

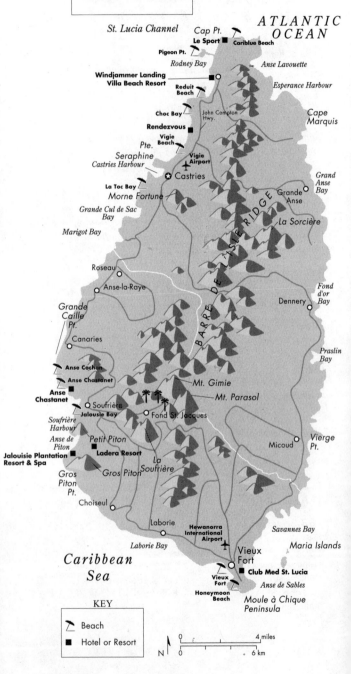

ST. LUCIA

ATLANTIC OCEAN

St. Lucia Channel

Cap Pt.

Le Sport ■

Cariblue Beach

Pigeon Pt.

Rodney Bay

Anse Lavouette

Windjammer Landing Villa Beach Resort ■

Esperance Harbour

Reduit Beach

Choc Bay

John Compton Hwy.

Cape Marquis

Rendezvous ■

Vigie Beach

Vigie Airport ✈

Pte. Seraphine

Castries Harbour

✪ **Castries**

Grand Anse Bay

La Toc Bay

Morne Fortune

Grande Anse

La Sorcière

Grande Cul de Sac Bay

Marigot Bay

Roseau

Anse-la-Raye

Fond d'or Bay

Dennery

Grande Caille Pt.

Canaries

Praslin Bay

Anse Cochon

Anse Chastanet

Anse Chastanet ■

Mt. Gimie

Soufrière

Jalousie Bay

Fond St. Jacques

Mt. Parasol

Soufrière Harbour

Anse de Piton

Petit Piton

Micoud

Vierge Pt.

Jalousie Plantation Resort & Spa ■

Ladera Resort

La Soufrière

Gros Piton Pt.

Gros Piton

Choiseul

Laborie

Hewanorra International Airport ✈

Savannes Bay

Maria Islands

Laborie Bay

Caribbean Sea

Vieux Fort ✈

Vieux Fort

■ Club Med St. Lucia

Anse de Sables

Honeymoon Beach

Moule à Chique Peninsula

BARRE DE L'ISLE RIDGE

KEY

⊼ Beach

■ Hotel or Resort

0 — 4 miles

0 — 6 km

N

ANSE CHASTANET

👨‍🍳	🛏️	🍴	☀️	**TOTAL**
62.5%	**65.6%**	**53.1%**	**75.0%**	**64.1%**

Stairs lead down to the beach at this 500-acre resort on the island's Caribbean coast, just north of Soufrière. Guests are accommodated in octagonal hillside gazebos and beachfront villas. The hotel was built in 1968 and renovated in 1993. The newest rooms date from 1990.

Reader Report

"Very nice, and the beach bar pours the best rum punch in the Caribbean."

FRED L. BENDER, CLEARWATER, FLORIDA

"Great diving program."

NAME WITHHELD, NEW YORK, NEW YORK

Address. Box 7000, St. Lucia, W.I., tel. 809/459–7000 or 800/223–1108, fax 809/459–7700.
Rooms. 48 rooms, including 12 beachside deluxe rooms. All have ceiling fans, coffee machines and refrigerators but showers only. Beachside rooms have a balcony or patio.
Facilities. 2 restaurants, 2 bars/lounges, unlighted tennis court, 2 boutiques, massages, dive center, windsurfing, 4 sailboats.
TV and VCR. No TVs.
No-smoking rooms. None.
Credit cards. AE, DC, D, MC, V.
Restrictions. Min. 3 nights Dec 20–Apr 16. No children under 2.
Wheelchair accessibility. No accessible rooms.
Prices. Dec 20–Apr 15: doubles $330–$430 MAP; beachside $495–$595 MAP. Low season: doubles $156–$240 EP; suites $260–$390 EP.

CLUB MED ST. LUCIA

👨‍🍳	🛏️	🍴	☀️	**TOTAL**
63.3%	**23.3%**	**63.3%**	**63.3%**	**53.3%**

Four-story beach and garden buildings make up this 95-acre all-inclusive resort on Savannes Bay on the Atlantic side of the island's southern tip.

Reader Report

"Beautiful location—our room overlooked the water. It has a laid-back atmosphere and good sports instruction. The staff is well organized, helpful, and friendly."

NAME WITHHELD, JERSEY CITY, NEW JERSEY

"Every aspect of the resort is magnificent, except for the rooms—they're stark, typical Club Med. It's great for couples

*or families; it accommodates all tastes. You have to take a
bus to the beach, but it's really only a hop away."*

CHERI ALBERT, NEW YORK, NEW YORK

Address. Box 246, Vieux Fort, St. Lucia, W.I., tel. 809/454–
6546 or 800/258-2633, fax 809/454–6017.
Affiliation. Club Med.
Rooms. 256 rooms. All have air-conditioning, but showers only.
Facilities. 3 restaurants, 2 bars/lounges, nightclub, theater, 8
lighted tennis courts, freshwater pool, horseback riding, exer-
cise room with weights and aerobic machines, aerobics classes,
supervised children's program, dive center, sailboats, circus
workshops.
TV and VCR. TV in public area only, with VCR.
No-smoking rooms. None.
Credit cards. AE, MC, V.
Restrictions. No children under 2.
Wheelchair accessibility. No accessible rooms.
Prices. Dec 10–Apr 30: $170–$230. Low season: $115. Prices
are all-inclusive and per person.

JALOUSIE PLANTATION RESORT & SPA

100.0%	86.7%	80.0%	100.0%	**TOTAL** 91.7%

Brown wooden cottages on a hillside by the sea accommodate
guests at this 320-acre all-inclusive resort opened in 1992. It's
set between the two Pitons, just south of Soufrière.

Reader Report

*"My wife works about 80 hours a week, and she chilled out
here more quickly than she ever has anywhere. Floating in
the intensely blue water off the beach she turned to me and
declared that we had to return here. When I asked her when,
she replied, 'Every year, for the rest of our lives.'"*

STEVEN MCCARTHY, MIDLOTHIAN, VIRGINIA

*"A beautiful hideaway with superb food. Our accommodations
were comfortable."*

NAME WITHHELD, GLENVIEW, ILLINOIS

Address. Box 251, Soufrière, St. Lucia, W.I., tel. 809/459–
7666 or 800/392-2007, fax 809/459–7667.
Affiliation. M Group Resort Services.
Rooms. 56 cottages, 28 suites, 12 rooms. All have air-conditioning, ceiling fans, and refrigerators; all cottages and suites
have private plunge pools.
Facilities. 4 restaurants, 4 bars/lounges, 3 lighted tennis courts,
1 unlighted, freshwater pool, horseback riding, exercise room
with weights and aerobic machines, aerobics classes, massages, sauna, salon, dry-cleaning, supervised children's program in season, dive center.

TV and VCR. TVs in all rooms, with 10 channels including CNN and cable movie channels. VCR in public area.
No-smoking rooms. None.
Credit cards. AE, DC, D, MC, V.
Restrictions. Min. 7 nights Dec 25–Dec 31.
Wheelchair accessibility. No accessible rooms.
Prices. Dec 22–Mar 31: doubles $600—$750; suites $800–$900. Low season: doubles $500–$600; suites $660–$730. All rates are all-inclusive.

LADERA RESORT

🍸	🛏	🍴	☀	**TOTAL**
71.4%	**85.7%**	**71.4%**	**85.7%**	**78.6%**

This low-rise, 3-acre resort is nestled in lush botanical gardens and overlooks the Pitons, the Caribbean sea, and Jalousie Plantation. Suites are decorated with handmade 19th-century French antiques and local artwork. Built in 1975, the hotel was restored and expanded in 1992.

Reader Report

"It was unique with an open-air room. The food at the restaurant was great. [It is] isolated though...there's not much to do in the resort area."

ROBERT WHITTEMORE, NORTH MERRICK, NEW YORK

"It was our favorite place on the island. It's very unusual; there's probably not another place like it. You have to have a little sense of adventure.... Each room has an open wall so that you can see right over the bay. Sometimes birds fly in."

DEBORAH MARIYA, KENSINGTON, MARYLAND

Address. Box 225, Soufrière, St. Lucia, W.I., tel. 809/459–7323, fax 809/459–5156.
Affiliation. Insignia Resorts.
Rooms. 13 suites, 6 villas. 8 suites have plunge pools, 5 villas have private swimming pools.
Facilities. Restaurant, bar/lounge, freshwater pool, massages.
TV and VCR. TV in public area only.
No-smoking rooms. None.
Credit cards. AE, D, DC, MC, V.
Restrictions. Min. 7 nights Dec. 18–Jan. 4. Not recommended for children under 8.
Wheelchair accessibility. No accessible rooms.
Prices. Dec. 18–Apr. 15: suites $450–$570 AP, $410–$530 MAP, $330–$450 EP; villas $595–$770 AP, $555–$730 MAP, $475–$650 EP. Low season: suites $315–$470 AP, $275–$430 MAP, $195–$350 EP; villas $415–$645 AP, $375–$605 MAP, $295–$525 EP.

LE SPORT

60.0%	60.0%	50.0%	70.0%	TOTAL 60.0%

This all-inclusive resort, built in 1971 and renovated 1989, sits on 14 acres on the northern tip of the island along a crescent-shaped beach. Included in the rate are various body treatments and fitness classes, including water aerobics, yoga, and meditation. The three-story hotel is modern, and the spa building is done in Spanish style.

Reader Report

"Nice, quiet location, very comfortable atmosphere."
KATHRYN GEBHARDT, UPPER SADDLE RIVER, NEW JERSEY

"It could be perfect—the location is ideal—but the place is run-down. The pool was not filtered, and the air conditioner in my room was broken. "
NAME WITHHELD, NEW YORK, NEW YORK

"The location was not to my liking—not enough beach to walk."
VERA SCHULTZ, MANSFIELD, OHIO

Address. Box 437, Cariblue Beach, Castries, St. Lucia, W.I., tel. 809/450–8551 or 800/544–2883, fax 809/450–0368.
Affiliation. SunSwept Resorts.
Rooms. 100 rooms including 2 suites. All have air-conditioning and small refrigerators.
Facilities. Restaurant, 2 bars/lounges, lighted tennis court, 9-hole golf course nearby, 3 freshwater pools, spa, golf school, dive center, sailboats.
TV and VCR. No TV.
No-smoking rooms. None.
Credit cards. AE, D, MC, V.
Wheelchair accessibility. No accessible rooms.
Prices. Dec 24–Apr 8: doubles $200–$260; suites $310. Low season: doubles $210–$230; suites $280. All rates are all-inclusive and per person.

RENDEZVOUS

69.2%	69.2%	76.9%	84.6%	TOTAL 75.0%

This all-inclusive resort for adult twosomes, formerly called Couples, is on the northwest Caribbean coast, just above Castries. It has a three-story main building with an oceanfront wing and was built in 1980, expanded in 1990, and renovated in 1992.

Reader Report

"We loved it. There are beautiful gardens, a nice beach, and open-air dining."

PATRICIA VRABEL, HERSHEY, PENNSYLVANIA

"The beachfront suites are lovely, though the older section needs to be redone. Mostly British guests. The somewhat rocky beach is public, and has dark sand and a steep dropoff. The food is good, with buffets at breakfast and lunch and a choice of two restaurants at dinner."

KIM TERRY, UPPERCO, MARYLAND

Address. Malabar Beach, Box 190, Castries, St. Lucia, W.I., tel. 809/452–4211 or 800/544–2883, fax 809/452–7419.
Affiliation. SunSwept Resorts.
Rooms. 89 rooms, 11 suites. All have air-conditioning. 70 rooms and 3 suites have ceiling fans. 3 suites have Jacuzzis.
Facilities. 2 restaurants, 3 bars/lounges, 2 lighted tennis courts, 2 freshwater pools, exercise room with weights and aerobic machines, aerobics classes, sauna, dive center, sailboats.
TV and VCR. No TVs.
No-smoking rooms. None.
Credit cards. AE, DC, MC, V.
Restrictions. Couples 17 and older only. No gay couples or singles.
Wheelchair accessibility. No accessible rooms.
Prices. Dec 17–Mar 2: doubles $1,230–$1,490 for 3 nights, extra night $355–$430; suites $1,495–$1,705 for 3 nights, extra night $425–$490. Low season: doubles $1,280–$1,475 for three nights, extra night $370–$420; suites $1,510–$1,660 for three nights, extra night $435–$475. Rates are all-inclusive.

WINDJAMMER LANDING VILLA BEACH RESORT

65.0%	75.0%	70.0%	85.0%	TOTAL 73.8%

The white stucco Mediterranean-style villas of this 55-acre resort are on a hillside above Labrelotte Bay on the northern end of the island's Caribbean coast. The hotel was built in 1971 and was last renovated in 1994.

Reader Report

"We loved this resort. It's very family-oriented with great atmosphere and room decor. We had a four-bedroom villa with a splash pool on the hillside, with a magnificent view of the ocean."

KAREN ROBICHAUD, GREENWICH, CONNECTICUT

"The food was good and the rooms were a good size. Though the beach was not large, it was still very nice."

JERRY BRUCE, SEAGOVILLE, TEXAS

Address. Labrelotte Bay, Box 1504, Castries, St. Lucia, W.I., tel. 809/452–0913 or 800/743–9609, fax 809/452–0907.

Affiliation. Robert Reid Associates.

Rooms. Superior and Deluxe rooms and 114 villas. All have air-conditioning and ceiling fans in the bedrooms. All villas have kitchenettes. 58 have shower only or tub only.

Facilities. 5 restaurants, 3 bars/lounges, 2 lighted tennis courts, 4 freshwater pools, health and beauty center, watersports, mini mart, 2 boutiques, conference center, supervised children's program, car rental, excursion desk, dive center.

TV and VCR. TVs in all rooms, villas with 13 channels including CNN. VCRs on request.

No-smoking rooms. None.

Credit cards. AE, MC, V.

Restrictions. Min. 10 nights Dec 25–31.

Wheelchair accessibility. No accessible rooms.

Prices. Dec 18–Apr 20: villas $310—$560 EP; rooms $230–$270 EP. Low season: villas $205–$460 EP; rooms $140–$270 EP.

ST. MARTIN/ST. MAARTEN

				TOTAL
68.5%	**56.8%**	**56.4%**	**53.6%**	**60.7%**

Reader Report

"In my opinion, the most beautiful island in the Caribbean—very lush with great beaches. It's more interesting, having a French and a Dutch half. There's something for everyone—water sports, beautiful resorts, beautiful scenery, nightlife, and gambling."

MARY JANE KOVALCIK, CLINTON TOWNSHIP, MICHIGAN

"Truly a food lover's paradise. From Grand Case on the French side to Philipsburg on the Dutch side, the quality of the meals is impressive. Prepare to spend a little more for casual elegance and memorable fare."

HETTIE D. MAIDMAN, KING OF PRUSSIA, PENNSYLVANIA

"Philipsburg has surpassed even Charlotte Amalie as the tacky souvenir capital of the Caribbean. Yet just a short and scenically stunning cab ride away lies Marigot, perhaps the most elegant shopping area between Worth Avenue and Caracas."

DON BYER, BROOKLYN, NEW YORK

"Get a room with a kitchen so you don't have to eat every meal out—food is expensive."

NAME WITHHELD, WESTLAKE, OHIO

"The only island we dare rent a car and drive all over. People seem genuinely friendly. No beach hawkers."

MAX ROBITZER, NEWBURY, VERMONT

Islands. St. Martin/St. Maarten is a 37-square-mile island that is home to both an independent protectorate of the Netherlands and an independent protectorate of France, with a combined population of about 32,000.

Language. Although English is widely spoken by the islanders, the official language of St. Martin is French and the official language of St. Maarten is Dutch.

Visitor Information

In the U.S. Contact the **St. Maarten Tourist Bureau** (675 Third Ave., New York, NY 10007, tel. 800/STMAARTEN, fax 212/986–3484) or call France-On-Call (tel. 900/990–0040; .50 a minute). Also call the **St. Martin Bureau of Tourism** (10 East 21 St., New York, NY 10010, tel. 212/838–7800, fax 212/838–7855; 9454 Wilshire Blvd., Beverly Hills, CA 90212, tel 310/271–6665, fax 310/276–2835; 676 N. Michigan Ave., Chicago, IL 60611, tel. 312/751–7800, fax 312/337–6339).

In Canada. Contact the **French Government Tourist Office** (Maison de la France, 1981 McGill College Ave., Suite 490,

ST. MARTIN/
ST. MAARTEN

Pt. du
Plum

Pte. du
Bluff

Baie Rouge

La Belle Creole

Pte. des
Pierres
a Chaux

Plum
Baie

Pt.
Arago

Baie de la
Potence

Baie de
Marigot

Marigot

Baie Longue

La Samanna

Cupecoy Beach

Simpson Bay Lagoon

Sentry
Hill

Mullet Bay

S T.

Juliana
International
Airport

Maho Bay

Port de Plaisance

Simpson
Bay

Koolbaai

*Caribbean
Sea*

Cole
Bay

KEY

Beach

Cruise Ship Dock

Ferry Route

■ Hotel or Resort

N

0   2 miles

0   3 km

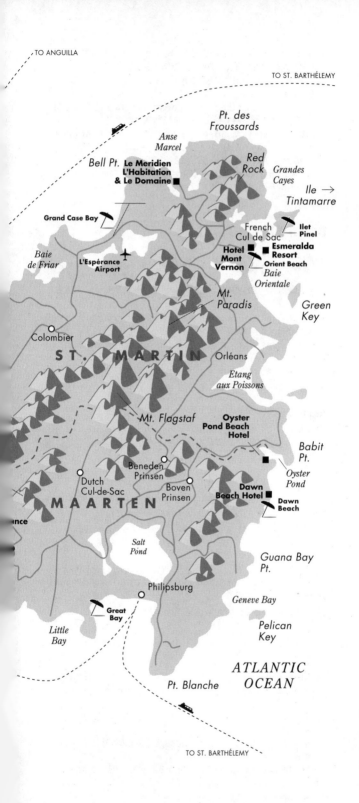

Montreal, Que. H3A 2W9, tel. 514/288–4264, fax 514/845–4868; **French Tourist Office** 30 St. Patrick St., Suite 700, Toronto, Ont. M5T 3A3, tel. 416/593–4723, fax 416/979–7587).

In the U.K. Contact the **French Government Tourist Office** (178 Picadilly, London W1V 0AL, tel. 071/491–7622).

In St. Martin/St. Maarten. Contact the **Tourist Information Bureau** (Cyrus Wathey Sq., Philipsburg, St. Maarten, Netherlands Antilles, tel. 599/52–2337, fax 599/52–4884) or **Saint Martin Tourist Office** (Port de Marigot, 97150 Marigot, St. Martin, F.W.I., tel. 590/87–57–21, fax 590/87–56–43).

DAWN BEACH HOTEL

👔	🛏	🍴	🌊	**TOTAL**
41.0%	**38.5%**	**43.6%**	**51.3%**	**43.6%**

Three-story hillside villas and single-story beach-level cabanas comprise this 17-acre resort on the Dutch end of the island's Atlantic coast. The beach has a reef offshore. The hotel was built in 1980 and expanded in 1982. During Hurricane Luis, the resort was seriously damaged and its opening was delayed; it will be reopened for the season by December.

Reader Report

"A little out of the way and at the base of a fairly steep hill— check your brakes before descending. Not the best location on the island, but enjoyable nonetheless."

STEPHEN B. FRIEDHEIM, DALLAS, TEXAS

"The beach is beautiful, and the beachfront cottages have a great view. Very hard to reach from the town but great for a secluded vacation."

JEAN BENOIT, PORTLAND, CONNECTICUT

"A lovely resort hotel with a beautiful beach and an excellent pool and dining rooms. Rooms in the hillside bungalows are large and nice. Far from town—after our first $10 cab ride to Philipsburg (maybe five miles!) we rented a car for $20 a day. "

DALE ROBERTS, CHICAGO, ILLINOIS

Address. Oyster Pond, Box 389, St. Maarten, Netherlands Antilles, tel. 599/52–2929 or 800/351–5656, fax 599/52–4421.

Rooms. 155 junior suites. All have air-conditioning and ceiling fans. 95 have showers only.

Facilities. 3 restaurants, 2 bars/lounges, 2 lighted tennis courts, freshwater pool.

TV and VCR. TVs in all rooms, with 30 channels including CNN and cable movie channels. No VCRs.

No-smoking rooms. None.

Credit cards. AE, DC, MC, V.

Wheelchair accessibility. No accessible rooms.

Prices. Dec 15–Apr 15: $200—$290 EP. Low season: $105–$195 EP.

ESMERALDA RESORT

 77.3%	 81.8%	 81.8%	 81.8%	**TOTAL** **80.7%**

Guest quarters of this 100-acre resort are in Creole-style villas. Built in 1991, the property is on Orient Beach, on the French side's Atlantic coast.

Reader Report

"Condos—new, clean, and simple but comfortable, with great food. Orient Beach is great and the people are friendly."

LARRY MABLE, SAN DIEGO, CALIFORNIA

"We like it because it is small, quiet, and relaxing with an excellent restaurant on site. The facilities are clean and spacious."

STEPHEN MARGA, PARAMUS, NEW JERSEY

Address. Box 5141, 97071 St. Martin, F.W.I., tel. 590/87–36–36 or 800/622–7836, fax 590/87–35–18.
Rooms. 44 rooms and 10 suites, in 14 villas. All have air-conditioning, ceiling fans, and Jacuzzis. 1 suite has tub only.
Facilities. Restaurant, 2 bars/lounges, 2 lighted tennis courts, 14 freshwater pools (1 per villa), horseback riding, massages, dive center, sailboats for an additional fee.
TV and VCR. TVs in all rooms, with 9 channels including CNN and cable movie channels. VCRs upon request.
No-smoking rooms. None.
Credit cards. AE, MC, V.
Restrictions. Min. 7 nights Dec 21–Feb 28.
Wheelchair accessibility. 3 rooms.
Prices. Dec 21–Apr 13: doubles $275–$400 CP; suites $450–$2,200 CP. Low season: doubles $180–$240 CP; suites $280–$1,240 CP.

HOTEL MONT VERNON

 47.4%	 63.2%	 36.8%	 68.4%	**TOTAL** **53.9%**

Ten two-story, Creole-inspired buildings sit on 70 hillside acres on Orient Beach, on the French side, along the Atlantic coast. The resort was built in 1989, enlarged in 1991, and renovated in 1995. During Hurricane Luis, the hotel sustained some serious damage and its opening was delayed; it is scheduled to be up and running for the season by December 18.

Reader Report

"The setting at the northeast edge of Orient Beach is lovely, with beautiful views—but it's rather remote unless you have a car. Rooms are large and comfortable."

VICTOR A. SANDERS, ARLINGTON, VIRGINIA

"Not super luxurious but reasonable. The pool is large and the beach outstanding. You can walk to several excellent restaurants."

JAY AND JOAN JACOBSON, ORANGEBURG, NEW YORK

Address. Chevrise Baie Orientale, Box 1174, 97150 St. Martin, F.W.I., tel. 590/87–62–00 or 800/223–0888, fax 590/87–37–27.

Affiliation. Jet Hotels.

Rooms. 357 junior suites, 37 1-bedroom suites. All suites have air-conditioning, refrigerators, private terraces.

Facilities. 2 restaurants, 2 bars/lounges, 2 lighted tennis courts, 18-hole golf course nearby, freshwater pool, horseback riding, exercise room with weights, dry-cleaning, conference center with business services, supervised children's program.

TV and VCR. TVs in all rooms, with 10 channels including CNN and cable movie channels. No VCRs.

No-smoking rooms. None.

Credit cards. AE, MC, V.

Restrictions. Min. 7 nights Dec 21–Jan 2.

Wheelchair accessibility. No accessible rooms.

Prices. Dec 18–Apr 3: junior suites $313; 1-bedroom suites $415. Low season: junior suites $140; 1-bedroom suites $263.

LA BELLE CREOLE

| 60.5% | 65.8% | 52.6% | 68.4% | **TOTAL** 61.8% |

A bluff across the bay from Marigot, the French side's capital, is the setting for this 25-acre Mediterranean-style village of one- to three-story villas built around a central plaza. The hotel was renovated and landscaped in 1995 and plans expansion in 1996. The resort sustained some serious damage during Hurricane Luis and it temporarily closed for repairs; it is scheduled to be up and running by December 1.

Reader Report

"Very attractive, with large, clean rooms and an efficient staff. They serve the best breakfast in the islands."

NAME WITHHELD, HOLLYWOOD, FLORIDA

"A stay at this unique resort is like stepping into another world. We felt as if we were in a Mediterranean village."

ROBERTA SANDRIN, DERWOOD, MARYLAND

Address. Box 4181 Marigot, 97065 St. Martin, F.W.I., tel. 590/87–66–00, fax 590/87–56–66.
Affiliation. Winfair Hospitality Group.
Rooms. 166 rooms, 22 suites. All have minibars. All have air-conditioning, and ceiling fans.
Facilities. 3 restaurants, 3 bars/lounges, outdoor jacuzzi, 4 lighted tennis courts, freshwater pool, casino nearby (on Dutch side), exercise room with weights and aerobic machines, aerobics classes, massages, croquet lawn, salon, dry-cleaning, supervised children's program in season, dive center, sailboats.
TV and VCR. TVs in all rooms, with 8 channels including CNN and cable movie channels. No VCRs.
No-smoking rooms. None.
Credit cards. AE, CB, DC, MC, V.
Wheelchair accessibility. 2 rooms.
Prices. Dec 22–Apr 2: doubles $315–$455 CP; suites $495–$1,410 CP. Low season: doubles $205–$280 CP; suites $340–$940 CP.

LA SAMANNA

				TOTAL
83.6%	77.0%	88.5%	90.2%	84.8%

This 55-acre Mediterranean-style resort is on the island's western coast, on the French side. It has a three-story main building and beach villas with one-, two-, and three-bedroom studios and villas. Built in 1973, the property was renovated in 1992. Note that the resort sustained some superficial damage during Hurricane Luis.

Reader Report

"Dining was sheer joy. Service was unhurried, waiters attentive to detail, and the food and wine absolutely wonderful."

G. AL CHIZ, MUNHALL, PENNSYLVANIA

"We found privacy, discreet and attentive service, and sunsets to kill for. The cuisine was not only pleasing to the palate but was presented with genuine friendliness. Not for the traveler who wants to be entertained, but absolutely fulfilling for those seeking soul-restorative quiet."

RICHARD JACOBS, JACKSON, TENNESSEE

"The private beach and updated rooms complete the experience here. Water sports and diving services are provided, and the staff is willing to direct you to isolated beach locations."

MARTIN HOLLAND, DALLAS, TEXAS

Address. Box 4077, 97064 St. Martin, F.W.I., tel. 590/87–64–00 or 800/854–2252, fax 212/832–5390.
Affiliation. Rosewood Hotels & Resorts.

Rooms. 80 rooms, 63 suites, 6 villas. All have minibars, air-conditioning, and ceiling fans.

Facilities. 2 restaurants, bar/lounge, 3 unlighted tennis courts, freshwater pool, fitness pavilion with weights and aerobic machines, aerobics classes, massages, 24-hr room service, dry-cleaning.

TV and VCR. TVs in public area only, with 3 channels including CNN. VCRs in public area and in rooms on request.

No-smoking rooms. None.

Credit cards. AE, MC, V.

Restrictions. Min. 14 nights Dec. 17–Jan 2.

Wheelchair accessibility. No accessible rooms.

Prices. Dec 17–Apr 16: doubles $490–$570 BP; suites $690–$1,300 BP; villas $1,850 BP. Low season: doubles $325–$380 BP; suites $480–$900 BP; villas $1,400 BP.

LE MERIDIEN L'HABITATION & LE DOMAINE

| 72.9% | 68.8% | 64.6% | 77.1% | TOTAL 70.8% |

This 150-acre resort complex on the French side (on the northeast point) has two- and three-story Creole-style gingerbread buildings, its own marina, and a hilltop sports club. It was built in 1986, expanded in 1992.

Reader Report

"Very pretty and upscale. The service is lovely."

CHERI ALBERT, NEW YORK, NEW YORK

"Beautiful location. The food was excellent, though prices were high. There is a beautiful beach and a marina."

TAGE NIELSEN, NEW LONDON, CONNECTICUT

Address. P.O. Box 581 Anse Marcel, 97056 St. Martin, F.W.I., tel. 590/87–67–00 or 800/543–4300, fax 590/87–30–38.

Affiliation. Forte/Meridien Hotels.

Rooms. L'Habitation: 189 rooms, 12 suites and 50 Marina suites. Le Domaine: 125 rooms and 20 ocean view suites. All have minibars, air-conditioning, and ceiling fans.

Facilities. 4 restaurants, 2 bars/lounges, 6 lighted tennis courts, 4 squash courts, 2 racketball courts, 2 freshwater pools, spa center, aerobics, supervised children's program (open during holidays if enough children on site), dive center, sailboats, deep sea fishing.

TV and VCR. TVs in all rooms, with 8 channels including CNN and cable movie channels.

No-smoking rooms. None.

Credit cards. AE, DC, EC, MC, V.

Restrictions. Min. 5 nights Dec 20–Jan 2.

Wheelchair accessibility. 12 rooms.

Prices. Dec 20–Jan 2: doubles $440–$560 EP; suites $590–$780 EP. Jan 3–Apr 9: doubles $280–$360 EP; suites $410–$520 EP. Low season: doubles $160–$220 EP; suites $240–$350 EP. Add $15 per person to include breakfast.

OYSTER POND BEACH HOTEL

| 74.2% | 74.2% | 71.0% | 77.4% | TOTAL 74.2% |

Twin towers and Moorish arches distinguish this two-story hotel, built in 1971 and renovated in 1990; adjacent are blocks of suites, constructed in 1990. The complex is on a cove near a mile-long beach, on the Atlantic coast of the Dutch side.

Reader Report

"A terrific hotel, small but elegant, with great food and a beautiful long beach. The rooms are exceptionally clean, and you can have fresh native fruit and French baked goods for breakfast every morning."

DOUGLAS JOHNSON, HADDONFIELD, NEW JERSEY

"The rooms have cool tile floors and light cottony materials, but the service is what makes it. Our flight was delayed and we didn't arrive until 11 o'clock at night—and we were starving! Though they had already locked up for the night, they opened the kitchen and fixed us a late supper."

CAROL BURK, BREMERTON, WASHINGTON

Address. Box 239, St. Maarten, Netherlands Antilles, tel. 5995/3–6206, fax 5995/3–6695.

Rooms. 16 rooms, 24 suites. All have air-conditioning, balconies or terraces, hair dryers, coffee makers, and ceiling fans. All rooms have showers only. All suites have refrigerators.

Facilities. Restaurant, bar/lounge, saltwater pool, massages, dry-cleaning, dive center.

TV and VCR. TVs in all rooms, with 28 channels including CNN and cable movie channels. No VCRs.

No-smoking rooms. None.

Credit cards. AE, MC, V.

Restrictions. Min. 7 nights Dec 20–Mar 31.

Wheelchair accessibility. No accessible rooms.

Prices. Dec 20–Mar 31: doubles $170–$275 BP; suites $290–$310 BP ($360 during holiday season). Low season: doubles $120–$175 BP; suites $190–$200 BP. Add $35 per person for MAP.

PORT DE PLAISANCE RESORT

				TOTAL
69.7%	75.8%	60.6%	66.7%	68.2%

Built in 1992, this three-story complex on its own island has large, modern suites with fully equipped kitchens; European-style bathrooms; and terrace views of gardens and Simpson Bay. The resort has a state-of-the-art, 6,500-square-foot spa; a tennis center; Mont Fortune Casino; and a marina built to dock some of the largest yachts in the Caribbean.

Reader Report

"We like it, but the prices are too steep normally. (We got a special once-in-a-lifetime deal.) But you could have anything you wanted...it was unbelievable."

CAROL DANZIGER, DIX HILLS, NEW YORK

"We enjoyed our stay there very much...it was very sumptuous.... It's sort of remote—you have to take a taxi or rent a car—but the resort is pretty much self-sufficient."

JOHN SMITH, JENKINGTOWN, PENNSYLVANIA

Address. Box 2089, Union Rd., Simpson Bay, St. Maarten, Netherlands Antilles, tel. 599/5–45222 or 800/732–9479, fax 599/5–42315.

Rooms. 88 suites. All have air-conditioning, ceiling fans, and kitchens.

Facilities. 3 restaurants, 5 bars/lounges, coffee shop, nightclub, 7 lighted tennis courts, 2 freshwater pools, casino, exercise room with weights and aerobic machines, salon, sauna, massages, conference center with business services, marina, sailboats, boat trips.

TV and VCR. TVs in all rooms, with 12 channels including CNN. VCRs in some rooms

No-smoking rooms. None.

Credit cards. AE, DC, V.

Wheelchair accessibility. No accessible rooms.

Prices. Dec. 22–Apr. 6: suites $335–$600 EP. Low season: suites $220–$385 EP. Children under 17 in parents' room free.

ST. VINCENT AND THE GRENADINES

    | **TOTAL**

77.3% | **45.5%** | **53.4%** | **59.1%** | **59.3%**

Reader Report

"St. Vincent offers some of the best sailing, best snorkeling and diving, and best amenities in the Caribbean—from the 'big' island of St. Vincent to the hundreds of smaller public and private islands (which include several of the most exclusive island resorts). There are enough 'new' places to discover here to keep you busy for a long time."

GARY MEDEN, JEFFERSONVILLE, INDIANA

"St. Vincent is like the Caribbean of the 1950s—see it now!"

JAY H. VAN VECHTEN, NEW YORK, NEW YORK

"Mustique is the Eden everyone talks about...as long as someone else is paying! Not the place if you are intimidated by snobs."

PAUL FRANCO, ROSEMEAD, CALIFORNIA

Islands. St. Vincent, which includes the Grenadine Islands, is a 150-square-mile independent protectorate of the United Kingdom with a population of about 170,000.
Language. English is the official language of St. Vincent and the Grenadines.

Visitor Information
In the U.S. Contact the **St. Vincent and the Grenadines Tourist Office** (801 2nd Ave., 21st floor, New York, NY 10017, tel. 212/687–4981 or 800/729–1726, fax 212/949–5946; 6505 Cove Creek Pl., Dallas, TX 75240, tel. 214/239–6451, fax 214/239–1002).
In Canada. Contact the **St. Vincent and the Grenadines Tourist Office** (32 Park Rd. Toronto, Ont. M4W 2N4, tel., 4126/924–5796, fax 416/924–5844).
In the U.K. Contact the **St. Vincent and the Grenadines Tourist Office** (10 Kensington Ct., London W8 5DL, tel. 071/937–6570, fax 071/937–3611).
In St. Vincent and the Grenadines. Contact the **St. Vincent Department of Tourism** (Box 834, Kingstown, St. Vincent, W.I., tel. 809/457–1502, fax 809/457–2880).

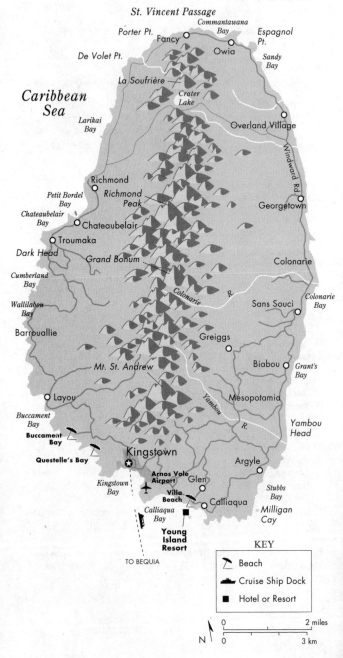

ST. VINCENT

ATLANTIC OCEAN

St. Vincent Passage

Porter Pt.
Fancy
Commantawana Bay
Espagnol Pt.

De Volet Pt.
Owia
Sandy Bay

Caribbean Sea

La Soufrière
Crater Lake

Larikai Bay

Overland Village

Windward Rd.

Richmond
Richmond Peak

Petit Bordel Bay
Chateaubelair Bay
Chateaubelair

Georgetown

Troumaka

Dark Head
Grand Bonum

Colonarie

Cumberland Bay
Colonarie R.

Wallilabou Bay
Sans Souci
Colonarie Bay

Barrouallie
Greiggs

Biabou
Grant's Bay

Mt. St. Andrew

Yambou R.
Mesopotamia

Layou
Yambou Head

Buccament Bay
Buccament Bay

Argyle

Questelle's Bay
Kingstown

Arnos Vale Airport
Glen
Stubbs Bay

Kingstown Bay
Villa Beach
Calliaqua
Milligan Cay

Calliaqua Bay
Young Island Resort

TO BEQUIA

KEY

⚓ Beach
🚢 Cruise Ship Dock
■ Hotel or Resort

N

| 0 | | 2 miles |
| 0 | | 3 km |

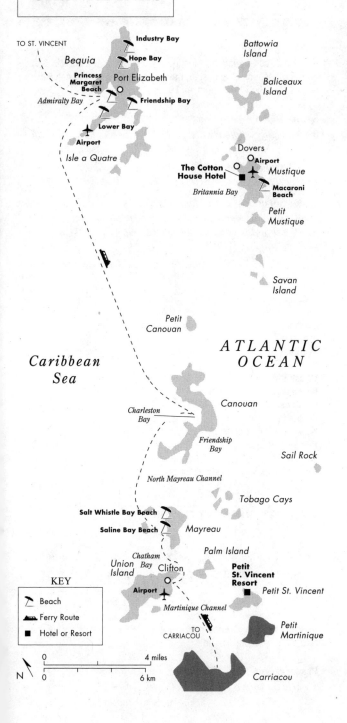

GRENADINES

TO ST. VINCENT

Bequia

Industry Bay

Hope Bay

Port Elizabeth

Princess Margaret Beach

Admiralty Bay

Friendship Bay

Lower Bay

Airport

Isle a Quatre

Battowia Island

Baliceaux Island

Dovers

Airport

The Cotton House Hotel

Mustique

Macaroni Beach

Britannia Bay

Petit Mustique

Savan Island

Petit Canouan

ATLANTIC OCEAN

Caribbean Sea

Canouan

Charleston Bay

Friendship Bay

Sail Rock

North Mayreau Channel

Tobago Cays

Salt Whistle Bay Beach

Saline Bay Beach

Mayreau

Palm Island

Chatham Bay

Clifton

Union Island

Airport

Petit St. Vincent Resort

Petit St. Vincent

Martinique Channel

Petit Martinique

TO CARRIACOU

KEY

🦅 Beach

🚢 Ferry Route

■ Hotel or Resort

N

0 ——— 4 miles
0 ——— 6 km

Carriacou

THE COTTON HOUSE HOTEL

87.5%	75.0%	75.0%	87.5%	TOTAL 81.3%

A renovated 18th-century great house and sugar mill are the core of this 12-acre resort on Mustique. Guests stay in cottages and outbuildings, some renovated, others new, and all with one or two stories. The hotel was built in 1972 and renovated in 1993-94.

Reader Report

"We were put completely at ease by the impeccable service and attention, and by the thoroughly romantic ambience of room #1, something straight out of Casablanca."

M. DAVID AND CATHY DIAL, DALLAS, TEXAS

"Rustic, not crowded, very laid back. This is an older property, good if you just want quiet relaxation. There are watersports available, and the white-sand beach in front of the hotel is fine, if a little rocky."

HARRY SEAGRAVES, SCOTTSDALE, ARIZONA

Address. Box 349, Mustique, St. Vincent and the Grenadines, W.I., tel. 809/456–4777, fax 809/456–5887.
Rooms. 10 rooms, 10 suites. All have minibars, air-conditioning, and ceiling fans.
Facilities. 2 restaurants, 3 bars/lounges, 2 unlighted tennis courts, freshwater pool, massages, dive center, sailboats.
TV and VCR. No TV.
No-smoking rooms. None.
Credit cards. AE, D, MC, V.
Restrictions. Min. 7 nights Dec 21–Jan 5.
Wheelchair accessibility. No accessible rooms.
Prices. Dec 16–Apr 15: doubles $475–$575 AP; suites $575–$760 AP. Low season: doubles $325 MAP; suites $450–$550 MAP. Every 7th night is free.

PETIT ST. VINCENT RESORT

88.9%	88.9%	83.3%	94.4%	TOTAL 88.9%

Twenty-two cottages, built of the local blue bitch stone, are set on the beach and hillsides of this 113-acre private island resort in the southern Grenadines, built in 1968. Guests arrive via launch from Union Island.

Reader Report

"A world all your own with a 360° view."

NORM SANTA, SHELTON, CONNECTICUT

"Though it is difficult to reach, I thought it was excellent. The service is not fawning, but you will promptly receive anything you ask for. The food was excellent, unusual in the Caribbean, and the watersports equipment was well maintained. It is a very private place, with lovely beaches and landscaping designed to hide the other cottages. The owner is a strong presence at the resort and the staff are all very nice. I would go back in a minute."

RITA D. BREVILLIER, COLORADO SPRINGS, COLORADO

Address. The Grenadines, St. Vincent, W.I., tel. 809/458–8801 or 800/654–9326, fax 809/458–8428.
Affiliation. Leading Hotels of the World.
Rooms. 22 cottages. All have minibars and ceiling fans, and all have showers.
Facilities. Restaurant, bar/lounge, lighted tennis court, sailboats.
TV and VCR. No TV.
No-smoking rooms. None.
Credit cards. AE, MC, V
Wheelchair accessibility. No accessible rooms.
Prices. Dec 18–Mar 16: $710 AP; Mar 17–Apr 13 $575 AP; Apr 14–Aug 31 and Nov 1–Dec 17 $450 AP. Prices are per cottage.

YOUNG ISLAND RESORT

				TOTAL
87.5%	79.2%	83.3%	87.5%	84.4%

This 35-acre private island resort lies just off Villa Beach, on St. Vincent's southwest end. Lodging is in Tahitian-style cottages surrounded by gardens. The hotel was built in 1965 and renovated in 1993.

Reader Report

"Young Island offers a touch of Polynesia in the Caribbean: unpretentious charm, privacy, peace, and beauty. Private cottages, leisurely dining, a friendly staff, security and inclusive rates combine to give guests a remarkable holiday rivaling that offered by any other resort of the same caliber in the Caribbean."

JAY H. VAN VECHTEN, NEW YORK, NEW YORK

Address. Box 211, Kingstown, St. Vincent, W.I., tel. 809/458–4826 or 800/223–1108, fax 809/457–4567.
Rooms. 30 rooms, 6 suites. All have ceiling fans and showers only. 2 rooms and 2 suites have Jacuzzis. 1 room has air-conditioning.
Facilities. 2 restaurants, 2 bars/lounges, lighted tennis court, saltwater pool, dry-cleaning, sailboats.
TV and VCR. No TV.
No-smoking rooms. None.

Credit cards. AE, MC, V.
Restrictions. Min. 7 nights Dec 23–Jan 3.
Wheelchair accessibility. No accessible rooms.
Prices. Dec 18–Apr 14: doubles $472 AP, $430 MAP; suites $632 AP, $590 MAP. Low season: doubles $325 AP, $275 MAP; suites $485 AP, $435 MAP.

TURKS AND CAICOS

				TOTAL
52.8%	41.7%	52.8%	65.3%	59.4%

Reader Report

*"[On Provo] we found absolutely beautiful water and a
seven-mile beach, with snorkeling near shore. It was very
laid-back, with some nightlife, friendly people, and reasonable
prices for most things. This is the Caribbean as it was 30
years ago—go now before it changes."*

KEITH E. GREENLAW, SOUTH HAMILTON, MASSACHUSETTS

*"A top beach destination. This pristine, undeveloped island is
for people who want total beach relaxation and incredible
snorkeling, in terms of geology and marine life. It's a quiet
island—no nightlife or shopping."*

ELLEN KEENAN, ROSLINDALE, MASSACHUSETTS

Islands. The Turks and Caicos form a 193-square-mile territory
of the United Kingdom with a population of about 14,000.
Language. The official language of the Turks and Caicos is
English.

Visitor Information
In the U.S. Contact the **Turks and Caicos Islands Tourist Board**
(tel. 800/241–0824), **Caribbean Tourism Organization** (20 E.
46th St., New York, NY 10017, tel. 212/682–0435, fax
212/697–4258).
In Canada. Contact the **Caribbean Tourism Organization** (512
Duplex St., Toronto, Ont. M4R 2E3, tel. 416/485–8724, fax
416/485–8256).
In the U.K. Contact the **Caribbean Tourist Organization** (120
Wilton Rd. Victoria London SW1 V16Z, tel. 71/233–8382, fax
71/873–8551).
In the Turks and Caicos Islands. Contact the **Turks and Caicos
Tourist Board** (Box 128, Pond St., Grand Turk, Turks and Caicos
Islands, B.W.I., tel. 809/946–2321, fax 809/946–2733).

CLUB MED TURKOISE

				TOTAL
64.1%	31.3%	64.1%	87.5%	61.7%

Three-story bungalows of this all-inclusive resort village range
along a mile-long beach on the windward side of Providenciales
island. The resortl was built in 1984, and expanded in 1987.

Reader Report

"Beautiful turquoise water surrounds this place—one of the best Club Meds. Excellent buffets with a different theme each night. Warm friendly atmosphere, beautiful flowers all around the grounds, and spacious, clean rooms."

LAUREL GLICKMAN, CHICAGO, ILLINOIS

"The buffets were the best ever, far superior to those on cruises. The athletics and water sports are fabulous."

SANDY OSHINSKY, ARLINGTON, VIRGINIA

"Beautiful beaches, nice resort layout, plenty of sports—good family fun!"

ELLIOTT A. REINFELD, SHERMAN OAKS, CALIFORNIA

"Club Med tends to feel confining after a full week's stay. The abundance of activities at the resort is like a Catch-22— although the vacation is both entertaining and relaxing you really do not experience the local culture."

GEOFFREY NEGIN, TAMPA, FLORIDA

Address. Grace Bay, Providenciales, Turks and Caicos Islands, B.W.I., tel. 809/946–5500 or 800/258–2633, fax 809/946– 5501.
Affiliation. Club Med.
Rooms. 298 rooms. All have air-conditioning and ceiling fans, but showers only.
Facilities. 3 restaurants, 3 bars/lounges, nightclub, theater, 4 lighted tennis courts, 4 unlighted, 18-hole golf course nearby, freshwater pool, exercise room with weights and aerobic machines, aerobics classes, massages, conference center with limited business services, dive center, sailboats, windsurfing, water skiing, intensive circus workshops.
TV and VCR. TV and VCR in public area only.
No-smoking rooms. None.
Credit cards. AE, MC, V.
Restrictions. No children under 12.
Wheelchair accessibility. No accessible rooms.
Prices. Dec 10–Apr 30: $175–$255. Low season: $125. Rates are all-inclusive and per person.

THE MERIDIAN CLUB

91.7%	50.0%	66.7%	100%	**TOTAL** 77.1%

This resort, built in 1974, occupies its own 800-acre island, Pine Cay, between Provo and North Caicos. Lodging is in Caribbean-style beach cottages, and there's a 500-acre nature reserve.

Reader Report

"A special place for those who want a laid-back place to do nothing—comfortable and relaxed."

NAME WITHHELD, WOODSTOCK, CONNECTICUT

"It's paradise for those who want to get away from it all—no TV, phones, or newspapers, but plenty of activities for those so inclined—tennis, snorkeling, biking, fishing, shelling, windsurfing, and kayaking and scuba can be arranged. The beach is gorgeous."

RITA QUINLAN, OYSTER BAY, NEW YORK

Address. Pine Cay, Turks and Caicos Islands, B.W.I., tel. 800/331–9154, fax 212/689–1598.
Rooms. 12 suites. All have ceiling fans but showers only.
Facilities. Restaurant, 2 bars/lounges, lighted tennis court, freshwater pool, sailboats.
TV and VCR. No TV.
No-smoking rooms. None.
Credit cards. No credit cards.
Restrictions. Min. 7 nights Dec 23–Jan 6. No children under 12.
Wheelchair accessibility. No accessible rooms.
Prices. Dec 16–Mar 16: $625 AP. Low season: $425 AP. Rates are per suite.

OCEAN CLUB, A BEACH & GOLF RESORT

				TOTAL
60.0%	60.0%	60.0%	60.0%	60.0%

Built in 1989 and expanded since, this seven-acre resort is located on the 12-mile beach of Grace Bay, on the leeward side of Providenciales island. It has three-story, Caribbean-style accommodations.

Reader Report

"Very nice. We would definitely stay there again. The accommodations and the beach were really lovely."

SHARON SCHNEIDER, CLEAR LAKE, IOWA

"A good spot for beach dives, thanks to the nearby dive shop and the really clear water."

MICHELLE HARTOUGH, SAN LOUIS OBISPO, CALIFORNIA

Address. Box 240, Providenciales, Turks and Caicos Islands, B.W.I., tel. 809/946–5880 or 800/457-8787, fax 809/946–5845.
Rooms. 60 suites. All have ceiling fans and a kitchen or a kitchenette and balcony.
Facilities. Restaurant, bar/lounge, lighted tennis court, 18-hole golf course nearby, 2 freshwater pools, exercise room with weights and aerobic machines, massages, dive center, sailboats, convenience store, car rental.
TV and VCR. TVs in all rooms, with 30 channels including CNN and cable movie channels. VCRs in rooms on request.
No-smoking rooms. None.
Credit cards. AE, D, MC, V.
Restrictions. Min. 7 nights Dec 18–Jan 6.

Wheelchair accessibility. No accessible rooms.
Prices. Dec 18–Apr 13: $190–$555 EP. Low season: $150–$405 EP. Rates are per suite.

TURQUOISE REEF RESORT & CASINO

48.0%	48.0%	40.0%	76.0%	**TOTAL** 53.0%

Each room of this seven-acre beachfront resort, a complex of 10 three-story buildings built in 1990 on Providenciales island, has its own pool-view patio or balcony. Overlooking part of the Princess Alexander National Marine Park, the resort has the island's only casino

Reader Report

"There's a helpful staff, a pretty pool, a fantastic endless beach, and very good snorkeling and scuba diving. The food is good, but not fabulous; this is a place to relax, not to dine. There's not much to do at night if you're not with someone you love."

NAME WITHHELD, PHILADELPHIA, PENNSYLVANIA

"It was beautiful, but there's not much to do there. There's a beach and a small casino, but very little shopping or restaurants. It has a lot of potential, but it needs to be developed more."

ANN DANA TRASK, PROVIDENCE, RHODE ISLAND

Address. Box 205, Providenciales, Turks and Caicos Islands, B.W.I., tel. 809/946–5555 or 800/223-6510, fax 809/946–5629. Reservations through Robert Reid Associates, Utell International and Charms
Rooms. 228 rooms, 2 suites. All have air-conditioning and ceiling fans. Both suites have minibars.
Facilities. 3 restaurants, 3 bars/lounges, 2 lighted tennis courts, 18-hole golf course nearby, freshwater pool, casino, exercise room with weights and aerobic machines, aerobics classes, massages, dry-cleaning, supervised children's program, dive center, sailboats, car rental, tour desk, specialty shops and convention facilities.
TV and VCR. TVs in all rooms, with 30 channels including CNN and cable movie channels.
No-smoking rooms. None.
Credit cards. AE, D, MC, V.
Restrictions. Min. 5 nights Dec 24–Jan 2.
Wheelchair accessibility. 2 rooms.
Prices. Dec 22–Apr 7: doubles $185–$295 EP; suites $410–$490 EP. Low season: doubles $125–$180 EP, suites $260 EP.

U.S. VIRGIN ISLANDS
St Croix

			🎎	**TOTAL**
65.9%	**48.1%**	**41.9%**	**46.3%**	**51.8%**

Reader Report

"St. Croix is back on her feet—the reconstruction after Hurricane Hugo is tasteful and appropriate, with modern condos dotting the hillsides. The mood (still of the '60s) remains laid-back and unselfconscious."

NAME WITHHELD, HANOVER, ILLINOIS

"It's easy to drive around to visit different parts of the island. Christiansted is charming with a variety of shops. Buck Island has the best snorkeling in the Caribbean."

JODI K. RUCQUOI, BRANFORD, CONNECTICUT

"Christiansted is rundown—uncomfortable for female business travelers at night."

NAME WITHHELD, FORT LAUDERDALE, FLORIDA

"St. Croix is beautiful, with a 'blast from the past' serenity."

MARY BRITTEN LYNCH, CHATTANOOGA, TENNESSEE

St. John

🐟	🏠	⛵	🎎	**TOTAL**
90.0%	**60.4%**	**60.4%**	**59.7%**	**70.8%**

Reader Report

"My favorite Virgin Island—mostly national park, it's beautifully preserved. There's a wide variety of accommodations and good shopping, but no nightlife (bring friends)."

TERRY CLARK, WAYZATA, MINNESOTA

"The climate is perfect—clear, sunny skies seasoned with dashes of cooling showers. Also, you have at least five world-class beaches."

JOHNNY W. CALLEBS, LEXINGTON, KENTUCKY

"The last of the uncommercialized islands in the Caribbean. Its beauty and beaches are unsurpassed. Tropical, enticing—you feel alone but secure."

GARY TAYLOR, GLEN ELLYN, ILLINOIS

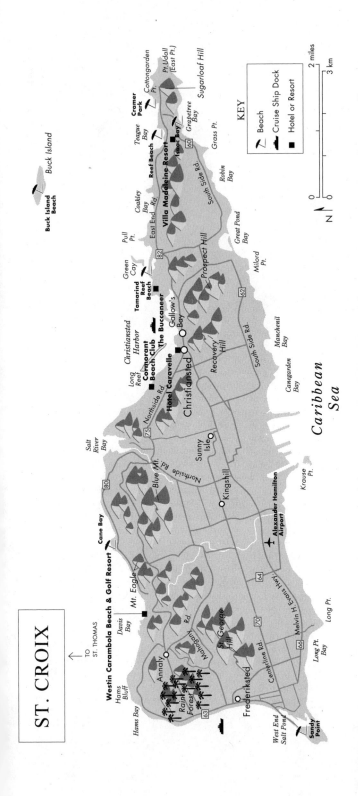

ST. CROIX

TO
ST. THOMAS

Hams Bluff

Hams Bay

Davis Bay

Westin Carambola Beach & Golf Resort

Mt. Eagle

Cane Bay

Blue Mt.

Annaly

Mahogany Rd.

Rain Forest

Sky George Hill

Frederiksted

West End Salt Pond

Sandy Point

Centerline Rd.

Melvin H. Evans Hwy.

Long Pt. Bay

Long Pt.

Salt River Bay

Northside Rd.

Kingshill

Sunny Isle

Alexander Hamilton Airport

Krause Pt.

Canegarden Bay

Caribbean Sea

Long Reef

Christiansted Harbor

Cormorant Beach Club

The Buccaneer

Hotel Caravelle

Gallow's Bay

Christiansted

Recovery Hill

South Side Rd.

Manchenil Bay

Milord Pt.

Great Pond Bay

Prospect Hill

Tamarind Reef Beach

Green Cay

Pull Pt.

Coakley Bay

East End Rd.

Reef Beach

Villa Madeleine Resort

Teague Bay

Cramer Park

Cottongarden Pt.

Pt. Udall (East Pt.)

Sugarloaf Hill

Grapetree Bay

Isaac Bay

Grass Pt.

South Side Rd.

Robin Bay

Buck Island

Buck Island

Buck Island Beach

KEY

- Beach
- Cruise Ship Dock
- ■ Hotel or Resort

N

0   2 miles
0   3 km

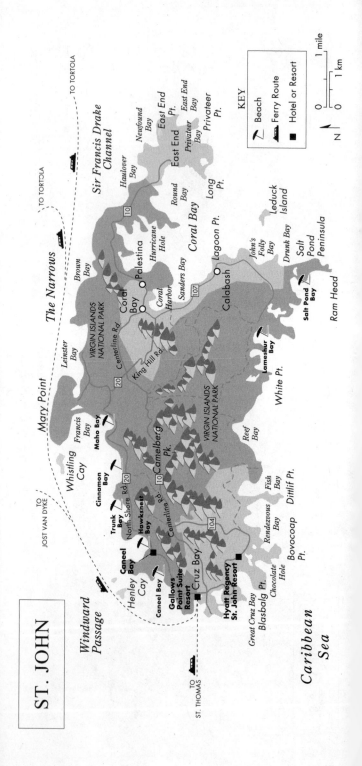

ST. JOHN

Windward Passage

The Narrows

TO
JOST VAN DYKE

TO
TORTOLA

TO
TORTOLA

TO
TORTOLA

Mary Point

Sir Francis Drake Channel

Leinster Bay

Brown Bay

Whistling Cay

Haulover Bay

Newfound Bay

East End Pt.

East End Bay

Privateer Bay

Privateer Pt.

Francis Bay

Maho Bay

Palestina

Coral Bay

VIRGIN ISLANDS NATIONAL PARK

Hurricane Hole

Round Bay

Long Pt.

East End

Coral Bay

Centerline Rd.

King Hill Rd.

Coral Harbor

Sanders Bay

Lagoon Pt.

Leduck Island

Cinnamon Bay

20

Camelberg Pk.

Calabash

107

John's Folly Bay

Trunk Bay

North Shore Rd. 20

Hawksnest Bay

10

Centerline Rd.

VIRGIN ISLANDS NATIONAL PARK

White Pt.

Drunk Bay

Salt Pond Peninsula

Caneel Bay

10

104

Reef Bay

Lameshur Bay

Salt Pond Bay

Henley Cay

Gallows
Point Suite Resort

Caneel Bay

Cruz Bay

Fish Bay

Ditlif Pt.

Ram Head

Hyatt Regency
St. John Resort

Rendezvous Bay

Bovocoap Pt.

Great Cruz Bay

Blasbalg Pt.

Chocolate Hole

TO
ST. THOMAS

Caribbean Sea

KEY

⚓ Beach
🚢 Ferry Route
■ Hotel or Resort

N

0   1 mile
0   1 km

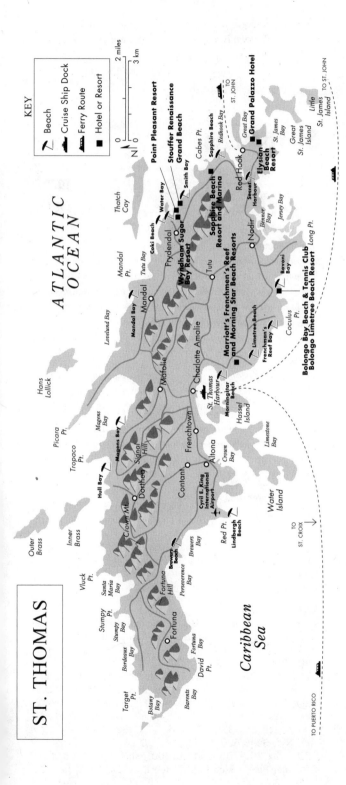

"The snorkeling was better on the Great Barrier Reef, but what the heck—St. John is a lot closer to home and a lot cheaper to get to."

NAME WITHHELD, MARSHFIELD, MASSACHUSETTS

St.Thomas

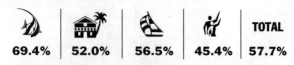

| 69.4% | 52.0% | 56.5% | 45.4% | **TOTAL** 57.7% |

Reader Report

"Mountainous, surrounded by beautiful blue waters and harbors studded with ships. Taxis crowd all the streets, especially the capital, Charlotte Amalie, the largest duty-free shopping area in the Caribbean. Dining is generally in open-air restaurants with great views."

SANDRA R. WRIGLEY, ABSECON, NEW JERSEY

"We thought this small island the most beautiful we have ever seen—and the people were very pleasant and helpful. Since our trip we have read about crime there, but we saw no signs of it."

HOWARD J. O'NEIL, CITRUS HEIGHTS, CALIFORNIA

"Crowded but fun—with the best shopping and lowest prices anywhere. Best when there are not too many ships in port."

WILLIAM M. O'HERN, CARDIFF, CALIFORNIA

"Heaven on earth. Affordable and tourist-friendly, with beautiful water and plenty to see and do. "

W. MACON RICHARDSON, RICHMOND, VIRGINIA

Islands. The U.S. Virgin Islands, consisting of St. Thomas, St. John and St. Croix, form a 133-square-mile territory of the United States, with a population of about 106,000.
Language. English is the official language.

Visitor Information
In the U.S. Contact the **U.S.V.I. Government Tourist Offices** (225 Peachtree St., Suite 760, Atlanta, GA 30303, tel. 404/688–0906, fax 404/525–1102; 500 N. Michigan Ave., Suite 2030, Chicago, IL 60611, tel. 312/670–8784, fax 312/670–8788; 3460 Wilshire Blvd., Suite 412, Los Angeles, CA 90010, tel. 213/739–0138, fax 213/739–2005; 2655 Le Jeune Rd., Suite 907, Coral Gables, FL 33134, tel. 305/442–7200, fax 305/445–9044; 1270 6th Ave., New York, NY 10020, tel. 212/332–2222, fax 212/332–2223; 900 17th Ave. NW, Suite 500 Washington, DC 20006, tel. 202/293–3707, fax 202/785–2542; 1300 Ashford Ave., Condado, Santurce, Puerto Rico 00907, tel. 809/724–3816, fax 809/724–7223).

In Canada. Contact the **Division of Tourism** (3300 Bloor St. W, Toronto, Ont. M8X 2X3, tel. 416/233–1414 or 800/465–8784, fax 416/233–9367).
In the U.K. Contact the **U.S.V.I. Government Tourist Office** (2 Cinnamon Row, Plantation Wharf, York Pl., London SW11 3TW, tel. 071/978–5262, fax 071/924–3171).
In the U.S. Virgin Islands. Contact the **Division of Tourism** (Box 4538, Christiansted, St. Croix, U.S.V.I. 00822, tel. 809/773–0495, fax 809/778–9259).

BOLONGO BAY BEACH & TENNIS CLUB

| 44.4% | 33.3% | 44.4% | 53.3% | **TOTAL** 43.9% |

* The above percentages apply to the former Bolongo Club Everything.

In 1995 Bolongo Club Everything separated into two sister properties, Bolongo Bay Beach & Tennis Club and Bolongo Limetree Resort. Bolongo Bay Beach & Tennis Club is a semi-inclusive resort on 9 acres of shoreline on southeast St. Thomas. Guests stay in two-story Caribbean-style clusters built in 1974 and renovated in 1995. Complimentary shuttles serve other Bolongo resorts. Serious hurricane damage delayed opening.

Reader Report

"Great scuba diving operation on the grounds. Suites were roomy for a family of four, with a nice kitchen and dining area. Convenient location."

LAWRENCE FLESH, VOORHEESVILLE, NEW YORK

"Our room had a poor view. The restaurant was pretty nice, though, and the staff was friendly."

NANCY MURRAY, NEW LONDON, CONNECTICUT

Address. 7150 Bolongo, St. Thomas, U.S.V.I. 00802, tel. 809/775–1800 or 800/524–4746, fax 809/775–3208.
Affiliation. Bolongo Beach Resorts.
Rooms. 77 rooms. All have air-conditioning and ceiling fans. All rooms have showers only.
Facilities. 2 restaurants, 2 bars/lounges, 2 lighted tennis courts, 2 unlighted, freshwater pool, exercise room with weights and aerobic machines, massages, dry cleaning, sauna, salon, conference center with business services, supervised children's program, dive center, 2 catamarans.
TV and VCR. TVs in all rooms, with 13 channels including cable movie channels. VCRs in all rooms.
No-smoking rooms. None.
Credit cards. AE, CB, DC, D, MC, V.
Wheelchair accessibility. No accessible rooms.
Prices. Dec 23–Apr 7: doubles $210–$235 EP. Low season: $140–$160 EP.

BOLONGO LIMETREE BEACH RESORT

An all-inclusive resort introduced by the split of Bolongo Club Everything. Located on Limetree Beach on the southeast coast of St. Thomas, the 26-acre resort has two-story, Caribbean-style buildings. Complimentary shuttles serve other Bolongo resorts. Serious hurricane damage delayed opening.

Address. 7150 Bolongo, St. Thomas, U.S.V.I. 00802, tel. 809/776–4770 or 800/524–4746, fax 809/775-3208.
Affiliation. Bolongo Beach Resorts.
Rooms. 84 rooms. All have air conditioning and ceiling fans. All rooms have showers only.
Facilities. 2 restaurants, 4 bars/lounges, 2 lighted tennis courts, freshwater pool, supervised children's program, excercise room with weights and aerobic machines, aerobics classes, massages, dry-cleaning, salon, sauna, sailboats.
TV and VCR. TV in all rooms, with 13 channels including cable movie channels. VCRs in all rooms.
Non-smoking rooms. None.
Credit cards. AE, CB, DC, D, MC, V
Wheelchair accessibility. No accessible rooms.
Prices. Dec 23–Apr 7: doubles $417–$433. Low season: doubles $384–$400. Rates are all-inclusive.

THE BUCCANEER

🍸	🛏	🍴	🌅	**TOTAL**
60.9%	**55.1%**	**55.1%**	**69.6%**	**60.1%**

This 300-acre resort, built in 1948 and renovated in 1994, is on a 17th-century sugar plantation. The main building sits on a hilltop; there's also a guest cottage. Three beaches face Christiansted harbor. It sustained superficial hurricane damage this fall.

Reader Report

"The championship golf course has views of the Caribbean from some hills; there are lighted tennis courts with an on-site pro. The rooms are elegantly decorated. The main beach has water sports, but the atmosphere is low-key. Service is excellent."

CINDY BENTZLER, WAUKESHA, WISCONSIN

"The best location on the island. Very spread-out and hilly, but with great views from the open-air restaurant."

CHRISTINA BRAUN, OCEANSIDE, NEW YORK

Address. Box 25200, Gallows Bay, St. Croix, U.S.V.I. 00824, tel. 809/773–2100 or 800/255-3881, fax 809/778–8215.
Rooms. 150 rooms, 12 suites, 12 villas. All have air-conditioning and ceiling fans.
Facilities. 4 restaurants, 2 bars/lounges, 2 lighted tennis courts,

18-hole golf course, 9-hole golf course, exercise room with weights and aerobic machines, massages, sauna, 24-hr room service, supervised children's program.

TV and VCR. TV in all rooms, with 33 channels including CNN and cable movie channels.

No-smoking rooms. None.

Credit cards. AE, DC, D, MC, V.

Restrictions. Min. 7 nights Dec 20–Jan 1 and Mar 26–Apr 3.

Wheelchair accessibility. 2 rooms.

Prices. Dec 20–Apr 1: doubles $210–$375; suites $375–$700. Low season: doubles $170–$235; suites $235–$325. All rates include breakfast.

CANEEL BAY

🏌️	🛏️	🍴	☀️	TOTAL
84.3%	73.9%	82.1%	95.5%	84.0%

This 170-acre resort, built in 1954 and renovated in 1994-95, is on the island's north shore. Rooms are in one- and two-story buildings. The hotel sustained superficial hurricane damage this fall.

Reader Report

"The seven beautiful beaches and the quiet elegant surroundings make this an ideal get-away-from-it-all spot. There's fabulous romantic dining under the stars at the Sugar Mill, one of my favorites. It's not a place for those who cannot tear themselves away from TV, telephone, or the outside world."

YVONNE NICHOLSON, SOUTH HADLEY, MASSACHUSETTS

"Lush, well-manicured grounds, numerous beaches, and wonderful food make Caneel Bay a regular vacation destination for many. The rooms in the tennis and garden areas lack privacy, though—sometimes you can hear your neighbor shower."

JAMES R. NERGER, BOUND BROOK, NEW JERSEY

"The understated elegance, the total comfort, the vistas, and the excellent food have appealed to us since the early 1960s. We've had memorable family vacations here."

RUTH E. FRANK, NEWTOWN, PENNSYLVANIA

Address. Box 720, Cruz Bay, St. John, U.S.V.I. 00831–0720, tel. 809/776–6111 or 800/928–8889, fax 809/693–8280.

Affiliation. Rosewood Hotels and Resorts.

Rooms. 168 rooms. All have minibars and ceiling fans. 160 have showers only.

Facilities. 3 restaurants, 2 bars/lounges, 11 unlighted tennis courts, freshwater pool, aerobic classes, massages, dry-cleaning, conference center with business services, gift shop, dive center, watersports center.

TV and VCR. TV in public area only. Nightly movie presentations.

No-smoking rooms. None.
Credit cards. AE, DC, MC, V.
Restrictions. Min. 10 nights Dec 20–Jan 1.
Wheelchair accessibility. 2 rooms.
Prices. Dec 20–Mar 31: singles/doubles $350–$750 EP; Apr 1–Apr 30 $300–$550. Low season: doubles $250–$550. Meal plans and vacation packages available.

CORMORANT BEACH CLUB

👔	🛏	✕	🌅	TOTAL
72.7%	63.6%	45.5%	63.6%	61.4%

This 12-acre resort 3 miles northwest of Christiansted sits on a 1,200-foot-long beach with an off-shore reef. There are two low-rise buildings and six adjacent condo blocks. The hotel was built in 1984 and renovated in 1990; it sustained superficial hurricane damage this fall.

Reader Report

"The resort itself is small, but the villas are spacious, the water beautiful, the beach well-maintained, and hammocks are hanging in all the right places. Breakfast served right at the edge of the ocean was worth jumping out of bed early for."

KELLY CUNNIFF, THOMASTON, CONNECTICUT

"The room was good, the sea views and beach pleasant. You really need a car to travel to town."

HAROLD SCHERER JR., CENTERVILLE, MASSACHUSETTS

"The atmosphere is very relaxed, very open. Upon arrival you are treated to a wonderful view through the lobby, past the bar. The room was perfect, with the best view outside the sliding glass door–a 50-foot walk and you're in the ocean. The food is also great!"

ERIC FERNANDEZ, GRAPEVINE, TEXAS

Address. 4126 La Grande Princesse, St. Croix, U.S.V.I. 00820–4441, tel. 809/778–8920 or 800/548–4460, fax 809/778–9218.
Rooms. 38 rooms, 4 suites, 12 villas. All suites have minibars. All villas include kitchen; 5 have jacuzzis.
Facilities. 2 restaurants, bar/lounge, 2 unlighted tennis courts, 2 freshwater pools, aerobics classes nearby, massages, dry-cleaning, conference center with business services, dive center.
TV and VCR. TVs in all rooms, with 45 channels including CNN. VCRs for rent.
No-smoking rooms. All rooms are no-smoking.
Credit cards. AE, CB, DC, MC, V.
Restrictions. Min. 7 nights Dec 20–Mar 15.
Wheelchair accessibility. Ground floor rooms accessible.
Prices. Dec 21–Apr 14: doubles $185–$265 EP; suites $295–$330 EP; villas $325–$475 EP. Low season: doubles $120–$230 EP; suites $250–$285 EP; villas $225–$365 EP.

ELYSIAN BEACH RESORT

 77.8%	 77.8%	 55.6%	 66.7%	TOTAL 69.4%

Accommodations at this eight-acre condo resort on Cowpet Bay, on the island's southeast corner, are in three-story Mediterranean-style buildings that are a distinctive coral hue. The hotel was built in 1989. Guests have privileges at other Bolongo resorts. Serious hurricane damage delayed opening.

Reader Report

"This hotel is gorgeous, with wonderful gardens. The beach isn't big, but it's a nice private area."

JoANN HOPKINS, CHARLOTTE, NORTH CAROLINA

"It's in a nice location, near good beaches. The restaurant, located right on the sand, was good and had lots of atmosphere. The rooms were clean and well-appointed. I recommend it."

JERI WEINSTEIN BLUM, LONG BEACH, NEW YORK

Address. 6800 #8–1 Estate Nazareth, St. Thomas, U.S.V.I. 00802, tel. 809/775–1000 or 800/524–4746, fax 809/776–0910.
Affiliation. Bolongo Beach Resorts.
Rooms. 160 rooms, 60 suites, 60 villas. All have minibars, air-conditioning, and ceiling fan.
Facilities. 2 restaurants, 3 bars/lounges, unlighted tennis court, freshwater pool, exercise room with weights and aerobic machines, aerobics classes, massages, conference center with business services, supervised children's program.
TV and VCR. TV in all rooms, with 13 channels including CNN and cable movie channels. VCRs in all rooms.
No-smoking rooms. None.
Credit cards. AE, CB, DC, D, MC, V.
Wheelchair accessibility. No accessible rooms.
Prices. Dec 23–Apr 17: doubles $285–$375; suites $425–$690. Low season: doubles $205–$255; suites $275–$475. All rates include Continental breakfast.

GALLOWS POINT SUITE RESORT

 69.6%	 78.3%	 63.0%	 93.5%	TOTAL 76.1%

The two-story grey villas of this five-acre resort on a bluff in the town of Cruz Bay were built in 1985 in the style of a 19th-century Danish manor house. Each contains four suites. The resort sustained superficial hurricane damage this fall.

Reader Report

"Small, quaint, and convenient to Cruz Bay. Great snorkeling."

NORM SANTA, SHELTON, CONNECTICUT

"Just steps outside Cruz Bay, on a bluff with fine views toward St. Thomas. The villas are simply furnished and have no air-conditioning (ceiling fans do the trick), but there is a nice pool and a terrific restaurant."

DENISE NOLTY, LAKE GROVE, NEW YORK

Address. Box 58, St. John, U.S.V.I., 00831–0058, tel. 809/776–6434 or 800/323–7229, fax 809/776–6520.
Affiliation. Inter Grande Hotels & Resorts.
Rooms. 60 suites, all with ceiling fans and showers only.
Facilities. Restaurant, bar/lounge, freshwater pool, gourmet shop and gifts
TV and VCR. TV in some rooms, with 2 channels. VCR in some rooms.
No-smoking rooms. None.
Credit cards. AE, DC, MC, V.
Restrictions. No children under 5.
Wheelchair accessibility. 2 accessible rooms; restaurant not accessible.
Prices. Dec 15–Mar 31: $275–$325 EP. Low season: $140–$180 EP.

GRAND PALAZZO HOTEL

				TOTAL
69.0%	88.1%	66.7%	90.5%	78.6%

This replica of a Venetian palace with three-story Italian Renaissance–style villas encircles a lily pond on 15 acres on Great Bay, at the island's east end near the Red Hook ferry. The hotel was built in 1992; serious hurricane damage this fall delayed opening.

Reader Report

"An elegant, beautiful new hotel on its own beach with views to St. John. European in feeling and nicely appointed with attractive rooms. The major problem here is the high cost per night!"

CANDICE GRASSI, GREENWICH, CONNECTICUT

" Quiet and luxurious with an outstanding view from main building."

NAME WITHHELD, GLENVIEW, ILLINOIS

Address. Great Bay, Estate Nazareth, St. Thomas, U.S.V.I. 00802, tel. 809/775–3333 or 800/545–0509, fax 809/775–4444.
Affiliation. Rockresorts.
Rooms. 152 rooms, 4 suites. All have minibars, air-conditioning, and ceiling fans.

Facilities. 3 restaurants, 3 bars/lounges, 4 lighted tennis courts, freshwater pool, exercise room with weights and aerobic machines, aerobics classes, massages, salon, 24-hr room service, dry-cleaning, conference center with business services, dive center, sailboats.

TV and VCR. TV in all rooms, with 12 channels including CNN and cable movie channels. VCR in rooms on request.

No-smoking rooms. 12 rooms.

Credit cards. AE, DC, D, MC, V.

Restrictions. Min. 8 nights Dec. 20–Jan 2. No children under 8 in one dining room.

Wheelchair accessibility. 2 accessible rooms.

Prices. Jan 2–Mar 31: doubles $590–$660 MAP, $450–$520 EP; suites $1,090–$1,565 MAP, $950–$1,425 EP. Low season: doubles $390–$415 MAP, $250–$275 EP; suites $660–$915 MAP, $520–$775 EP.

HOTEL CARAVELLE

				TOTAL
38.5%	53.8%	46.2%	69.2	51.9%

Located on a main thoroughfare in downtown Christiansted, this small, moderately priced, three-story, European-style hotel has rooms with refrigerators; several rooms have water views. Note that the hotel sustained superficial hurricane damage this fall.

Reader Report

"Rooms are spacious and clean. There's a pleasant shopping arcade and free off-street parking, a real plus. This is one of the nicest hotels in the heart of Christiansted—if you have a reason to stay there—but the fact that there's no beach on the property is a drawback."

NAME WITHHELD, BAYSIDE , NEW YORK.

"It's strictly for scuba diving. We enjoyed it, but our main purpose was scuba diving—it's definitely oriented in that direction."

EDWARD WEIMER, DALLAS, TEXAS

Address. 44A Queen Cross St., Christiansted, St. Croix, U.S.V.I. 00820, tel. 809/773–0687, 800/524–0410, or 800/595–9505, fax 809/778-7004.

Rooms. 43 rooms, 1 suite. All have air-conditioning; 20 rooms and the suite have ceiling fans.

Facilities. Restaurant, bar/lounge, freshwater pool, horseback riding, exercise room with weights and aerobic machines, aerobics classes, massages, salon, sauna, dry-cleaning, conference center with business services, dive center.

TV and VCR. TV in all rooms, with 31 channels including CNN and cable movie channels. VCR in public area, and in rooms on request.

No-smoking rooms. 20 rooms, 1 suite.
Credit cards. AE, D, DC, MC, V.
Wheelchair accessibility. No accessible rooms.
Prices. Dec. 15–Apr. 14: doubles $109–$139 EP, suite $275 EP. Low season: doubles $89–$109 EP, suite $200 EP.

HYATT REGENCY ST. JOHN RESORT

👔	🛏	✕	🌅	**TOTAL**
69.1%	**74.8%**	**61.0%**	**85.4%**	**72.6%**

A modern, two-story atrium building is the center of this 34-acre resort on Great Cruz Bay, south of the town of Cruz Bay. Contemporary low-rise accommodations are set around the grounds. The hotel was built in 1986 and renovated in 1994. Serious hurricane damage delayed opening until December 15.

Reader Report

"A great place to relax; or, if you prefer, there's snorkeling, scuba, the ferry to St. Thomas, et cetera. I loved the layout of the rooms."

JANICE L. SCHUYLER, COLLEGEVILLE, PENNSYLVANIA

"Beautiful rooms and grounds and no nightlife except for moonlight strolls. The scuba diving is fabulous—boats leave right from the hotel. The food is expensive."

LAWRENCE H. FLESH, VOORHEESVILLE, NEW YORK

Address. Box 8310, Great Cruz Bay, St. John, U.S.V.I. 00831, tel. 809/693–8000 or 800/233–1234, fax 809/693–8888.
Affiliation. Hyatt Hotels and Resorts.
Rooms. 285 rooms, 21 suites. All have minibars and air-conditioning. All suites and 48 rooms have ceiling fans. All suites have Jacuzzis.
Facilities. 3 restaurants, 2 bars/lounges, 6 lighted tennis courts, freshwater pool, conference center with business services, supervised children's program, dive center, fitness center.
TV and VCR. TV in all rooms, with 10 channels including CNN, cable movie channels, and pay movies. No VCR.
No-smoking rooms. 94 rooms.
Credit cards. AE, CB, DC, MC, V.
Wheelchair accessibility. 4 accessible rooms.
Prices. Dec 22–Apr 15: doubles $340–$520 EP; suites $635–$975 EP. Low season: doubles $225–$320 EP; suites $425–$605 EP. Add $64 per person for MAP.

MARRIOTT'S FRENCHMAN'S REEF RESORT, ST. THOMAS

62.6%	58.6%	56.2%	76.4%	**TOTAL** 63.4%

This contemporary eight-story hotel complex, on the coast just southeast of the Charlotte Amalie harbor, shares a beach with Marriott's Morning Star Beach Resort. Frenchman's Reef was built in 1973, expanded in 1981, and renovated in 1990. The resort sustained some serious hurricane damage, and its opening was delayed until December 22.

Reader Report

"At sunrise each morning, you can open your drapes to view a magnificent procession of cruise ships entering the channel for the Charlotte Amalie harbor. Take advantage of the resort's 'Reefer' boat service—the easiest way to get to and from the center of town."

SUSAN K. CHAMBERS, ROCKVILLE, MARYLAND

"Marriott has done wonders with the place. Great rooms— some with Jacuzzi—a huge beach, pools, shops, and lots of activities. There are nice views of the town of Charlotte Amalie, as the resort sits out on a point."

JOEL CHUSID, IRVING, TEXAS

"The resort had excellent service, spacious rooms, and great vistas—love it!"

NAME WITHHELD, ROCKVILLE, MARYLAND

Address. #5 Estate Bakkeroe, St. Thomas, U.S.V.I. 00801, tel. 809/776–8500 or 800/524–2000, fax 809/776–3054.
Affiliation. Marriott.
Rooms. 407 rooms, 18 suites. All have minibars and air-conditioning.
Facilities. 5 restaurants, 5 bars/lounges, 4 lighted tennis courts, 2 freshwater pools, exercise room with weights and aerobic machines, aerobics classes, massages, salon, dry-cleaning, conference center with business services, dive center.
TV and VCR. TV in all rooms, with 12 channels including CNN and cable movie channels. No VCRs.
No-smoking rooms. 210 rooms.
Credit cards. AE, CB, DC, D, MC, V.
Wheelchair accessibility. 4 accessible rooms.
Prices. Dec 18–Apr 16: doubles $265–$298 EP; suites $428–$855 EP. Low season: doubles $175–$198 EP; suites $248–$495 EP. Add $64 per person for FAP, $52 for MAP, $15 for breakfast.

MARRIOTT'S MORNING STAR BEACH RESORT

				TOTAL
88.9%	84.4%	75.6%	91.1%	85.0%

The beachfront sister of Marriot's Frenchman's Reef is a group of two- and three-story contemporary buildings, just southeast of Charlotte Amalie's harbor. The resort was built in 1986 and renovated in 1993. Serious hurricane damage delayed opening.

Reader Report

"Rooms are very nice and located right on the beach, which is a great one for sunbathing."

JoAnn Hopkins, Charlotte, North Carolina

"I liked it very much, and prefer it over Frenchman's Reef. The rooms are a good size and are very nicely decorated; those looking out over the water are especially nice."

Frances Baum, Weston, Connecticut

Address. #5 Estate Bakkeroe, St. Thomas, U.S.V.I. 00801, tel. 809/776–8500 or 800/524–2000, fax 809/776–3054.
Affiliation. Marriott.
Rooms. 96 rooms. All have minibars, air-conditioning, and ceiling fans.
Facilities. 2 restaurants, 3 bar/lounges, 4 lighted tennis courts, dry-cleaning, conference center with business services, dive center, full use of facilities at Marriott's Frenchman's Reef Resort.
TV and VCR. TVs in all rooms, with 12 channels including CNN and cable movie channels. No VCRs.
No-smoking rooms. 48 rooms.
Credit cards. AE, CB, DC, D, MC, V.
Wheelchair accessibility. No accessible rooms.
Prices. Dec 18–Apr 17: $325–$395 EP. Low season: $220–$270 EP. Add $64 per person for FAP, $52 for MAP, $15 for breakfast.

POINT PLEASANT RESORT, ST. THOMAS

				TOTAL
51.5%	66.7%	54.5%	75.8%	62.1%

Built in 1977 and renovated in 1994, this resort overlooks Smith Bay on the island's northeast coast. Accommodations are in condo units on a steep hillside, and there are nature trails on its 15 acres. Serious hurricane damage delayed opening.

Reader Report

"The restaurant was very nice—the food and service were good. The view of the bay and the fishing boats below set a tranquil tone."

Mike de Haas, Diekirch, Luxembourg

*"Location was gorgeous and the views were great, with
wonderful sunsets. It was a nice, restful place to be . . . ."*

NAME AND ADDRESS WITHHELD

Address. 6600 Estate Smith Bay #4, St. Thomas, U.S.V.I. 00802,
tel. 809/775-7200 or 800/524-2300, fax 809/776-5694.

Rooms. 134 suites, all with air-conditioning and ceiling fans.

Facilities. 2 restaurants, 2 bars/lounges, lighted tennis court,
golf course nearby, 3 freshwater pools, exercise room with
weights, massages, dive center, sailboats.

TV and VCR. TVs in all rooms, with 9 channels including cable
movie channels. No VCRs.

No-smoking rooms. None.

Credit cards. AE, CB, DC, D, MC, V.

Wheelchair accessibility. No accessible rooms.

Prices. Dec 23–Apr 22: $275–$380 EP. Low season:
$200–$280 EP. Add $55 per person for MAP, $10 for breakfast.

SAPPHIRE BEACH RESORT AND MARINA, ST. THOMAS

🍸	🛏	✕	☀	**TOTAL**
74.6%	**73.2%**	**56.3%**	**85.9%**	**72.5%**

On the island's east end near the Red Hook ferry, this 35-acre
all-suite resort complex has modern hotel blocks and villas and
its own marina. The hotel was built in 1988, expanded two
years later, and renovated in 1994. It sustained some superficial hurricane damage.

Reader Report

*"One of the most breathtaking beaches on the island. Sundays
are the best, when the island's best reggae band performs live
at the beach.*

JEANNE LeGUILLOU, EAST NORTHPORT, NEW YORK

*"The views of neighbor islands rising above the sapphire-blue
sea and far-stretching, white-sand beach are soothing to the
soul. Children's programs make the place even more
relaxing, and kitchen facilities, although spartan, add to the
comforts. Performers at beach bar on Sunday afternoons
attract so many islanders that the beach is barely accessible
to hotel guests."*

SANDRA R. WRIGLEY, ABSECON, NEW JERSEY

*"My favorite location, with beautiful views from the beach.
Good snorkeling and swimming, and great windsurfing to
watch from the beach, the lunch veranda, or the open bar. Be
sure you book your room away from the volleyball area—it
can be very noisy in the day if you want a nap!"*

CANDICE GRASSI, GREENWICH, CONNECTICUT

Address. Box 8088, St. Thomas, U.S.V.I. 00801, tel. 809/775–6100 or 800/524–2090, fax 809/775–4024.

Rooms. 114 suites, 57 villas. All have air-conditioning and ceiling fans.

Facilities. 3 restaurants, 3 bars/lounges, 4 unlighted tennis courts, 18-hole golf course nearby, 9-hole golf course nearby, freshwater pool, massages, dry-cleaning, conference center with business services, dive center.

TV and VCR. TVs in all rooms, with 10 channels including cable movie channels. No VCRs.

No-smoking rooms. None.

Credit cards. AE, DC, MC, V.

Restrictions. Min. 5 nights over Christmas Day, New Year's Day, and Presidents' Day.

Wheelchair accessibility. No accessible rooms.

Prices. Dec 23–Apr 11: suites $310–$475 EP; Low season: $190–$280 EP. Add $70 per person in high season for MAP; $60 per person in low season. Children under 13 receive free meals.

STOUFFER RENAISSANCE GRAND BEACH RESORT, ST. THOMAS

				TOTAL
66.7%	67.9%	58.3%	76.2%	67.3%

Like a staggered series of two-story beach houses, this 34-acre resort climbs a hill from a 1,000-foot-long beach on Smith Bay on the island's northeast coast. The property was built in 1984 and renovated in 1989.

Reader Report

"A beautiful hotel with a view of St. John. The water on this part of the island is more turquoise than in other areas."

JoAnn Hopkins, Charlotte, North Carolina

"A fun place! Wonderful rooms and great food—and a very accommodating staff. Clean and fresh."

E. Tish Brissette, Wilmington, North Carolina

Address. Box 8267, St. Thomas, U.S.V.I. 00801, tel. 809/775–1510, fax 809/775–2185.

Affiliation. Renaissance Hotels and Resorts.

Rooms. 254 rooms, 24 1-bedroom suites, 12 2-bedroom town houses. All have air-conditioning, direct dial telephones, patio or balcony, coffee maker, hairdryers and refrigerators. All suites and town houses have ceiling fans and jacuzzis.

Facilities. 2 restaurants, 2 bars/lounges, coffee shop, 6 lighted tennis courts, 18-hole golf course nearby, 2 freshwater pools, watersports center, private dock, exercise room with weights and aerobic machines, aerobics classes, massages, sauna, salon, 24-hr room service, dry-cleaning, conference center with business services, supervised children's program, dive center, sailboats.

TV and VCR. TVs in all rooms, with about 20 channels including CNN and cable movie channels.

No-smoking rooms. Available upon request.

Credit cards. AE, CB, DC, D, MC, V.

Restrictions. Min. 10 nights Dec 23–Jan 1.

Wheelchair accessibility. No accessible rooms.

Prices. Dec 23–Apr 5: doubles $325–$435 EP; suites $595 EP; town houses $895 EP. Apr 6–May 25 and Oct 26–Dec 20: doubles $265–$355 EP; suites $475 EP; town houses $675 EP. Low season: doubles $225–$315 EP; suites $450 EP; townhouses $550 EP. Add $65 per person for AP; $55 for MAP.

VILLA MADELEINE RESORT

				TOTAL
62.5%	75.0%	75.0%	75.0%	71.9%

This resort's main building is atop a hill and is patterned after a turn-of-the-century West Indian, plantation great house. Private villas—each with its own pool and kitchen—are scattered down both sides of the hill. Built in 1989, the resort is on the eastern end of St. Croix, about ¼ mile from the nearest beach. It sustained superficial hurricane damage this fall.

Reader Report

"This is a beautiful property, the last word in luxury and exquisite privacy. Even if you're not staying here, the rich decor of the plantation house is alone worth a visit to the east of the island. The Great House is a fine restaurant with a lovely view of the water. Having your own private pool is great because the beach isn't that close."

NAME WITHHELD, CORAM, NEW YORK

"It was one of the nicest experiences I've had in the Caribbean. You have your own villa with your own pool.... Since it's so private, you can just fall out of bed and into the pool.... [The main house] is like visiting a really cultured person's home...like something out of the 1920s. My only problem was leaving!"

SYBIL TAYLOR, NEW YORK CITY, NEW YORK

Address. Box 3109, 19A-4 Teague Bay, Christiansted, St. Croix, U.S.V.I. 00820, tel. 809/778–7377 or 800/548–4461, fax 809/773–7518.

Rooms. 43 villas. All have air-conditioning, ceiling fans, and full kitchens.

Facilities. Restaurant; bar/lounge; unlighted tennis court; 9-hole golf course nearby; 43 private freshwater pools; billiards room; conference center with business services; water sports (parasailing, snorkeling, and waterskiing) nearby.

TV and VCR. TV in all rooms, with 38 channels including CNN and cable movie channels. VCRs in all rooms.

No-smoking rooms. 10 villas.
Credit cards. AE, D, DC, MC, V.
Wheelchair accessibility. No accessible rooms.
Prices. Dec. 15–Apr. 14: villas $425 EP. Low season: villas $300 EP.

WESTIN CARAMBOLA BEACH & GOLF RESORT

| 61.4% | 77.3% | 68.2% | 72.7% | TOTAL 69.9% |

On the northwest coast at Davis Bay, this 28-acre resort is made up of clusters of two-story, red-roofed villas, each containing six rooms. Built in 1986, the resort was renovated in 1991 after Hurricane Hugo; it sustained further superficial hurricane damage this fall.

Reader Report

"In a lush valley at the edge of St. Croix's rain forest, Carambola is somewhat removed from the less savory side of the island. The beach is fine, as is the golf, but you'll need a car to get anywhere."

DENISE NOLTY, LAKE GROVE, NEW YORK

"A nice resort. The beach was very pretty, and the grounds were spacious, with gardens all the way to the sand.

CHERI ALBERT, NEW YORK, NEW YORK

"The resort was well laid-out, with a spectacular setting but lacked a Caribbean resort necessity—poolside drink service!"

NAME WITHHELD, NEW YORK, NEW YORK

Address. Estate Davis Bay, St. Croix, U.S.V.I. 00851, tel. 809/778–3800 or 800/228–3000, fax 809/778–1682.
Affiliation. Westin Hotels International.
Rooms. 150 rooms including 2 suites. All have air-conditioning and ceiling fans but showers only. The suites have a minibar; 1 has a private porch and the other a balcony.
Facilities. 2 restaurants, bar/lounge, coffee shop, 2 lighted tennis courts, 2 unlighted, 18-hole golf course, 9-hole golf course, freshwater pools, exercise room with weights and aerobic machines, aerobics classes, massages, conference center with business services, dive center.
TV and VCR. TVs in all rooms, with 13 channels including CNN and cable movie channels. VCR in public area.
No-smoking rooms. 80 rooms.
Credit cards. AE, CB, DC, D, MC, V.
Restrictions. Min. 7 nights Dec 22–Dec 29.
Wheelchair accessibility. 3 rooms.
Prices. Nov 2–Apr 23: doubles $165–$330 EP; suite $520–$580 EP. Low season: doubles $109–$250 EP; suite $380 EP.

WYNDHAM SUGAR BAY RESORT

| 47.5% | 52.6% | 50.0% | 52.6% | **TOTAL** 50.7% |

Originally built as a Holiday Inn Crowne Plaza in 1993, this large four-story hotel on 31 acres has rooms with balconies, many of them with water views. The resort has a small beach, a giant free-form pool with waterfalls, a plethora of water sports, and a tennis stadium. Hurricane damage delayed opening.

Reader Report

"The resort was nice.... The breakfast buffet was great, especially the pineapple."

WILLIAM ROBERTSON, BETHESDA, MARYLAND

"It has a gorgeous pool with waterfalls and a grotto bar...our room almost felt like a boat since the balcony hung out so far towards the ocean."

KAREN FELLIN, NORTH WALES, PENNSYLVANIA

Address. 6500 Estate Smith Bay, St. Thomas, U.S.V.I. 00802, tel. 809/777–7100 or 800/WYNDHAM, fax 809/777–7200.
Affiliation. Wyndham Hotels and Resorts.
Rooms. 300 rooms, 9 suites. All have air-conditioning and ceiling fans.
Facilities. 2 restaurants, 2 bars/lounges, 7 lighted tennis courts, 3 freshwater pools, exercise room with weights and aerobic machines, aerobic classes, massages, dry-cleaning, supervised children's program, conference center with business services, dive center.
TV and VCR. TV in all rooms, with 10 channels including CNN and cable movie channels.
No-smoking rooms. 60 rooms, 3 suites.
Credit cards. AE, D, DC, MC, V.
Restrictions. Min. 4 nights Dec. 24–Jan. 1.
Wheelchair accessibility. 3 accessible rooms.
Prices. Dec 15–Apr 14: villas $425 EP. Low season: villas $300 EP.

The Cruise
Lines

AMERICAN CANADIAN CARIBBEAN LINE

64.3%	**38.1%**	**61.9%**	**54.8%**	**TOTAL**

Address. Box 368, Warren, RI 02885, tel. 401/247–0955 or 800/556–7450.

Reader Report

"Small sixty-passenger cruise ships, superb crew, excellent meals. Small enough that you can get to know all passengers and crew."

ELTON JONES, ADDRESS WITHHELD

"They cover New England–area canals in the summer and out-of-the-way spots in the Caribbean in the winter. Using small boats (smaller than the Clipper boats), with informal dining et cetera, the cruising is inexpensive and fun."

NAME WITHHELD, SAN FRANCISCO, CALIFORNIA

Mayan Prince

Size. 92 tons
Outside cabins. 87%
Crew. 18 (American)
Passenger/crew ratio. 5 to 1
Number of cabins. 46
Passengers. 92
Officers. American
Year built. 1992
Cost per day. Outside double $184–$219, inside double $122–$181.
Itinerary. *Winter:* First twelve-day cruise from Nassau to the Caicos Islands, stopping at Allans Cay, Normans Cay, Georgetown, Long Island, Crooked Island, Mayaguana and Providenciales. Subsequent twelve-day cruises from Colon to the San Blas Islands, the Pearl Islands, and the Darien jungle.

Niagara Prince

Size. 99 tons
Outside cabins. 95%
Crew. 17 (American)
Passenger/crew ratio. 5 to 1
Number of cabins. 42
Passengers. 84
Officers. American
Year built. 1994
Cost per day. Outside double $117–$208; inside double $150–$175.
Itinerary. *Winter:* Twelve-day Virgin Island loops depart St. Thomas, calling at St. John; Tortola; Virgin Gorda; Prickly Pear; Anegada; Beef Island; Jost Van Dyke; Sandy Cay; and Norman Island. Twelve-day Venezuelan cruise between Trinidad and Tobago calls at Ciudad Guayana (for Angle Falls) and sails the Macareo and Orinoco rivers. Twelve-day southern Caribbean cruises include calls at Aruba, Bonaire, and Curaçao.

Caribbean Prince

Size. 89 tons
Outside cabins. 82%
Crew. 17 (American)
Passenger/crew ratio. 5 to 1
Number of cabins. 39
Passengers. 78
Officers. American
Year built. 1983
Cost per day. Ouside double $187–$210; inside double $99–$164.
Itinerary. Winter: Twelve-day cruises from Belize City, calling at several destinations along the Barrier Reef, including the Rio Dulce and Lago Izabal in Guatemala. Twelve-day cruises between Belize City and Roatan, stopping at the Rio Dulce; Lake Izabal; Omoa Beach; Fortaleza de San Fernando; Utila and Roatan in Honduras.

CARNIVAL CRUISE LINES

🕴️	🚢	✗	🗑️	TOTAL
55.3%	45.7%	49.7%	53.3%	54.7%

Address. Carnival Pl., 3655 NW 87 Ave., Miami, FL 33178, tel. 305/599–2600.

Reader Report

"A Carnival cruise is the best stress-reduction activity I've found. No matter what your age is, you can act like a kid or act like an idiot and not worry about what other people think, because they're all doing their own thing, too!"

JULIE MOCIULEWSKI, STERLING HEIGHTS, MICHIGAN

"We've come to enjoy most of the Carnival fleet. Perhaps our good fortune has been to have the most personable waiters they hire. We've always received more than our money's worth for the three- and four-day cruises."

RICHARD L. HUGGINS, ALTAMONTE SPRINGS, FLORIDA

"A nightmare of undisciplined young people! A cruise line only for the brave and hardy."

GARY L. GABBERT, VAN NUYS, CALIFORNIA

"[Our trip on the Celebration*] seemed like a seven-day floating prom. . . "*

ELMER W. HANNERS, MONTGOMERY, ALABAMA

"The service [on the Fantasy*] was Carnival all the way . . . which is to say party, eat, sleep, party, eat, party, eat, sleep . . ."*

DAVID P. NEAL, JACKSONVILLE, FLORIDA

MS Celebration

Size. 47,262 tons
Outside cabins. 61%
Crew. 670 (international)
Number of cabins. 743
Passengers. 1,486
Officers. Italian

Passenger/crew ratio. 2.2 to 1   **Year built.** 1987
Cost per day. Suite $333–$347; outside double $231–$264, inside double $217–$250. (Rates include airfare.)
Itinerary. *Year-round:* Seven-day Caribbean loops depart Miami Saturdays, calling at San Juan, St. Thomas, and St. Maarten/St. Martin.

MS Ecstasy

Size. 70,367 tons   **Number of cabins.** 1,020
Outside cabins. 60.7%   **Passengers.** 2,040
Crew. 920 (international)   **Officers.** Italian
Passenger/crew ratio. 2.2 to 1   **Year built.** 1991
Cost per day. Suite $285–$390; outside double $230–$320, inside double $217–$300. (Rates include airfare.)
Itinerary. *Year-round:* Three-day Bahamas loops depart Miami Fridays, calling at Nassau. Four-day Mexican Yucatan loops depart Miami Monday, calling at Key West and Cozumel/Playa del Carmen.

MS Fantasy

Size. 70,367 tons   **Number of cabins.** 1,022
Outside cabins. 60.7%   **Passengers.** 2,044
Crew. 920 (international)   **Officers.** Italian
Passenger/crew ratio. 2.2 to 1   **Year built.** 1990
Cost per day. Suite $285–$390; outside double $230–$320, inside double $217–$300. (Rates include airfare.)
Itinerary. *Year-round:* Three-day Bahamas loops depart Port Canaveral, Florida, Thursdays, calling at Nassau. Four-day Bahamas loops depart Port Canaveral Sundays, calling at Freeport/Lucaya and Nassau.

MS Fascination

Size. 70,367 tons   **Number of cabins.** 1,020
Outside cabins. 60.7%   **Passengers.** 2,040
Crew. 920 (international)   **Officers.** Italian
Passenger/crew ratio. 2.2 to 1   **Year built.** 1994
Cost per day. Suite $318–$347; outside double $231–$264, inside double $217–$250. (Rates include airfare.)
Itinerary. *Year-round:* Seven-day Caribbean loops depart San Juan Saturdays, calling at St. Thomas, Guadeloupe, Grenada, La Guaira/Caracas, and Aruba.

TSS Festivale

Size. 38,175 tons   **Number of cabins.** 580
Outside cabins. 47%   **Passengers.** 1,146
Crew. 580 (international)   **Officers.** Italian
Passenger/crew ratio. 1.9 to 1   **Year built.** 1961
Cost per day. Suite $290–$347; outside double $231–$271, inside double $217–$250. (Rates include airfare.)
Itinerary. *Year-round:* Seven-day Caribbean loops depart San Juan Sundays, calling at St. Thomas/St. John; St. Maarten/St.

Martin; Dominica; Barbados; and Martinique. Beginning in April, seven-day cruises will depart San Juan and call at St. Thomas; Antigua; Barbados; St. Lucia; St. Kitts; and St. Barts.

MS Holiday

Size. 46,052 tons **Number of cabins.** 726
Outside cabins. 61.5% **Passengers.** 1,452
Crew. 660 (international) **Officers.** Italian
Passenger/crew ratio. 2.2 to 1 **Year built.** 1985
Cost per day. Suite $310–$390; outside double $230–$320, inside double $217–$300. (Rates include airfare.)
Itinerary. *Year-round:* Three-day cruises depart Los Angeles Fridays calling at Ensenada, Mexico. Four-day loops depart Los Angeles Mondays, calling at Ensenada, Mexico, and Catalina Island.

MS Jubilee

Size. 47,262 tons **Number of cabins.** 743
Outside cabins. 61% **Passengers.** 1,486
Crew. 670 (international) **Officers.** Italian
Passenger/crew ratio. 2.2 to 1 **Year built.** 1987
Cost per day. Suite $333–$347; outside double $231–$264, inside double $217–$250. (Rates include airfare.)
Itinerary. *Year-round:* Seven-day Mexican Riviera loops depart Los Angeles Sundays, calling at Puerto Vallarta; Mazatlan; and Cabo San Lucas.

MS Sensation

Size. 70,367 tons **Number of cabins.** 1,020
Outside cabins. 60.7% **Passengers.** 2,040
Crew. 920 (international) **Officers.** Italian
Passenger/crew ratio. 2.2 to 1 **Year built.** 1993
Cost per day. Suite $318–$347; outside double $231–$264, inside double $217–$250. (Rates include airfare.)
Itinerary. *Year-round:* From Miami, seven-day eastern Caribbean loops depart alternate Sundays calling at St. Croix, San Juan, and St. Thomas. Seven-day western Caribbean loops depart alternate Sundays, calling at Playa del Carmen/Cozumel, Mexico; Grand Cayman; and Ocho Rios, Jamaica.

MS Tropicale

Size. 36,674 tons **Number of cabins.** 511
Outside cabins. 63% **Passengers.** 1,022
Crew. 550 (international) **Officers.** Italian
Passenger/crew ratio. 1.9 to 1 **Year built.** 1981
Cost per day. Suite $332–$340; outside double $238–$257, inside double $224–$243. (Rates include airfare.)
Itinerary. *Year-round:* From New Orleans, seven-day western Caribbean cruises depart on Sundays, stopping at Tampa; Grand Cayman; and Cozumel/Playa del Carmen, Mexico. Sunday departures from Tampa call at Grand Cayman; Playa del

Carmen/Cozumel; and New Orleans. *Spring:* 16-day Panama Canal cruise calls at Cartagena, Colombia; Panama Canal transit; Caldera, Costa Rica; Acapulco, Zihuatanejo/Ixtapa, Puerto Vallarta and Cabo San Lucas, Mexico; and Vancouver. Fall: 14-day cruise departs Los Angeles and calls at Puerto Vallarta, Zihuatanejo/Ixtapa and Acapulco, Mexico; Caldera, Costa Rica; Panama Canal transit; Curaçao; Netherlands Antilles; St. Thomas, U.S. Virgin Islands; and San Juan.

CELEBRITY CRUISES

				TOTAL
85.4%	74.9%	83.2%	63.2%	79.1%

Address: 5200 Blue Lagoon Dr., Miami, FL 33126, tel. 800/437–3111.

Reader Report

"After 20 cruises, Celebrity gets our vote—for food and entertainment, and a mix of passengers of all age groups. Immaculate ships and outstanding personnel."

ELSIE AND JACK HAAG, GLEN ROCK, NEW JERSEY

"Go on a diet before sailing—Celebrity has the finest food of any line offering 7- to 10-day cruises."

AL IKENBERG, ATLANTA, GEORGIA

"When the officer in charge of housekeeping [on the Zenith] 'white gloves' the deck and poolside chaises twice a day or more, and gets immediate action; when the personnel smiles and is courteous; and when everyone is ready to make your trip a treasured memory—that is a good ship!"

MARJORIE H. BRAENDER, VERO BEACH, FLORIDA

"This [trip in the Horizon] is not a laugh-a-minute type of cruise but rather a first-class cruise experience for people who like the finer things in life."

JEFF AND LAUREL CHANDLER, CINCINNATI, OHIO

MV Century

Size. 70,000 tons   **Number of cabins.** 875
Outside cabins. 64%   **Passengers.** 1,750
Crew. 853 (international)   **Officers.** Greek
Passenger/crew ratio. 2.1 to 1   **Year built.** 1995
Cost per day. Suites $442–$556; outside double $285–$378, inside double $239–$278.
Itinerary. *Year-round:* Seven-night eastern Caribbean loops depart Fort Lauderdale alternate Saturdays, calling at San Juan, St. Thomas, St. Maarten, and Nassau. Seven-night western Caribbean cruises depart Fort Lauderdale alternate Saturdays, calling at Ocho Rios, Jamaica; Grand Cayman; Cozumel/Playa del Carmen, Mexico; and Key West.

MV Horizon

Size. 46,811 tons
Outside cabins. 84%
Crew. 642 (international)
Passenger/crew ratio. 2.1 to 1
Number of cabins. 677
Passengers. 1,354
Officers. Greek
Year built. 1990
Cost per day. Suites $327–$542; outside double $285–$349, inside double $239–$278.
Itinerary. *Fall:* 14- or 15-day Transcanal cruises stopping at Aruba; Cartagena; the Panama Canal; Puerto Caldera; Acapulco; Cabo San Lucas; San Diego, and Los Angeles. *Late fall–winter:* Seven-day deep Caribbean series calls at San Juan, Martinique, Barbados, St. Lucia, Antigua, St. Thomas. *Spring–summer:* 7-day Caribbean cruises (same as winter).

SS Meridian

Size. 30,440 tons
Outside cabins. 54%
Crew. 580 (international)
Passenger/crew ratio. 1.9 to 1
Number of cabins. 553
Passengers. 1,106
Officers. Greek
Year built. 1967
Cost per day. Suite $377–$404; outside double $254–$331, inside double $180–$231.
Itinerary. *Fall:* Ten-day Caribbean trips calling at Aruba, La Guaira, Grenada, Barbados, St. Lucia, Martinique, St. Maarten, and St. Thomas. Eleven-day cruises call at La Cuaira, the Panama Canal, San Blas Cartagena, Martinique, St. John, and St. Thomas. Another eleven-day cruise stops at Nassau, Tortola, St. Maarten, Antigua, Martinique, Barbados, Grenada, and St. Thomas. *Winter:* Same as fall. *Spring–summer:* Twelve-day Caribbean cruise stopping at Grenada, Barbados, St. Lucia, Martinique, Antigue, St. Barts, St. Maarten, St. Thomas, and Nassau. Seven-day Bermuda sailings to King's Wharf.

MV Zenith

Size. 47,255
Outside cabins. 84%
Crew. 670 (international)
Passenger/crew ratio. 2.1 to 1
Number of cabins. 687
Passengers. 1,374
Officers. Greek
Year built. 1992
Cost per day. Suite $327–$542; outside double $285–$349, inside double $239–$278.
Itinerary. *Fall:* Seven-day Bermuda cruise stopping at Hamilton, St. George. Seven-day southern Caribbean route through St. Thomas, Guadeloupe, Grenada, La Guaira, and Aruba. *Winter:* Seven-day southern Caribbean cruise (same as fall). *Spring-Summer:* Seven-day Caribbean trip stopping at St. Thomas, St. Maarten, and Bermuda. Seven-day Bermuda cruise (same as fall).

CLIPPER CRUISE LINE

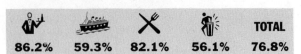

				TOTAL
86.2%	59.3%	82.1%	56.1%	76.8%

Address. 7711 Bonhomme Ave., St. Louis, MO 63105, tel. 800/325–0010.

Reader Report

"Young staff and a crew that's fun to be around. The food is unsurpassed and the attention to detail unflagging. Not for tourists who want nighttime entertainment."

JANELLE G. SHAW, NORTH CONWAY, NEW HAMPSHIRE

"The American crew of these small ships is enthusiastic and made the cruise one of the best we've taken."

KENT SHAMBLIN, AFTON, MINNESOTA

"What more could one ask? Chefs from the Culinary Institute of America, a young, energetic, and eager American crew, visits to ports and islands overlooked by larger cruise vessels, and to top it off, Clipper Chipper Cookies served fresh daily at 4 PM. A happy ship [Yorktown Clipper]."

WILLIAM G. BAILEY, LONGBOAT KEY, FLORIDA

MV Nantucket Clipper

Size. 96 tons
Outside cabins. 100%
Crew. 32 (American)
Passenger/crew ratio. 3.2 to 1
Cost per day. Double per person $243–$362.
Number of cabins. 51
Passengers. 102
Officers. American
Year built. 1984

Itinerary. *Winter:* Eight-day Caribbean cruises depart Crown Bay Marina, St. Thomas, calling at Salt Island; Tortola; Norman Island; Virgin Gorda; Jost Van Dyke; Soper's Hole; Christmas Cove and St. Thomas/St. John.

MV Yorktown Clipper

Size. 97 tons
Outside cabins. 100%
Crew. 40 (American)
Passenger/crew ratio. 3.5 to 1
Cost per day. Double $259–$386.
Number of cabins. 69
Passengers. 138
Officers. American
Year built. 1988

Itinerary. *Winter:* Eleven-day Orinoco River, Venezuela, cruises between Curaçao and Trinidad call at Mochima National Park, Venezuela; Ciudad Guayana/Angel Falls, Venezuela; Tobago; and Bonaire. Eleven-day Caribbean cruises between St. Martin and Grenada call at Anguilla; Saba; St. Kitts; Iles des Saintes, Guadeloupe; Dominica; St. Lucia; Bequia and Union Island, Grenadines.

CLUB MED

👨‍✈️	🚢	✕	🗑️	TOTAL
77.5%	82.5%	75.0%	70.0%	80.0%

Address. 40 W. 57th St., New York, NY 10019, tel. 800/CLUB–MED.

Reader Report

"A nice small ship, with a sports deck off the back. I'd recommend it highly for a romantic getaway."

—Elliott A. Reinfeld, Sherman Oaks, California

"The honeymoon suite (there are only two on board) was very small and not what we expected, compared to other ships. Mostly foreigners on board."

Victor M. Renteria, San Antonio, Texas

Club Med 1

Size. 14,000 tons
Outside cabins. 100%
Crew. 207 (international)
Passenger/crew ratio. 2.1 to 1
Number of cabins. 188
Passengers. 399
Officers. French
Year built. 1990
Cost per day. Suite $467; double $291–$338.
Itinerary. *Mid-fall–mid-spring:* Four different seven-day alternating Caribbean loops depart Fort-de-France, Martinique Saturdays, calling at such islands as Marie-Galant; Dominica; St. Maarten/St. Martin; Puerto Rico; Virgin Gorda; Jost Van Dyke; St. Kitts; St. Barts; St. Thomas; and Nevis; or St Lucia; Tobago; Mayreau; Barbados;and Venezuela.

COMMODORE CRUISE LINE

👨‍✈️	🚢	✕	🗑️	TOTAL
51.9%	33.0%	49.5%	41.5%	47.1%

Address. 800 Douglas Rd., Coral Gables, FL 33134, tel. 305/529–3000.

Reader Report

"Good value with a friendly crew."

Jan Cleary, Huntington Beach, California

"Best of the economy-priced cruises. The New Orleans departure [for the Enchanted Seas*] is a nice touch."*

Name Withheld, Long Island, New York

"Wonderful, nonstop fun [on the Enchanted Seas*]. The cruise will give you as much excitement as you can stand."*

ALICE R. LUCAS, ST. LOUIS, MISSOURI

SS Enchanted Seas

Size. 23,500 tons
Outside cabins. 79%
Crew. 330 (international)

Number of cabins. 364
Passengers. 726
Officers. European and American

Passenger/crew ratio. 2.2 to 1
Year built. 1958
Cost per day. Outside double $101–$184, inside double $93–$108.
Itinerary. As of Dec 17 1995. *Year-round:* Seven-day western Caribbean loops depart from New Orleans on Sundays, calling at Playa del Carmen and Cozumel, Mexico; Roatan, Honduras and Puerto Cortes, Honduras.

SS Enchanted Isle

Size. 23,395 tons
Outside cabins. 78%
Crew. 350 (international)

Number of cabins. 367
Passengers. 729
Officers. European and American

Passenger/crew ratio. 2.0 to 1
Year built. 1958
Cost per day. Outside double $101–$184, inside double $93–$108.
Itinerary. *Year-round:* Seven-day Caribbean loops depart New Orleans on Saturdays, stopping at Playa del Carmen and Cozumel, Mexico; Grand Cayman and Montego Bay, Jamaica.

COSTA CRUISE LINES

64.7%	53.6%	64.2%	48.1%	TOTAL 62.7%

Address. World Trade Center, 80 S.W. 8th St., Miami, FL 33130, tel. 800/462–6782.

Reader Report

"This cruise line gives new meaning to the idea of fun with elegance. Marvelous food, fabulous on-board activities, and some of the friendliest crew members I have ever met."

KEVIN MAGUIRE, AUSTIN, TEXAS

"Outstanding food and service on an intimate ship [the Allegra*]. Perfect for people who have tried a cruise or two and are ready for cruising Italian style. The streamlined, ultra-modern decor without a hint of Hollywood or Vegas is a refreshing change."*

MARY M. GODDARD, WATERFORD, MICHIGAN

"Except for the pasta, the food was mediocre, as was the service."

EDNA MACALUSO, ABINGTON, PENNSYLVANIA

"What a deal! The food is excellent and the ships are clean."

LOUISE HENNING, READING, PENNSYLVANIA

"Service on the Romantica *is uncoordinated but willing, and cabins are roomy with excellent bathrooms. Recreation is unimaginative."*

VICTOR AND MILDRED GIANDANA, COCONUT CREEK, FLORIDA

"Nice ship [the Classica*]. Food is very good, especially the pasta. Cabins are nice sized, and the oversized portholes in the outside cabins are really neat."*

EWALD WIBERG, BOCA RATON, FLORIDA

MS CostaAllegra

Size. 30,000 tons **Number of cabins.** 405
Outside cabins. 55% **Passengers.** 800
Crew. 450 (international) **Officers.** Italian
Passenger/crew ratio. 2 to 1 **Year built.** 1992
Cost per day. Suite $385–$427; minisuite $299–$342; outside double $199–$299, inside double $113–$235. (Rates include airfare.)
Itinerary. *Mid-fall–mid-spring:* Seven-day southern Caribbean loops depart San Juan on Saturdays, calling at St. Thomas/St. John, St. Maarten, Guadeloupe, St. Lucia, Tortola/Virgin Gorda, Serena Cay (Costa's private island); and Casa de Campo, Dominican Republic.

CostaRomantica

Size. 54,000 tons **Number of cabins.** 678
Outside cabins. 68% **Passengers.** 1,350 .
Crew. 650 (international) **Officers.** Italian
Passenger/crew ratio. 2 to 1 **Year built.** 1993
Cost per day. Suite $335–$427; outside double $227–$306, inside double $135–$243. (Rates do not include airfare.)
Itinerary. *Late fall–mid-spring:* Seven-day alternating eastern and western Caribbean loops depart Miami Sundays. The eastern loop calls at San Juan; St. Thomas/St. John; Serena Cay (Costa's private island); Casa de Campo, Dominican Republic; and Nassau. The western route calls at Key West; Playa del Carmen/Cozumel, Mexico; Montego Bay, Jamaica; and Grand Cayman.

CRYSTAL CRUISES

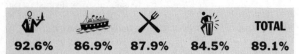

👨‍💼	🚢	✕	🗑️	**TOTAL**
92.6%	**86.9%**	**87.9%**	**84.5%**	**89.1%**

Address. 2121 Ave. of the Stars, Suite 200, Los Angeles, CA 90067, tel. 800/446–6620.

Reader Report

"We have cruised on a variety of vessels and Crystal Harmony *is the best. A large vessel but with less than a thousand passengers. We especially like the cabins with verandas. Food excellent, entertainment outstanding."*

NAME WITHHELD, ANNAPOLIS, MARYLAND

"[The Crystal Harmony *is] the most elegant 'lady' to ply the seven seas. Large enough for the discriminating cruiser, but small enough to be friendly and comfortable. Not your veritable 'city at sea' like so many of the huge liners, but with same or better amenities."*

MARY M. DIDZUN, SEATTLE, WASHINGTON

"We have been cruising for many years—always looking for new ships—and found a home on the Crystal Harmony. *We are planning a fourth cruise on this fabulous ship. Everything is first-class."*

BEATRICE MICHALSKI, ALTAMONTE SPRINGS, FLORIDA

"Affordable luxury; superior cuisine and food service; all the ship's staff give friendly, impeccable service. Many passengers are repeaters—does this tell you something?"

JAMES F. SUESS, JACKSON, MISSISSIPPI

Crystal Harmony

Size. 49,400 tons
Outside cabins. 96%
Crew. 545 (International)

Number of cabins. 480
Passengers. 960
Officers. Norwegian and Japanese

Passenger/crew ratio. 1.7 to 1
Year built. 1990

Average cost per day. Suite $683; outside double with verandah $455, outside double without verandah $416. (Rates do not include airfare.)

Itinerary. *Winter:* Eleven-day Panama Canal transit between Fort Lauderdale and Acapulco calls at Nevis/Monserrat; Playa del Carmen/Cozumel and Huatulco, Mexico; Grand Cayman; and Puerto Limón, Costa Rica. Ten and eleven-day Panama Canal transit between Acapulco and San Juan calls at Puerto Caldera, Costa Rica; Aruba; St. Thomas; Curaçao; San Blas Islands; Huatulco, Mexico; and St. Maarten. Eleven-day Caribbean/Amazon cruises between San Juan and Manaus, Brazil, stop at Barbados; Grenada; Devil's Island, French Guiana; Belem, Alter de Chao, Macapa, or Santerem, Brazil.

Twelve-day Panama Canal tour between Acapulco and New Orleans calls at Puerto Quetzal, Guatamela; Puerto Caldera, Costa Rica; San Blas Islands; and Playa del Carmen/Cozumel, Mexico. *Spring:* Ten and twelve-day Panama Canal cruises (same as winter). 13-day Panama Canal trip between San Juan and Los Angeles calls at Curaçao, Aruba, and Huatulco and Acapulco, Mexico.

Crystal Symphony

Size. 50,000 tons
Outside cabins. 100%
Crew. 530 (European)
Number of cabins. 480
Passengers. 960
Officers. Norwegian and Japanese
Passenger/crew ratio. 1.8 to 1
Year built. 1995
Average cost per day. Suite $683; outside double with verandah $455; outside doubles without verandah $416.
Itinerary. *Winter:* Seven-day Mexican Riviera loop departs Los Angeles calling at Puerto Vallarta, Mazatlán, and Cabo San Lucas. 96-day world cruise departs Los Angeles calling at 38 ports including Honolulu and Lahania, Hawaii.

CUNARD LINE LIMITED

Percentages are listed below for specific divisions.

SS CUNARD CROWN DYNASTY

				TOTAL
67.8%	56.3%	57.1%	51.0%	64.1%

RMS QUEEN ELIZABETH 2

				TOTAL
72.3%	59.6%	65.7%	63.8%	70.4%

MS ROYAL VIKING SUN

				TOTAL
92.7%	84.5%	85.0%	76.8%	87.1%

SEA GODDESS I

				TOTAL
86.0%	75.4%	80.7%	62.3%	79.2%

Address. 555 5th Ave., New York, NY 10017, tel. 800/221–4770.

Reader Report

"[The QE 2*] is not a glitzy resort on the water but a comfortable home on the sea. Its service staff is professional and its rooms in the least expensive category smaller, but the ride is a true cruising experience."*

YVONNE L. SANDOVAL, STEWART MANOR, NEW YORK

"Choose a cruise to nowhere, Caribbean sail, or trans-Atlantic crossing [on the QE 2*] and you'll find standards of service, food, cabins, and public spaces distinctive in their quiet elegance and world-class appeal. This is* not *a cruise ship; the* QE 2 *is an ocean liner."*

JAY H. VAN VECHTEN, NEW YORK, NEW YORK

"[The Sagafjord *and the* Vistafjord*] appeal to a sophisticated, older crowd who appreciate dressing for afternoon tea and dinner. The staff remembers repeat passengers (of which there are many)."*

JANELLE MCDONALD AND ROBERT REID, CAMPBELL, CALIFORNIA

"We've been on the Royal Viking *six times...that's the only one we've gone on [repeatedly]. Everything else just doesn't measure up."*

BETTY MOORE, FLUSHING, MISSISSIPPI

MV Cunard Countess

Size. 17,593 tons
Number of cabins. 398
Outside cabins. 66%
Passengers. 796
Crew. 350 (mainly British)
Officers. British
Passenger/crew ratio. 2.3 to 1
Year built. 1976
Average cost per day. Suites $234–$318; outside double $140–$205, inside double $109–$170. (Rates do not include airfare.)
Itinerary. *Year-round:* Alternating seven-day Caribbean loops depart San Juan Saturdays. One loop calls at Tortola; Antigua; Martinique; Barbados; and St. Thomas. The second round-trip stops at St. Maarten; Guadeloupe; Grenada; St. Lucia; St. Kitts; and St. Thomas. After April 20, two new itineraries will be introduced: the first round-trip from San Juan calls at St. Maarten; Grenada; Dominica; St. Lucia; St. Kitts; and St. Thomas. The following round-trip departs San Juan and stops at Tortola; Antigua; Martinique; Barbados; and St. Thomas.

SS Cunard Crown Dynasty

Size. 20,000 tons
Number of cabins. 400
Outside cabins. 69.5%
Passengers. 800
Crew. 320 (Filipino)
Officers. Northern European
Passenger/crew ratio. 2.5 to 1
Year built. 1993
Average cost per day. Suite $194–$442; outside double $140–$357, inside double $109–$273. (Rates do not include airfare.)

Itinerary. *Spring:* Ten-day Panama Canal sailing calls at Acapulco, Mexico; Puerto Caldera, Costa Rica; the Panama Canal; Ocho Rios, Jamaica; Key West; and Fort Lauderdale. 14-day Panama Canal cruise departs Fort Lauderdale and calls at Grand Cayman, Mexico; Cartagena, Colombia; the Panama Canal; Puerto Caldera, Costa Rica; Acapulco, Mexico; and Los Angeles. *Early fall–winter:* Eleven-day Panama Canal sailing departs Fort Lauderdale and calls at Cozumel and Grand Cayman, Mexico; the Panama Canal; Puerto Caldera, Costa Rica; and Acapulco, Mexico. Seven-day round-trip western Caribbean sailing departs Fort Lauderdale and calls at Ocho Rios, Jamaica; Grand Cayman, Cancun, and Cozumel, Mexico.

RMS Queen Elizabeth 2

Size. 70, 327 tons	**Number of cabins.** 963
Outside cabins. 70%	**Passengers.** 1,810
Crew. 1,000 (international)	**Officers.** British
Passenger/crew ratio. 1.8 to 1	**Year built.** 1969

Average cost per day. Suite $3,915–$5,108; outside double $313–$1,397, inside double $239–$348. (Rates include airfare.)

Itinerary. The 1996 world cruise calls at Cozumel, Mexico; Cartagena, Colombia; the Panama Canal; and Acapulco, Mexico.

MS Royal Viking Sun

Size. 38,000 tons	**Number of cabins.** 370
Outside cabins. 94.8%	**Passengers.** 756
Crew. 460 (European)	**Officers.** Norwegian
Passenger/crew ratio. 1.6 to 1	**Year built.** 1988

Average cost per day . Suite $953–$1,281; outside double $498–$740, inside double $423–$463. Christmas cruise: suite $1,038–$1,397; outside double $541–$805, inside double $459–$503. (Rates include airfare.)

Itinerary. The 1996 world cruise calls at Oranjestad, Aruba; the Panama Canal; Puerto Caldera, Costa Rica; and Acapulco, Mexico. The Christmas transcanal sailing calls at Cozumel, Mexico; Oranjestad, Aruba; the Panama Canal; Puerto Caldera, Colombia; Acapulco and Mazatlan, Mexico.

MS Sagafjord

Size. 24,474 tons	**Number of cabins.** 321
Outside cabins. 90%	**Passengers.** 589
Crew. 352 (mostly Scandinavian)	**Officers.** Norwegian
Passenger/crew ratio. 1.7 to 1	**Year built.** 1965

Average cost per day. Suite $640–$1,505; outside double $315–$933, inside double $275–$481. Christmas cruise: suite $903–$1,403; outside double $433–$806, inside double $374–$409. (Rates include airfare.)

Itinerary. The 1996 world cruise will call at St. Croix. *Spring:* 14-day cruise departs Fort lauderdale and calls at Cancun, Mexico; Isla de San Andres; Oranjestad, Aruba; St. George's, Grenada; Castries; and St. John's, Antigua. Following 14-day cruise departs Fort Lauderdale and calls at San Juan; St. Croix;

Gustavia; Fort-de-France, Martinique; Bridgetwon, Barbados; St. John's, Antigua; Philipsburg, St. Martin; and St. Thomas. Seven-day cruise calls at Bridgetown, Barbados; St. John's, Antigua; Philipsburg, St. Martin; and St. Thomas. *Winter:* 13-day round-trip cruise departs Fort Lauderdale and calls at Kralendijk, Bonaire; Oranjestad, Aruba; Santa Marta; Cartagena, Colombia; the San Blas Islands; Puerto Limón; Isla de San Andres; and Cozumel, Mexico. Christmas sailing departs Fort Lauderdale and calls at San Juan; Philipsburg, St. Martin; St. John's, Antigua; Fort-de-France, Martinique; Willemstad, Curaçao; Puerto La Cruz; Castries; and St. Thomas.

Sea Goddess I

Size. 4,250 tons

Outside cabins. 100%

Crew. 89 (American and European)

Passenger/crew ratio. 1.3 to 1

Number of cabins. 58

Passengers. 116

Officers. Norwegian

Year built. 1984

Average cost per day. $643–$743 for seven-day cruises; $707 for 14-day cruises. (Rates include airfare.)

Itinerary. *Late fall–winter:* Seven-day Caribbean loops depart St. Thomas, calling at St. John; St. Maarten/St. Martin; St. Barts; Antigua; Virgin Gorda; and Jost Van Dyke. Two 14-day cruises; the first calls at Barbados; Mayreau; Isla Margarita; Aruba; Cartagena, Colombia; the San Blas Islands; Panama Canal transit; Puerto Caldera, Costa Rica; Puerto Escondido; and Acapulco, Mexico. The second calls at all ports in reverse order. Seven-day cruise calls at Barbados; Mayreau; St. Lucia; Martinique; Antigua; St. Barts; Jost Van Dyke; and St. Thomas.

SS Vistafjord

Size. 24,492 tons

Outside cabins. 81%

Crew. 379 (mainly Scandinavian)

Passenger/crew ratio. 1.9 to 1

Number of cabins. 387

Passengers. 736

Officers. Norwegian

Year built. 1973

Average cost per day. Suite $622–$1,054; outside double $305–$1,096, inside double $289–$326. Christmas cruise: suite $748–$1,166; outside double $363–$1,213, inside double $344–$356. (Rates include airfare.)

Itinerary. *Winter:* A 14 day cruise departs Fort Lauderdale and stops at St. Thomas; St. John's, Antigua; Gustavia; Philipsburg, St. Martin; Montserrat; Bridgetown, Barbados; Kingstown, St. Vincent; Oranjestad, Aruba; and Grand Cayman. 16-day cruise departs Fort Lauderdale and calls at Grand Cayman; Cartagena, Colombia; Panama Canal transit; Puerto Caldera, Costa Rica; Acapulco, Puerto Vallarta, and Cabo San Lucas, Mexico. Christmas cruise departs Fort Lauderdale and calls at San Juan; St. Croix; St. George's, Grenada; Castries; Bridgetown, Barbados; Scarborough, La Guaira; Oranjestad, Aruba; and St. Thomas.

DOLPHIN CRUISE LINE

68.0%	39.8%	68.9%	46.3%	**TOTAL** 58.6%

Address. 901 South America Way, Miami, FL 33132, tel. 800/992–4299.

Reader Report

"Although [the Dolphin *is] outdated by today's cruise standards, the crew's service and meals made up for it. When we first boarded I was somewhat disappointed at the room— by the end of four days I didn't want to leave."*

JULIANN KOCH, LEICESTER, NEW YORK

"Enjoyed the smaller ship [the Dolphin*] versus getting lost on a larger one. The wooden decks with the old-style wooden deck chairs are a reminder of travel via ship several years ago—elegant and personable."*

BONNIE HIATT, WALTON, KENTUCKY

"Good if you don't have to have everything new and fancy. The food [on the SeaBreeze*] is the best and the ports of call are the same as other boats—for far less money. Bargain cruising at its best."*

BRIAN DUBES, WATERLOO, IOWA

SS Dolphin IV

Size. 13,007 tons
Outside cabins. 70.4%
Crew. 285 (international)
Passenger/crew ratio. 2.1 to 1
Cost per day. Rates not yet established.

Number of cabins. 294
Passengers. 588
Officers. Greek
Year built. 1956

Itinerary. *Year-round:* Two-night cruises from Port Canaveral to Grand Bahama Island.

SS OceanBreeze

Size. 21,486 tons
Outside cabins. 61.3%
Crew. 310 (international)
Passenger/crew ratio. 2.5 to 1

Number of cabins. 384
Passengers. 776
Officers. Greek
Year built. 1955

Cost per day. Suite $213–$363; outside double $106–$299, inside double $89–$256.

Itinerary. *Winter:* Alternating seven-night Caribbean or Panama Canal loops depart Aruba Sundays, calling at Dominica, Barbados, Martinique, and Curaçao; or Cartagena in Colombia, the San Blas Islands (near Panama), and Curaçao. They also sail Gatun Lake (Panama Canal). Beginning May 3 1996; Year-round: Three-night Bahamas loops depart Miami Fridays, calling at Nassau and Blue Lagoon Island. Four-night Bahamas loops depart Miami Mondays, calling at Nassau, Blue Lagoon Island and Key West.

SS SeaBreeze

Size. 21,000 tons
Outside cabins. 62.5%
Crew. 400 (international)
Passenger/crew ratio. 2.1 to 1
Number of cabins. 421
Passengers. 840
Officers. Greek
Year built. 1958
Cost per day. Suite $179–$250; outside double $79–$227, inside double $73–$192.

Itinerary. *Year-round:* Alternating seven-day eastern and western Caribbean loops depart Miami Sundays, calling at Nassau and Blue Lagoon Island in the Bahamas, San Juan, and St. Thomas/St. John. The second route calls at Grand Cayman; Montego Bay, Jamaica; and Cozumel/Playa del Carmen, Mexico.

HOLLAND AMERICA LINE

				TOTAL
86.3%	76.6%	79.7%	68.5%	80.7%

Address. 300 Elliott Ave. W, Seattle, WA 98119, tel 206/281–3535.

Reader Report

"This line is the crème de la crème. Food, service, decor, entertainment, officers and crew—five-plus stars. Bravo!"

E. A. KEATING, NAPA, CALIFORNIA

"Although the Filipino and Indonesian staff expect no tips, the service on this line is clearly superior. The style of service is different from most ships—it is quiet and efficient and not meant to be entertaining."

JEFF AND LAUREL CHANDLER, CINCINNATI, OHIO

"The Rotterdam is one of the last remaining 'great ships' of the traditional nature. It has a great variety of cabins, due to the old transatlantic class structure. Old World charm. Super service!"

EWALD WIBERG, BOCA RATON, FLORIDA

"Loved the ship itself [the Westerdam]. If all you want to do is eat and gamble, go for it. But there was no nightlife or dancing, the music was very dull; and ship's officers cannot mingle. Deadly dull for singles."

CAROL SCANDURA, ALTA LOMA, CALIFORNIA

MS Maasdam

Size. 55,451 tons
Outside cabins. 77%
Crew. 571 (Indonesian/Filipino)
Passenger/crew ratio. 2.2 to 1
Number of cabins. 633
Passengers. 1,266
Officers. Dutch
Year built. 193
Cost per day. Minimum rate $300–$322, maximum rate $535–$787 (Rates do not include airfare.)

Itinerary. *Late fall–early winter:* 14-day round-trip Caribbean sailing departs New Orleans and calls at Playa del Carmen/Cozumel, and Montego Bay, Mexico; Curaçao; Aruba; St. Thomas. Ten-day Panama Canal cruise departs New Orleans and calls at Playa del Carmen/Cozumel, Mexico; Grand Cayman; the Panama Canal; and Puerto Quetzal. Following ten-day Panama Canal cruise follows same course in reverse order. Three ten-day Panama Canal cruises depart Fort Lauderdale and visit Grand Cayman; the Panama Canal; Puerto Caldera, Costa Rica; and Puerto Quetzal. Two ten-day Panama Canal cruises loop between New Orleans and Acapulco and call at Puerto Quetzal; the Panama Canal; Grand Cayman; and Playa del Carmen/Cozumel. Ten-day Panama Canal cruise departs Acapulco and stops at Puerto Quetzal; Puerto Caldera, Costa Rica; the Panama Canal; and Grand Cayman.

MS Nieuw Amsterdam

Size. 33,930 tons	**Number of cabins.** 605
Outside cabins. 68%	**Passengers.** 1,214
Crew. 542 (Indonesian and Filipino)	**Officers.** Dutch
Passenger/crew ratio. 2.2 to 1	**Year built.** 1983

Cost per day. Minimum rate $162–$262, maximum rate $300–$413. (Rates do not include airfare.)

Itinerary. *Fall:* Two seven-day loops depart from New Orleans and call at Montego Bay; Grand Cayman; and Playa del Carmen/Cozumel, Mexico. 20-day Panama Canal cruise departs Vancouver and calls at Seattle, San Francisco, Cabo San Lucas and Acapulco, Mexico; Puerto Caldera, Costa Rica; the Panama Canal; Aruba; and Ocho Rios, Jamaica. *Winter:* Ten-day holiday cruise departs New Orleans and visits Playa del Carmen/Cozumel, Mexico; Grand Cayman; Puerto Limón; and Montego Bay. The following ten-day cruise departs New Orleans and calls at St. Thomas; Montego Bay; Grand Cayman; and Playa del Carmen/Cozumel, Mexico. *Spring:* 19-day Panama Canal cruise departs New Orleans and calls at Montego Bay; Cartagena, Colombia; the San Blas Islands; the Panama Canal; Puerto Caldera, Costa Rica; Acapulco and Cabo San Lucas, Mexico.

MS Noordam

Size. 33,930 tons	**Number of cabins.** 605
Outside cabins. 68%	**Passengers.** 1,214
Crew. 542 (Indonesian and Filipino)	**Officers.** Dutch
Passenger/crew ratio. 2.2 to 1	**Year built.** 1984

Cost per day. Minimum rate $147–$263, maximum rate $300–$415. (Rates do not include airfare.)

Itinerary. *Fall:* Seven-day western Caribbean cruises depart Tampa and call at Key West; Playa del Carmen/Cozumel, Mexico; Ocho Rios, Jamaica; and Grand Cayman. 19-day Panama Canal cruise departs Vancouver and calls at Victoria, San Francisco, San Diego; Cabo San Lucas and Acapulco, Mexico; Puerto Caldera, Costa Rica; the Panama Canal; Cartagena, Colomiba; and Grand Cayman. *Winter:* Seven-day western Caribbean loops depart Tampa, calling at Key West, Cozumal/Playa del Carmen, Mexico; Ocho Rios, Jamaica; and Grand Cayman. *Spring:* 17-day Panama Canal cruise departs Tampa and calls at Grand Cayman; Cartagena, Colombia; the

Panama Canal; Puerto Caldera, Colombia; Acapulco and Cabo San Lucas, Mexico.

SS Rotterdam

Size. 38,645 tons

Outside cabins. 53%

Crew. 603 (Indonesian and Filipino)

Passenger/crew ratio. 1.8 to 1

Number of cabins. 575

Passengers. 1,075

Officers. Dutch

Year built. Constructed in 1959; renovated in 1989

Cost per day. Minimum rate $170–$274, maximum rate $274–$428. (Rates do not include airfare.)

Itinerary. *Winter:* Ten-day Caribbean cruise departs Fort Lauderdale and stops at Aruba; Cartegena, Colombia; the San Blas Islands; the Panama Canal; and Puerto Limón. 15-day holiday Caribbean cruise departs Fort Lauderdale and calls at St. John/St. Thomas; Antigua; Martinique; St. Lucia; Trinidad; Barbados; Curaçao; and Jamaica. 14-day Panama Canal tour departs Fort Lauderdale and calls at Grand Cayman; the Panama Canal; Puerto Quetzal; Acapulco and Cabo San Lucas, Mexico. *Spring:* 23-day Panama Canal tour departs New York and visits Fort Lauderdale; Curaçao; Aruba; Cartagena, Colombia; the San Blas Islands; the Panama Canal; Puerto Caldera, Costa Rica; Acapulco, Mazatlan, and Cabo San Lucas, Mexico.

MS Ryndam

Size. 55,451 tons

Outside cabins. 79%

Crew. 571 (Indonesian/Filipino)

Passenger/crew ratio. 2.2 to 1

Number of cabins. 633

Passengers. 1,266

Officers. Dutch

Year built. 1994

Cost per day. Minimum rate $175–$284, maximum rate $449–$546. (Rates do not include airfare.)

Itinerary. *Fall:* Two ten-day Caribbean cruises depart from Fort Lauderdale. The first visits St. Maarten; St. Lucia; Barbados; Dominica; St. Thomas; and Nassau. The second follows the same route but substitutes Antigua for Dominica. 20-day Panama Canal transit from Vancouver to Fort Lauderdale calls at Los Angeles; Puerto Vallarta, Zihuatanejo, and Acapulco, Mexico; Puerto Caldera, Costa Rica; the Panama Canal; St. Thomas; and Nassau. *Winter:* Seven-day eastern Caribbean Christmas cruise departs Fort Lauderdale and calls at Nassau; San Juan; and St. John/St. Thomas. Seven-day western Caribbean New Year's cruise departs Fort Lauderdale and calls at Playa del Carmen/Cozumel, Mexico; Grand Cayman; Ocho Rios, Jamaica; and Key West. Spring: 20-day Panama Canal cruise departs Fort Lauderdale and calls at Nassau; San Juan; Aruba; the Panama Canal; Puerto Quetzal; Acapulco and Cabo San Lucas, Mexico; Los Angeles, Seattle, and Vancouver.

MS Statendam

Size. 55,451 tons

Outside cabins. 79%

Crew. 571 (Indonesian/Filipino)

Passenger/crew ratio. 2.2 to 1

Number of cabins. 633

Passengers. 1,266

Officers. Dutch

Year built. 1993

Cost per day. Minimum rate $169–$284, maximum rate $449–$546.

Itinerary. *Fall:* 10-day Caribbean cruise departs Fort Lauderdale and visits Curaçao; Caracas; Grenada; Martinique; St. Thomas; and Nassau. Ten-day Caribbean cruise departs Fort Lauderdale and calls at St. John/St. Thomas; Dominica; Grenada; Caracas; and Curaçao. 21-day Panama Canal cruise departs Vancouver and visits Victoria, San Francisco, San Diego; Cabo San Lucas, Puerto Vallarta, and Acapulco, Mexico; Puerto Quetzal; the Panama Canal; Cartagena,Colombia; Catalina Island; and Nassau. *Winter:* Seven-day western Caribbean Christmas cruise departs Fort Lauderdale and calls at Grand Cayman; Ocho Rios, Jamaica; and Playa del Carmen/Cozumel, Mexico. Seven-day eastern Caribbean New Year's cruise departs Fort Lauderdale and calls at St. Thomas; St. John; and Nassau. Ten-day Caribbean cruise departs Fort Lauderdale and calls at St. John/St. Thomas; Dominica; Grenada; Caracas; and Curaçao. Spring: 20-day Panama Canal cruise departs Fort Lauderdale and visits Grand Cayman; Cartagena, Colombia; the San Blas Islands; the Panama Canal; Puerto Caldera; Costa Rica; Acapulco and Cabo San Luca, Mexico; San Diego, San Francisco, and Victoria.

MS Veendam

Size. 55,451 tons   **Number of cabins.** 633
Outside cabins. 77%   **Passengers.** 1,266
Crew. 571 (Indonesian and Filipino)   **Officers.** Dutch
Passenger/crew ratio. 2.2 to 1   **Year built.** 1996
Cost per day. Minimum rate $175–$284, maximum rate $449–$546. (Rates do not include airfare.)
Itinerary. *Spring–summer:* Alternating seven-day eastern or western Caribbean loops depart Fort Lauderdale Saturday or Sunday, calling at Key West, Cozumel/Playa del Carmen, Mexico; Ocho Rios, Jamaica; and Grand Cayman or Nassau, San Juan, and St. Thomas/St. John. Seven-day eastern Caribbean cruise departs Fort Lauderdale and calls at Nassau; San Juan; and St. John/St. Thomas.

MS Westerdam

Size. 53,872 tons   **Number of cabins.** 747
Outside cabins. 66%   **Passengers.** 1,494
Crew. 620 (Indonesian and Filipino)   **Officers.** Dutch
Passenger/crew ratio. 2.4 to 1   **Year built.** 1986
Cost per day. Minimum rate $185–$172, maximum rate $398–$$431. (Rates do not include airfare.)
Itinerary. *Mid-fall–spring:* Seven-day eastern Caribbean loops depart Fort Lauderdale Saturdays, calling at St. Maarten/St. Martin, St. Thomas/St. John, and Nassau. Seven-day western Caribbean Christmas cruise departs Fort Lauderdale and visits Key West; Ocho Rios, Jamaica; Grand Cayman; and Cozumel, Mexico. Seven-day eastern Caribbean New Year's cruise departs Fort Lauderdale and calls at St. Maarten; St. John/St. Thomas; and Nassau. 18-day Panama Canal cruise departs Fort Lauderdale and visits Curaçao; the San Blas Islands; the Panama Canal; Puerto Quetzal; Acapulco and Cabo San Lucas, Mexico. 20-day Panama Canal tour departs Vancouver and calls at Los Angeles; Puerto Vallarta, Zihuatanejo, and Acapulco, Mexico; Puerto Quetzal; the Panama Canal; Cartagena, Colombia; Grand Cayman; and Ocho Rios, Jamaica.

MAJESTY CRUISE LINE

 82.8%	 69.4%	 81.1%	 65.0%	TOTAL 73.3%

Address. 901 South America Way, Miami, FL 33132, tel. 800/645–8111.

Reader Report

"What a relief to take a cruise on a small ship that has the amenities of the larger boats—without sacrificing personalized service. My state room was pleasant with lots of space. It's great to have breakfast and lunch outside on the deck at table rather than in a cafeteria. The dining room was intimate, and the service was excellent."

MIDGE GIARRUSSO, MT. SINAI, NEW YORK

"I fell in love with the ship—it was brand-new.... Everybody was so upbeat. I also went at Christmas and that was really special. It's a beautiful ship."

MARY CALANNINO, REVERE, MASSACHUSETTS

MV Royal Majesty

Size. 32,400 tons   **Number of cabins.** 528
Outside cabins. 65%   **Passengers.** 1,056
Crew. 500 (international)   **Officers.** Greek
Passenger/crew ratio. 2.1 to 1   **Year built.** 1992
Cost per day. Suite $285–$436; outside double $202–$300; inside double $123–$229.
Itinerary. *Late spring–early fall:* Seven-night Bermuda loops depart Boston, calling at St. George's. *Mid-fall–mid-spring:* Three-night Bahamas loops depart Miami, calling at Nassau, with a beach party excursion to Royal Isle.

NORWEGIAN CRUISE LINE

 72.8%	 54.3%	 67.2%	 67.7%	TOTAL 68.5%

Address. 95 Merrick Way, Coral Gables, FL 33134, tel. 800/327–7030.

Reader Report

"The [Norway's] entertainment is first-rate; the food and service ranges from very good to okay. While the design is classical, it is also inconvenient."

P. J. FAGLEY, WEXFORD, PENNSYLVANIA

"The Norway *has delightful ambience and excellent*

entertainment. This is a tremendous ship, but the staterooms are on the small side."

NAME WITHHELD, RICHMOND, VIRGINIA

"The Norway is huge, so there's no feeling of confinement, and the cabins are more than adequate. The service is perfect. The entertainment is spectacular."

GAIL HABER, GREENSBORO, NORTH CAROLINA

"The Dreamward is an outstanding mid-size ship—fewer passengers equals more space per passenger. The many floor-to-ceiling windows mean spectacular views. Cabins are very spacious and dining rooms intimate, with windows all around for perfect views."

STEPHEN MCLEAN, LINCOLN PARK, MICHIGAN

MS Dreamward

Size. 41,000 tons **Number of cabins.** 623
Outside cabins. 85% **Passengers.** 1,242
Crew. 483 (international) **Officers.** Norwegian
Passenger/crew ratio. 2.6 to 1 **Year built.** 1992
Cost per day. Suite $350–$571; outside double $271–$335, inside double $238–$298. (Rates include airfare.)
Itinerary. *Fall–spring:* Seven-day western Caribbean loops depart Fort Lauderdale Sundays, calling at Grand Cayman; Cozumel/Playa del Carmen, Mexico; Cancun; and Great Stirrup Cay, Bahamas. *Summer:* Seven-day Bermuda loops depart New York Saturdays, calling at St. George's and Hamilton.

MS Leeward

Size. 25.000 tons **Number of cabins.** 482
Outside cabins. 67% **Passengers.** 950
Crew. 400 **Officers.** Norwegian
Passenger/crew ratio. 2.4 to 1 **Year built.** 1992
Cost per day. Suite $300–$552; outside double $235–$366, inside double $192–$260. (Rates include airfare.)
Itinerary. *Year-round:* weekly alternating three-day and seasonal four-day loops depart Miami on Fridays and Mondays. First three-day loop calls at Nassau and Great Stirrup Cay, Norwegian Cruise Line's private island in the Bahamas. The second three-day calls at Key West and Great Stirrup Cay. *Summer:* Four-day cruise calls at Playa del Carmen, Cozumel and Key West. *Winter:* Three-day loop visits Key West, Cancun and Cozumel, Mexico.

SS Norway

Size. 76,049 tons **Number of cabins.** 1,024
Outside cabins. 56.9% **Passengers.** 2,032
Crew. 900 (international) **Officers.** Norwegian
Passenger/crew ratio. 2.3 to 1 **Year built.** 1961
Cost per day. Suite $364–$778; outside double $271–$364, inside double $210–$278. (Rates include airfare.)

Itinerary. *Fall:* Seven-day eastern Caribbean loops depart Miami, calling at Ocho Rios, Grand Cayman, Playa del Carmen, Cozumel, and Great Stirrup Cay in the Bahamas.

MS Seaward

Size. 42,000 tons	**Number of cabins.** 767
Outside cabins. 67.7%	**Passengers.** 1,504
Crew. 630 (international)	**Officers.** Norwegian
Passenger/crew ratio. 2.4 to 1	**Year built.** 1988

Cost per day. Suite $335–$400; outside double $271–$364, inside double $200–$276. (Rates include airfare.)

Itinerary. *Year-round:* Alternating seven-day Caribbean loops depart San Juan Sundays. First loop calls at Barbados, Martinique, St. Maarten, Antigua and St. Thomas. The second loop calls at Aruba, Curaçao, Tortola and St. Thomas.

MS Windward

Size. 41,000 tons	**Number of cabins.** 623
Outside cabins. 85%	**Passengers.** 1,246
Crew. 483 (international)	**Officers.** Norwegian
Passenger/crew ratio. 2.6 to 1	**Year built.** 1993

Cost per day. Suite $378–$600; outside double $300–$364, inside double $268–$321. (Rates include airfare.)

Itinerary. *Fall–mid-spring:* Alternating seven-day Caribbean loops depart San Juan Sundays. The first loop calls at Barbados, Martinique, St. Maarten/St. Martin, and St. Thomas/St. John. The second route calls at Aruba, Curaçao, Tortola/Virgin Gorda, and St. Thomas/St. John.

PREMIER CRUISE LINES

				TOTAL
65.6%	44.4%	58.9%	57.9%	55.5%

Address. Box 573, Cape Canaveral, FL 32920, tel. 407/783-5061.

Reader Report

"The Oceanic *is a surprisingly good deal. The staff is exceptionally helpful."*

NONA STARR, WALTHAM, MASSACHUSETTS

"A short four-day cruise on the Atlantic *on Premier is great for someone who is not sure cruising is for them. The service is excellent, and there's plenty to do for both adults and children. Interior cabins small but very clean."*

ROBERT E. GLASSFORD, JR., EFFINGHAM, NEW HAMPSHIRE

"This four-day cruise on the Oceanic *(the 'Big Red Boat') was very good: The food was excellent and sophisticated, the*

cabins comfortable, the service impeccable . . . and the price most extraordinarily reasonable!"

MARC MOGIL, GREAT NECK, NEW YORK

"The ship [the Oceanic] is old, but the cabins are large and the food is exceptional. And most importantly, the crew go out of their way for you."

DAVID P. NEAL, JACKSONVILLE, FLORIDA

Star/Ship Atlantic

Size. 35,143 tons
Outside cabins. 73%
Crew. 535 (international)
Passenger/crew ratio. 3.1 to 1
Number of cabins. 549
Passengers. 1,550
Officers. Greek
Year built. 1982
Cost per day. Apartment suite $443–$332, suite $297–$396; deluxe outside $284–$379; outside double $274–$366, inside double $244–$326. (Rates include airfare.)
Itinerary. *Year-round:* Three- and four-day Bahamas loops depart Port Canaveral Thursdays and Sundays, calling at Nassau and Port/Lucaya.

Star/Ship Oceanic

Size. 38,772 tons
Outside cabins. 44%
Crew. 565 (international)
Passenger/crew ratio. 3 to 1
Number of cabins. 590
Passengers. 1,800
Officers. Greek
Year built. 1965
Cost per day. Apartment suite $443–$332, suite $297–$396; deluxe outside $284–$379; outside double $274–$366, inside double $244–$326. (Rates include airfare.)
Itinerary. Same as for *Star/Ship Atlantic,* above, except departures every Friday and Monday.

PRINCESS CRUISES

				TOTAL
76.7%	70.5%	68.8%	72.9%	76.0%

Address. 10100 Santa Monica Blvd., Los Angeles, CA 90067, tel. 310/553–1770.

Reader Report

"We love to travel on the Princess Line! Other passengers are about our age (50 and over), middle-class, and interesting to talk to. Food, service, and entertainment are very very good."

NAME WITHHELD, OAKLAND, CALIFORNIA

"The Crown Princess is elegant and clean, with cabins that were large for a cruise ship. Service was great, and there were lots of activities on the ship while at sea."

DEBORAH HUGHES, ALBANY, NEW YORK

"The dining room [of the Crown Princess*] was awfully noisy and the food was never hot by the time it was served. Facilities were very nice, and the decor was lovely. The recreation was great—there was always something to do."*

ELIZABETH PUGLISI, SUNNYVALE, CALIFORNIA

MV Crown Princess

Size. 70,000 tons
Outside cabins. 80%
Crew. 696 (international)
Passenger/crew ratio. 2.4 to 1
Number of cabins. 795
Passengers. 1,590
Officers. Italian
Year built. 1990
Cost per day. Suite $478–$485; minisuite $421–$428; outside double $257–$368, inside double $193–$271. (Rates include airfare.)
Itinerary. *Mid-fall–early spring:* Seven-day western Caribbean loop departs Fort Lauderdale calling at Princess Cays, Bahamas; Montego Bay, Jamaica; Grand Cayman, and Playa del Carmen/Cozumel, Mexico. Ten-day western Caribbean route departs Fort Lauderdale and calls at Nassau, St. Thomas, Guadeloupe, Barbados, Dominica, St. Maarten, and the Princess Cays.

MV Pacific Princess

Size. 20,000 tons
Outside cabins. 77.5%
Crew. 350 (international)
Passenger/crew ratio. 1.8 to 1
Number of cabins. 305
Passengers. 640
Officers. British
Year built. 1971
Cost per day. Prices for spring cruises only: suite $710–$728; minisuite $605–$640; outside double $365–$518; inside double $314–$370. (Rates include airfare.) Prices for winter cruises to be announced.
Itinerary. *Spring:* Eleven-day Amazon cruise from San Juan to Manaus, Brazil, calls at St. Thomas/St. John, Martinique, Barbados, and Devil's Island, and sails along the Amazon River to Santana, Santarém, Alter do Cháo, and Boca do Valer. 14-day South American loop from Manaus to Buenos Aires, cruising the Amazon river and stopping at Recife, Rio de Janeiro, and Montevideo. *Winter:* 14-day Panama Canal loop from San Juan to New Orleans, stopping at St. Thomas; Guadaloupe; Grenada; La Guaira; Aruba; the Panama Canal, Limón, Costa Rica; Playa del Carmen, and Cozumel, Mexico.

MV Regal Princess

Size. 70,000 tons
Outside cabins. 80%
Crew. 696
Passenger/crew ratio. 2.4 to 1
Number of cabins. 795
Passengers. 1,590
Officers. Italian
Year built. 1991
Cost per day. Suite $485–$535; minisuite $428–$478; outside double $264–$418, inside double $200–$321. (Rates include airfare.)
Itinerary. *Fall-spring:* Seven-day southern Caribbean loop departs San Juan calling at Barbados, Princess Bay,

Martinique, St. Maarten, and St. Thomas.

MV Star Princess

Size. 63,500 tons
Number of cabins. 735
Outside cabins. 78%
Passengers. 1,490
Crew. 600 (international)
Officers. Italian
Passenger/crew ratio. 2.5 to 1
Year built. 1989
Cost per day. Suite $471–$521; minisuite $414–$464; outside double $264–$378, inside double $185–$307. (Rates include airfare.)
Itinerary. *Fall–spring:* Seven-day eastern Caribbean loop departs Fort Lauderdale calling at Nassau, St. Thomas, St. Maarten, and the Princess Cays.

RADISSON SEVEN SEAS CRUISES

				TOTAL
95.2%	93.7%	92.9%	69.8%	91.0%

Address. 600 Corporate Dr., Suite 410, Ft. Lauderdale, FL 33334, tel. 800/333–3333.

Reader Report

"All outside suites, most with verandas. Wonderful meals, with open seating."

MARY K. ELLENWOOD, FORT WORTH, TEXAS

"Very upscale and low-key. There's not much nightlife . . . mostly piano bar and the occasional comedian, but there are VCRs in the cabins. I really liked the ship because every cabin has either a wall-size window or a balcony. Good for veteran cruisers who have sailed a great deal and want to see more exotic ports on a smaller ship. There are no set seatings . . .you can even be served in your cabin by candlelight if you prefer. It has the feel of a small, European hotel. The catamaran design makes the ship more stable than most single-hull ships."

HEIDI WALDROP, NEW YORK, NEW YORK

MS Hanseatic

Size. 9,000 tons
Number of cabins. 90
Outside cabins. 100%
Passengers. 188
Crew. 125 (European)
Officers. European
Passenger/crew ratio. 1.5
Year built. 1993
Cost per day. $525 (Rates include airfare.)
Itinerary. *Fall:* Eight-day Caribbean cruise from Philippsburg to San Juan, Costa Rica, calling at Roadtown, British Virgin Islands; Santo Domingo, Dominican Republic; Port Antonio,

Jamaica; Great Inagua, Bahamas; and Cayo Levantado, Dominican Republic. From San Juan, Costa Rica to Philippsburg, port of call are Basseterre, St. Kitts; Roseau, Dominica; St. George's, Grenada; Port Elizabeth; Bequia; Bridgetown, Barbados; and Pointe-à-Pitre, Guadeloupe. 13-day tour of the Panama Canal and the Galapagos Islands from Philippsburg to Esmeraldas.

SSC Radisson Diamond

Size. 20,000 tons
Outside cabins. 100%
Crew. 192 (international)
Passenger/crew ratio. 1.8 to 1
Cost per day. $570. (Rates include airfare.)
Number of cabins. 177
Passengers. 350
Officers. Finnish
Year built. 1992

Itinerary. Late fall–winter: Three-night Caribbean loops depart San Juan, calling at St. Maarten/St. Martin and St. Thomas. Four-night Caribbean loops from San Juan call at St. Kitts, Montserrat and St. John or St. Thomas, St. Bart and St. Maarten. Five-night cruises call at St. Thomas, St. Barts, St. Maarten and Tortola. Six-night Caribbean transits between San Juan and Barbados call at Tortola; St. Kitts; Antigua; Martinique; and Carriacou. Seven-night cruises stop at St. Thomas; St. Barts; Bequia; and St. George's. Seven-, eight-, and nine-night Panama Canal cruises between Bridgetown, Barbados and San Juan, Costa Rica call at Curaçao; Cartagena, Colombia; the San Blas Islands; and Puerto Caldera, Costa Rica.

REGENCY CRUISES

				TOTAL
60.8%	47.3%	55.0%	38.7%	57.5%

Address. 260 Madison Ave., New York, NY 10016, tel. 212/972–4499.

Reader Report

"Food [on the Regent Sun] is superb; service is fine and friendly. Unusual itineraries, roomy cabins—always a fun, classy trip."

EDNA MACALUSO, ABINGTON, PENNSYLVANIA

"These cruises provide good value for the dollar. They need bigger entertainment budgets."

ROBERT E. HUGHES, TAVARES, FLORIDA

"[Our trip on the Regent Sun was] the best-priced cruise I've found. Smaller ships like this stop more and it's fun to see more places. The rooms were modest, the decor simple (don't spend the money on a nicer room—none of them are great)."

TERRY CLARK, WAYZATA, MINNESOTA

*"The itineraries are excellent, but the cruise staff is not
knowledgeable about the ports of call."*

JOHN B. INGLE, HONEOYE, NEW YORK

Regent Sun

Size. 25,500 tons **Number of cabins.** 422
Outside cabins. 81.9% **Passengers.** 830
Crew. 410 (European/international) **Officers.** Greek
Passenger/crew ratio. 2 to 1 **Year built.** 1964
Cost per day. Suite $295–$330; outside double $195–$280,
inside double $170–$190.
Itinerary. *Winter–spring:* Seven-day southern Caribbean loops
depart San Juan. One loop calls at St. Lucia; St. Kitts;
Barbados; St. Croix; and St. Maarten/St. Martin. An alternate
route calls at St. Barts; Antigua; Martinique; Grenada; and St.
Thomas/St. John.

RENAISSANCE CRUISES

| 80.5% | 94.2% | 73.2% | 36.2% | TOTAL 77.4% |

Address. 1800 Eller Dr., Suite 300, Box 350307, Fort
Lauderdale, FL 33335–0307, tel. 800/525-5350.

Reader Report

*"We prefer these smaller ships—we do not need the
entertainment and nightlife, and we enjoy the opportunity to
dine by ourselves without having to play 'cruise one-up-man-
ship.'"*

WILLIAM F. RUCK, SAN FRANCISCO, CALIFORNIA

*"We were skeptical at first—such a small ship [the
Renaissance III]! But after the first day, we made friends and
found a great variety of people in our age range (35 to 45).
Great rooms and food. Tours were very well done and in
small groups."*

MARY ANNE WINSCHEL-SPANN, NAPLES, FLORIDA

*"High quality cruising at affordable prices. Excellent food and
very interesting land options."*

EVERETT AND BARBARA ALLEN, VILLANOVA, PENNSYLVANIA

"[The Renaissance III is] a comfortable ship, with good food."

NAME WITHHELD, SMITHSBURG, MARYLAND

Renaissance IV

Size. 4,500 tons **Number of suites.** 50
Outside cabins. 100% **Passengers.** 100

Crew. 67 (European)
Officers. Italian
Passenger/crew ratio. 1.6 to 1
Year built. 1990
Cost per day. Renaissance Suite $499, Veranda Suite $456, Premium Suite $414, Deluxe Suite $371, Superior Suite $328, Standard Suite $286.
Itinerary. *Late fall–early spring:* Seven-day alternating northern Caribbean loops depart Antigua Sundays, calling at Montserrat; Martinique; Grenada; Tobago; Trinidad; St. Lucia; and Barbados.

ROYAL CARIBBEAN CRUISE LINE

				TOTAL
84.1%	57.6%	77.2%	76.3%	76.3%

Address. 1050 Caribbean Way, Miami, FL 33132, tel. 305/539–6000.

Reader Report

"If food is your top priority, Royal Caribbean is your choice."
TROY AND JANET DUNGAN, DALLAS, TEXAS

"The Sun Viking *is the ideal size—it's large enough to provide all the amenities, but still feels like a friendly ship rather than a mall that had floated out to sea."*
VAL CHERNI, BRANFORD, CONNECTICUT

*"[*Song of Norway *and* Sun Viking*] are a little old (built in the early 1970s) but their staffs are genuinely happy. You know you are dealing with a happy crew when the guy polishing the brass in the stairway gives you a big smile and wishes you good morning."*
JEFF AND LAUREL CHANDLER, CINCINNATI, OHIO

"Normally herd scenes are anathema to me but the Monarch of the Seas *was amazingly well-run; from the captain to the room steward, everyone was great."*
MICHAEL FLANAGAN, WINTERVILLE, NORTH CAROLINA

"The Sovereign of the Seas *is a large and grand ship, but what a shame that the rest doesn't match—we found mediocre food service, and generally small cabins (although cabin personnel are good)."*
JAMES F. SUESS, JACKSON, MISSISSIPPI

MS Majesty of the Seas

Size. 73,941 tons
Number of cabins. 1,177
Outside cabins. 63%
Passengers. 2,744
Crew. 822 (international)
Officers. Norwegian

Passenger/crew ratio. 2.8 to 1   **Year built.** 1992

Cost per day. Suite $354; outside double $299, inside double $264. (Rates include airfare.)

Itinerary. *Year-round:* Seven-day western Caribbean loops depart Miami Sundays, calling at Grand Cayman; Cozumel/Playa del Carmen, Mexico; Ocho Rios, Jamaica; and Labadee.

MS Monarch of the Seas

Size. 73,941 tons   **Number of cabins.** 1,177

Outside cabins. 63%   **Passengers.** 2,744

Crew. 822 (international)   **Officers.** Norwegian

Passenger/crew ratio. 2.8 to 1   **Year built.** 1991

Cost per day. Suite $368; outside double $314, inside double $278. (Rates include airfare.)

Itinerary. *Year-round:* Seven-day southern Caribbean loops depart San Juan Sundays, calling at Martinique; Barbados; Antigua; St. Maarten/St. Martin; and St. Thomas/St. John.

MS Nordic Empress

Size. 48,563 tons   **Number of cabins.** 800

Outside cabins. 60%   **Passengers.** 2,020

Crew. 671 (international)   **Officers.** International

Passenger/crew ratio. 2.3 to 1   **Year built.** 1990

Cost per day. Suite $358; outside double $309, inside double $275. (Rates include airfare.)

Itinerary. *Year-round:* Four-day Bahamas loops depart Miami Mondays, calling at Nassau; CocoCay, Bahamas; and Freeport/Lucaya. Three-day Bahamas loops depart Miami Fridays, calling at Nassau and CocoCay, Bahamas.

MS Song of America

Size. 37,584 tons   **Number of cabins.** 701

Outside cabins. 57%   **Passengers.** 1,552

Crew. 535 (international)   **Officers.** Norwegian

Passenger/crew ratio. 2.6 to 1   **Year built.** 1982

Cost per day. Suite $394; outside double $292, inside double $256. (Rates include airfare.)

Itinerary. *Winter:* Seven-day southern Caribbean loops depart San Juan Saturdays, calling at St. Croix; St. Kitts; Guadeloupe; St. Maarten; St. John; and St. Thomas. *Summer:* Seven-night Bermuda loops depart from New York Sundays, stopping at St. George's and Hamilton.

MS Song of Norway

Size. 23,005 tons   **Number of cabins.** 502

Outside cabins. 65.2%   **Passengers.** 1,138

Crew. 423 (international)   **Officers.** Norwegian

Passenger/crew ratio. 2.4 to 1   **Year built.** 1970

Cost per day. Suite $372; outside double $309, inside double $270.

Itinerary. *Winter:* Seven-day Mexican Riviera transits depart Los Angeles and stop at Cabo San Lucas, Mazatlan, and Puerto Vallarta, Mexico.

MS Sovereign of the Seas

Size. 73,192 tons
Number of cabins. 1,138
Outside cabins. 63%
Passengers. 2,524
Crew. 808 (international)
Officers. Norwegian
Passenger/crew ratio. 2.8 to 1
Year built. 1988
Cost per day. Suite $347; outside double $300, inside double $264. (Rates include airfare.)
Itinerary. *Year-round:* Seven-day eastern Caribbean loops depart Miami Saturdays, calling at Labadee, CocoCay, Bahamas; San Juan; and St. Thomas/St. John.

ROYAL CRUISE LINE

				TOTAL
80.4%	69.4%	68.8%	60.4%	75.8%

Address. 1 Maritime Plaza, San Francisco, CA 94111, tel. 415/956-7200.

Reader Report
"Everybody does an outstanding job at trying to please the customers—from the booking to final homeward journey."

NAME AND ADDRESS WITHHELD

MS Crown Odyssey

Size. 34,250 tons
Number of cabins. 526
Outside cabins. 78%
Passengers. 1,052
Crew. 470 (Greek)
Officers. Greek
Passenger/crew ratio. 2.2 to 1
Year built. 1988
Cost per day. Suite $857–$503; outside double $472–$311, inside double $272–$285.
Itinerary. *Winter:* 14-day Panama Canal tour departs San Juan and calls at Oranjestad, Aruba; transits the Panama Canal, Caldera; Acapulco; Zihuatanejo, Puerta Vallarta; Los Angeles. Second 14-day Panama Canal loop same as first but arrives in San Diego. Twelve-day round-trip Panama Canal cruise departs San Juan and calls at Acapulco; Caldera; transits the Panama Canal; Aruba; Curaçao; St. Croix, and St. Thomas.

MS Queen Odyssey

Size. 10,000 tons
Number of cabins. 106
Outside cabins. 100%
Passengers. 212
Crew. 142 (international)
Officers. Greek
Passenger/crew ratio. 1.6 to 1
Year built. 1992
Cost per day. Owner's Suite $1,405; suites $714; outside double $471–$315; inside doubles $279.
Itinerary. *Winter:* Seven-day Caribbean sailings between Barbados and San Juan stopping at Jost Van Dyke, British Virgin Islands; Marigot; Cabrits and Roseau Dominica; Union

Island; St. George's, Grenada; and Bridgetown, Barbados. Ten-day Caribbean cruises between Barbados and San Juan stop at Bridgetown; St. George's, Grenada; Fort-de-France, Martinique; Plymouth, Montserrat; St. John's, Antigua; Basseterre, St. Kitts; Gustavia, St. Barts; Virgin Gorda, British Virgin Islands; St. John, and St. Thomas. Ten-day Panama Canal cruises between San Juan and Caldera, calling at San Juan; Bonaire; Oranjestad, Aruba; the San Blas Islands; the Panama Canal; Puerto Amuelles, Panama; and Puerto Quepos and Santa Rosa, Costa Rica.

MS Royal Odyssey

Size. 28,000 tons
Outside cabins. 87%
Crew. 410 (Greek)
Passenger/crew ratio. 1.8 to 1

Number of cabins. 399
Passengers. 750
Officers. Greek
Year built. 1973

Cost per day. Suite $553–$805; outside double $291–$471, inside double $250–$285.

Itinerary. *Spring:* 17-day Panama Canal cruise departs Fort Lauderdale and calls at Playa del Carmen, Cozumel, Isla San Andreas, Mexico; transits the Panama Canal; Caldera; Acapulco; Puerta Vallarta; Los Angeles, and San Francisco. *Fall-winter:* Ten-day Panama Canal cruise departs Fort Lauderdale and stops at Playa del Carmen; Puerto Limón, Costa Rica; transits Panama Canal; Caldera; Acapulco. Second ten-day Panama Canal cruise departs Acapulco and calls at Caldera; transits Panama Canal; the San Blas Islands, Curaçao; Aruba. Two twelve-day Panama Canal loops between Aruba, Acapulco and Fort Lauderdale, calling at San Jose; transits Panama Canal; Zihuatanejo, Mexico; the San Blas Islands; Ocho Rios, Jamaica; Grand Cayman; and Key West. Twelve-day holiday Caribbean round-trip loop departs Fort Lauderdale and stops at Key West; Grand Cayman; Curaçao;

MS Star Odyssey

Size. 28,000 tons
Outside cabins. 88%
Crew. 410 (Greek)
Passenger/crew ratio. 1.8 to 1

Number of cabins. 401
Passengers. 750
Officers. Greek
Year built. 1972

Cost per day. Suite $805–$651; outside doubles $315–$471, inside doubles $279.

Itinerary. *Fall:* Ten-day western Caribbean–Central America loops depart Fort Lauderdale, calling at Key West; Cozumel/Playa del Carmen, Mexico; Limón, Costa Rica; and Grand Cayman. 16-day Christmas/New Year's cruise from Fort Lauderdale to Key West, Playa del Carmen and Cozumel, Mexico; Isla San Andreas, the Panama Canal; San Jose, Acapulco, Zihuatanejo, and Puerta Vallarta, Mexico; and San Diego.

SEABOURN CRUISE LINE

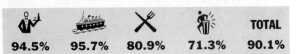

👔	🚢	✕	🗑️	**TOTAL**
94.5%	**95.7%**	**80.9%**	**71.3%**	**90.1%**

Address. 55 Francisco St., San Francisco, CA 94133, tel. 415/391–7444 or 800/929–9696.

Reader Report

"After you've done the main tourist stops, try a Seabourn cruise for a relaxing tour to out-of-the-way spots only a small ship can reach. Roomy, all suites; gourmet dining; and intimate, subdued entertainment. A joyful experience!"

SHERRY SWEELEY, DISCOVERY BAY, CALIFORNIA

"The Seabourn Pride *is a small, private yacht-like ship, very upscale—with beautiful cabins, one-seating dining, and excellent water sports, but limited on-board entertainment."*

NAME WITHHELD, BETHESDA, MARYLAND

"The Seabourn Pride *is a super deluxe ship with outstanding service—the staff anticipates your every need."*

LESLEY HOHEB, PORT WASHINGTON, NEW YORK

"The Seabourn Pride is the most luxurious of any of the many cruise ships we have sailed. The cabins (suites) are roomy; open seating at all meals and absolutely excellent food."

JOSEPH FRIEND, RANCHO MIRAGE, CALIFORNIA

Seabourn Pride

Size. 10,000 tons
Outside cabins. 100%
Crew. 140 (international)
Passenger/crew ratio. 1.5 to 1
Number of cabins. 106
Passengers. 204
Officers. Norwegian
Year built. 1988
Cost per day. Owner's suite $1,240–$1,320; suite $715–$737. (Rates include airfare.)
Itinerary. *Late fall–winter:* Four- to 16-day Caribbean and Caribbean–Amazon cruises depart Fort Lauderdale, St. Thomas, or Manaus, Brazil. Caribbean sailings may call at Tortola; St. Croix; Virgin Gorda; Jost Van Dyke; St. Maarten/St. Martin; St. Barts; St. Kitts; the Grenadines; Antigua; San Juan; or Guadeloupe. Caribbean–Amazon cruises may also call at Parintina and Alter do Cháo, Brazil, and Devil's Island.

SEAWIND CRUISE LINE

👤	🚢	✕	🗑	TOTAL
71.2%	53.4%	67.1%	41.1%	66.2%

Address. 1750 Coral Way, Miami, FL 33145, tel. 305/854–7800.

Reader Report

"With its sweeping grand staircases and fantastic hand-painted murals, the Seawind Crown *was once an elegant transatlantic ship, but the beautiful public areas are just a little frayed around the edges. Be sure to choose a cabin that was in the original first-class section of the ship (the top deck)."*

JEFF AND LAUREL CHANDLER, CINCINNATI, OHIO

"The ship itself [the Seawind Crown*] was not a #1, but the choice of islands, the food, and the ship's personnel all made for a great trip. The price was right."*

GERALD KRAMER, VENICE, FLORIDA

TSS Seawind Crown

Size. 24,000 tons
Outside cabins. 68%
Crew. 364 (international)

Number of cabins. 371
Passengers. 728
Officers. Greek and Portuguese

Passenger/crew ratio. 2 to 1
Year built. 1961

Cost per day. Suite $335–$406; outside double $242–$320, inside double $178–$235. (Rates include airfare.)

Itinerary. *Year-round:* Alternating seven-day Caribbean loops; the first departs Aruba and calls at Curaçao; Grenada; Barbados; and St. Lucia. Second departs Aruba and stops at Antigua; Guadeloupe; Barbados; and Dominica. Special Aruba land stay program offered.

SILVERSEA CRUISES

👤	🚢	✕	🗑	TOTAL
89.7%	97.4%	66.7%	87.2%	90.6%

Address. 110 E. Broward Blvd., Fort Lauderdale, FL 33301, tel. 305/522–4477 or 800/722–6655.

Reader Report

"There are no minuses...we'd never cruised before we went on the Silver Cloud, *and I was extraordinarily pleased. The crew is phenomenal.... Make sure there's a Viennese chef on board for the pastries!"*

NAME WITHHELD, EASTON, CONNETICUT

"The accommodations were excellent. The crew is more than eager to please, and the captain was most cordial. The only problem was that there was no cold water for the showers. The water was so hot you couldn't stand under it.... Except for that one problem, I would go back in a minute."

ROBERT GILLIS, LAKE WYLIE, SOUTH CAROLINA

Silver Cloud and Silver Wind

Size. 16,800 tons
Outside cabins. 100%
Crew. 196 (international)
Passenger/crew ratio. 1.5 to 1
Number of cabins. 148
Passengers. 296
Officers. Italian
Year built. 1994

Cost per day. Outside suites: $189–$1,188 (rates include airfare.)

Itinerary. *Late fall–spring:* A six-day cruise between Barbados and Fort Lauderdale calls at Antigua and Virgin Gorda. A seven-day cruise between Fort Lauderdale and Barbados calls at St. Martin, St. Barts, Guadeloupe, and Dominica. A 10-day cruise between Nassau and Fort Lauderdale calls at Cozumel, Aruba, Guadeloupe, Iles des Saintes, and Virgin Gorda. A 14-day loop departs Fort Lauderdale and calls at St. Martin, Martinique, Barbados, St. Lucia, Guadeloupe, Iles des Saintes, and La Romana (Casa de Campo). Another 14-day loop departs Fort Lauderdale and calls at Key West, Grand Cayman, Aruba, Barbados, Antigua, St. Martin, and Virgin Gorda. A 14-day cruise between Barbados and Fort Lauderdale calls at Tobago, St. Lucia, Martinique, Dominica, Guadeloupe, Iles des Saintes, Antigua, Montserrat, St. Martin, and La Romana (Casa de Campo). A 14-day cruise between Fort Lauderdale and Barbados calls st Key West, Galveston, New Orleans, Cozumel, Grand Cayman, Aruba, Los Roques, and Bequia.

STAR CLIPPERS

				TOTAL
69.8%	61.9%	54.0%	47.6%	68.0%

Address. 4101 Salzedo Ave., Coral Gables, FL 33146, tel. 800/442–0551.

Reader Report

"Provides an authentic sailing experience, despite that it is actually a cruise ship—that's its primary appeal. It is especially inviting for those who prefer a casual yacht-like experience, as opposed to the traditional formality, anonymity, and structured environment offered by most cruise ships."

NAME AND ADDRESS WITHHELD

Star Clipper

Size. 3,025 tons

Outside cabins. 91%

Crew. 72 (international)

Passenger/crew ratio. 2.6 to 1

Number of cabins. 85

Passengers. 170

Officers. International

Year built. 1991

Cost per day. Outside double $192–$342, inside double $159.

Itinerary. *Year-round:* Alternating seven-day loops. First round-trip departs Barbados Saturdays and calls at Tobago; Grenada; Carriacou; St. Vincent; St. Lucia. Second round trip departs Barbados and stops at the Tobago Cays; Bake; Dominica; Martinique; and St. Lucia.

Star Flyer

Size. 3,025 tons

Outside cabins. 91%

Crew. 72 (international)

Passenger/crew ratio. 2.6 to 1

Number of cabins. 85

Passengers. 170

Officers. International

Year built. 1992

Cost per day. Outside double $185–$364, inside double $149–$206.

Itinerary. *Winter:* Alternating seven-day Caribbean loops depart St. Maarten Sundays. First round trip calls at Monserrat or Nevis; Dominica; Iles des Saintes; Antigua; St. Kitts; and St. Barts. Second round trip calls at Anguilla; Soper's Hole; Tortola; Sandy Cay or Jost Van Dyke; Norman Island; Virgin Gorda; and St. Barts.

SUN LINE CRUISES

| 71.2% | 40.1% | 63.5% | 39.2% | **TOTAL** 60.9% |

Address. 1 Rockefeller Plaza, Suite 315, New York, NY 10020, tel. 800/872–6400, or 800/368–3888 in Canada.

Reader Report

"The Stella Solaris *is an intimate size, yet large enough for even their three-week cruises. The service is excellent and always personalized and friendly. I like the diversity of their ports and the enrichment lecture series."*

BARBARA DEAN, ST. LOUIS, MISSOURI

"The Stella Solaris *was great because it was small, and the Greek crew was excellent."*

SUE C. DAVIS, MART, TEXAS

"We had a sad experience [on the Stella Solaris*]. Food was not good; the staff spoke little English; there was poor entertainment (many of our 24 days at sea had no shows)."*

MARION E. KLUPKA, NEW HYDE PARK, NEW YORK

"The Stella Solaris*, though an older ship, was lovely, clean,*

and spacious. All of the employees that we encountered were friendly and fun. We especially loved the location of the casino, as we could enjoy the shows while playing.

ANN BONNEY KINNEAR, MORRISVILLE, PENNSYLVANIA

TSS Stella Solaris

Size. 18,000 tons
Outside cabins. 76%
Crew. 310 (Greek)
Passenger/crew ratio. 2 to 1

Number of cabins. 329
Passengers. 620
Officers. Greek
Year built. 1953 (rebuilt 1973)

Cost per day. Deluxe suite $275–$525; outside double $215–$375, inside double $130–$315. (Rates include airfare.)

Itinerary. *Winter:* Eleven-day holiday cruise round-trip from Fort Lauderdale calls at Nassau; St. Barts; St. Maarten; Iles des Saintes; Guadeloupe; Grenada; Barbados; and St. Croix. Two 14-day Caribbean/Amazon River loops depart from Fort Lauderdale and stop st St. Thomas; St. Lucia; Barbados; Grenada; Tobago; the Amazon River; Curuna-Una; Boca da Valeria; and Manaus. Two 13-day Caribbean/Amazon River loops depart from Manaus, Brazil and call at Boca da Valeria; Santarem; the Amazon River; Trinidad; St. Vincent; Antigua; and San Juan. Two twelve-day Panama Canal cruises round-trip from Galveston, Texas call at Grand Cayman; Cristobal; the Panama Canal; the San Blas Islands; Port Limón; Cozumel and Playa del Carmen, Mexico. Seven-day western Caribbean cruise loop departs Galveston, Texas and stops at Cozumel; Grand Cayman; and Key West.

WINDJAMMER BAREFOOT CRUISES

				TOTAL
65.8%	35.6%	52.4%	60.9%	62.7%

Address. 1759 Bay Rd., Miami Beach, FL 33139–1413, tel. 305/534–7447 or 800/327–2601.

Reader Report

"These are for folks who enjoy unstructured, casual sailing, seeing small islands, and excellent snorkeling throughout the Windward and Leeward Caribbean. Attentive, amiable crew."

LOUISE HORN, JACKSONVILLE BEACH, FLORIDA

"Go to party, don't go to sail. On our last trip [on the Flying Cloud*], a typical day was two hours sailing, twenty-two hours partying."*

ROBERT E. HUGHES, TAVARES, FLORIDA

"The airline lost my luggage—all I had was my bathing suit, one pair of shorts, and two T-shirts. The week [on the Yankee Clipper*]was wonderful; I never missed my clothes."*

MARY CRICHLOW, DARIEN, ILLINOIS

"The Amazing Grace *is one of the best bargains out there. Big-big with the older set, and singles fit in from day one. This is a commissary ship; it's fun to meet up with the 'tall ships' and mingle with the youngsters sailing on the windjammers."*

THOMAS DANDO, ALEXANDRIA, VIRGINIA

M/V Amazing Grace

Size. 1,585 tons
Outside cabins. 47
Crew. 40 (West Indian)

Passenger/crew ratio. 2.4 to 1

Number of cabins. 48
Passengers. 94
Officers. British and Australian
Year built. 1955 (refurbished 1989)

Cost per day. Owner's suite $223; suite $98–$105; cabin $86–$90.
Itinerary. *Year-round:* Alternating 13-day Caribbean loops depart Freeport or Grenada and call at such ports as Nassau; Martinique; Tortola; St. Maarten; Antigua; St. Lucia; St. Vincent; St. Barts; or Montserrat at the captain's discretion.

S/V Fantome

Size. 676 tons
Outside cabins. 54
Crew. 45 (West Indian)

Passenger/crew ratio. 2.8 to 1

Number of cabins. 64
Passengers. 128
Officers. British and Australian
Year built. 1927

Cost per day. Suite $162–$178; cabin $145.
Itinerary. *Year-round:* A Caribbean loop departs Antigua and calls at such islands as St. Kitts; Nevis; St. Barts; St. Maarten; Montserrat; Guadeloupe; Isle des Saintes; or Dominica.

S/V Flying Cloud

Size. 400 tons
Outside cabins. 33
Crew. 25 (West Indian)

Passenger/crew ratio. 3.1 to 1

Number of cabins. 33
Passengers. 74
Officers. British and Australian
Year built. 1927

Cost per day. Suite $195–$162; cabin $116–$145.
Itinerary. *Year-round:* Seven-day Caribbean cruise departs Tortola and calls at a selection of ports, among them Tortola, Salt Island, Virgin Gorda, Beef Island, Green and Sandy cays, and Norman and Cooper islands.

S/V Mandalay

Size: 420 tons
Outside cabins. 36
Crew. 28 (West Indian)

Number of cabins: 36
Passengers. 72
Officers. British and Australian

Passenger/crew ratio. 2.6 to 1
Year built. 1923
Cost per day. Suite $142; cabin $122–$134.
Itinerary. *Year-round:* A 13-day Caribbean cruise departs Grenada or Antigua and calls at such ports as Palm Island; Mayreau; Tobago Cays; Bequia; St. Vincent; St. Lucia; Martinique; Dominica; Montserrat; or Nevis.

S/V Polynesia

Size: 430 tons
Outside cabins. 17
Crew. 45 (West Indian)

Number of cabins: 57
Passengers. 126
Officers. British and Australian

Passenger/crew ratio. 2.8 to 1
Year built. 1927
Cost per day. Suite $178; cabin $116–$145.
Itinerary. *Year-round:* Six-day Caribbean loops depart St. Maarten and call at a selection of ports such as St. Barts; St. Kitts; Saba; Statia; Anguilla; Nevis; and Montserrat.

S/V Yankee Clipper

Size: 327 tons
Outside cabins. 32
Crew. 29

Number of cabins: 32
Passengers. 64
Officers. British and Australian

Passenger/crew ratio. 2.2 to 1
Year built. 1927
Cost per day. Cabin $145–$162.
Itinerary. *Year-round:* Six-day Caribbean cruises depart Grenada and sail through the Grenadines, calling at ports such as Tobago Cays; Bequia; Mayreau; Palm, Union, and Young islands; and Canouan or Carriacou.

WINDSTAR CRUISES

				TOTAL
94.2%	88.7%	89.8%	69.5%	89.3%

Address. 300 Elliott Ave. W, Seattle, WA 98119, tel. 800/258-7245.

Reader Report

"Sailing on any of the Windstar ships is an excellent way to see the islands, especially if you haven't been there before—it's a great way to 'try them on.' The three ships are all clean, elegant, and restful."

CAROL AND MIKE McGUIRE, POWELL, OHIO

"Excellent service, friendly atmosphere, well-designed itineraries with plenty of sports activities. No regimentation, open seating—the Wind Star *is a five-star ship without a restricting dress code. Casual elegance."*

ROLF M. LUDWIG, YUCAIPA, CALIFORNIA

"The design of the Wind Spirit *is a benchmark for other ships to strive for. Fresh fruit, French toiletries, and a VCR and film library added to the cabin's beauty."*

JAMES SWEET, SAN DIEGO, CALIFORNIA

"Friendly and laid-back. They have all the amenities of large cruise ships but none of the 'pomp.' The kind of atmosphere where a single traveler is absorbed into the community."

MARY M. DIDZUN, SEATTLE, WASHINGTON

Wind Spirit

Size. 5,350 tons
Outside cabins. 100%
Crew. 91 (Indonesian/Phillipine)

Number of cabins. 74
Passengers. 148
Officers. British and Norwegian

Passenger/crew ratio. 1.6 to 1
Year built. 1988
Cost per day. Owner's suite $593–$611; suite $456–$470.
Itinerary. *Fall-winter:* Seven-day eastern Caribbean loops depart St. Thomas Sundays, calling at St. Croix; Saba; Montserrat; St. Barts; Virgin Gorda; and St. John. Longer holiday cruises available.

Wind Star

Size. 5,350 tons
Outside cabins. 100%
Crew. 91 (British)

Number of cabins. 74
Passengers. 148
Officers. British and Norwegian

Passenger/crew ratio. 1.6 to 1
Year built. 1986
Cost per day. Owner's suite $573–$620; cabin $441–$477.
Itinerary. *Late fall:* Alternating seven-day Caribbean loops depart Barbados Saturdays. One loop calls at Nevis; St. Martin; St. Barts; Montserrat; and Martinique. The alternate loop stops at Bequia; Carriacou; Grenada; Tobago; the Tobago Cays; and St. Lucia. Longer holiday cruises available.

WINDSTAR CRUISES

DIRECTORY 1: HOTELS AND RESORTS

A

Almond Beach Club, Barbados, 41
Americana Aruba Beach Resort & Casino, Aruba, 21
Anse Chastanet, St. Lucia, 171
Ariel Sands Beach Club, Bermuda, 53
Aruba Sonesta Resort Casino at Sea Port Village, Aruba, 21
Atlantis, Bahamas, 32
Auberge de la Vieille Tour, Guadeloupe, 106
Avila Beach Hotel, Curaçao, 89

B

Bahamas Princess Resort & Casino, Bahamas, 33
Bavaro Beach Resort Hotels, Golf & Casino, Dominican Republic, 94
Belmont Hotel, Golf & Country Club, Bermuda, 54
Best Western Talk of the Town Resort, Aruba, 22
Biras Creek, Virgin Gorda, British Virgin Islands, 75
Bitter End Yacht Club, Virgin Gorda, British Virgin Islands, 78
Blue Waters Beach Hotel, Antigua, 11
Bobscobel Beach Hotel, Jamaica, 114
Bolongo Bay Beach & Tennis Club, St. Thomas, U.S. Virgin Islands, 203
Bolongo Limetree Beach Resort, St. Thomas, U.S. Virgin Islands, 204
The Buccaneer, St. Croix, U.S. Virgin Islands, 204

C

Calabash Hotel, Grenada, 102
Cambridge Beaches, Bermuda, 55
Caneel Bay, St. John, U.S. Virgin Islands, 205
Cap Juluca, Anguilla, 3
Captain's Quarters, Saba, 153
Caribe Hilton and Casino, Puerto Rico, 141
Casablanca Resort, Anguilla, 5
Casa de Campo Resort, Dominican Republic, 96
Castelets Hotel, St. Barthélemy, 156
Ciboney Ocho Rios, Jamaica, 115
Cinnamon Reef Beach Club, Anguilla, 6
Club Med Buccaneer's Creek, Martinique, 134
Club Med Columbus Isle, Bahamas, 33
Club Med Eleuthera, Bahamas, 34
Club Med La Caravelle, Guadeloupe, 107
Club Med Paradise Island, Bahamas, 35
Club Med Punta Cana, Dominican Republic, 97
Club Med St. Lucia, St. Lucia, 171
Club Med Turkoise, Turks and Caicos, 193
Club on the Green, Dominican Republic, 98
Cobblers Cove, Barbados, 41
Coccoloba, Anguilla, 7
Colony Club Hotel, Barbados, 44
Condado Beach Hotel and Casino, Puerto Rico, 141

Hyatt Regency St. John Resort, St. John, U.S. Virgin Islands, 210

W

Y

DIRECTORY 2: CRUISE SHIPS

A

M/V Amazing Grace, Windjammer Barefoot Cruises, 257

C

Caribbean Prince, American Canadian Caribbean Line, 221
MS Celebration, Carnival Cruise Lines, 221
MV Century, Celebrity Cruises, 224
Club Med 1, Club Med, 227
MS CostaAllegra, Costa Cruise Lines, 229
CostaRomantica, Costa Cruise Lines, 229
MS Crown Odyssey, Royal Crown Line, 250
MV Crown Princess, Princess Cruises, 244
Crystal Harmony, Crystal Cruises, 230
Crystal Symphony, Crystal Cruises, 231
MV Cunard Countess, Cunard Line Limited, 232
SS Cunard Crown Dynasty, Cunard Line Limited, 232

D

SS Dolphin IV, Dolphin Cruise Line, 235
MS Dreamward, Norwegian Cruise Line, 241

E

MS Ecstasy, Carnival Cruise Lines, 222
SS Enchanted Isle, Commodore Cruise Line, 228
SS Enchanted Seas, Commodore Cruise Line, 228

F

MS Fantasy, Carnival Cruise Lines, 222
S/V Fantome, Windjammer Barefoot Cruises, 257
MS Fascination, Carnival Cruise Lines, 222
TSS Festivale, Carnival Cruise Lines, 222
S/V Flying Cloud, Windjammer Barefoot Cruises, 257

H

MS Hanseatic, Radisson Seven Seas Cruises, 245
MS Holiday, Carnival Cruise Lines, 223
MV Horizon, Celebrity Cruises, 225

J

MS Jubilee, Carnival Cruise Lines, 223

L

MS Leeward, Norwegian Cruise Line, 241

M

MS Maasdam, Holland America Line, 236
MS Majesty of the Seas, Royal Caribbean Cruise Line, 248
S/V Mandalay, Windjammer Barefoot Cruises, 258

Mayan Prince, American Canadian Caribbean Line, 220
SS Meridian, Celebrity Cruises, 225
MS Monarch of the Seas, Royal Caribbean Cruise Line, 249

N

MV Nantucket Clipper, Clipper Cruise Line, 226
Niagara Prince, American Canadian Caribbean Line, 220
MS Nieuw Amsterdam, Holland America Line, 237
MS Noordam, Holland America Line, 237
MS Nordic Empress, Royal Caribbean Cruise Line, 249
SS Norway, Norwegian Cruise Line, 242

O

SS OceanBreeze, Dolphin Cruise Line, 235

P

MV Pacific Princess, Princess Cruises, 244
S/V Polynesia, Windjammer Barefoot Cruises, 258

Q

RMS Queen Elizabeth 2, Cunard Line Limited, 233
MS Queen Odyssey, Royal Cruise Line, 250

R

SSC Radisson Diamond, Radisson Seven Seas Cruises, 246
MV Regal Princess, Princess Cruises, 244
Regent Sun, Regency Cruises, 247
Renaissance IV, Renaissance Cruises, 247
SS Rotterdam, Holland America Line, 238
MV Royal Majesty, Majesty Cruise Line, 240
MS Royal Odyssey, Royal Cruise Line, 251
MS Royal Viking Sun, Cunard Line Limited, 233
MS Ryndam, Holland America Line, 238

S

MS Sagafjord, Cunard Line Limited, 233
Seabourn Pride, Seabourn Cruise Line, 252
SS SeaBreeze, Dolphin Cruise Line, 236
Sea Goddess 1, Cunard Line Limited, 234
MS Seaward, Norwegian Cruise Line, 242
TSS Seawind Crown, Seawind Cruise Line, 253
MS Sensation, Carnival Cruise Lines, 223
Silver Cloud and Silver Wind, Silversea Cruises, 254
MS Song of America, Royal Caribbean Cruise Line, 249
MS Song of Norway, Royal Caribbean Cruise Line, 249
MS Sovereign of the Seas, Royal Caribbean Cruise Line, 250
Star Clipper, Star Clippers, 255
Star Flyer, Star Clippers, 255
MS Star Odyssey, Royal Cruise Line, 251
MV Star Princess, Princess Cruises, 245
Star/Ship Atlantic, Premier Cruise Lines, 243
Star/Ship Oceanic, Premier Cruise Lines, 243
MS Statendam, Holland America Line, 238
TSS Stella Solaris, Sun Line Cruises, 256

NOTES

NOTES

NOTES

NOTES

NOTES

NOTES

NOTES

NOTES

NOTES

NOTES

NOTES

What's hot, where it's hot!

Condé Nast Traveler CARIBBEAN RESORT AND CRUISE SHIP FINDER

"It's not often you can call on the opinions of 12,000 vacationers when you need a little travel advice. But if your destination is the Caribbean, you're in luck." —*Hartford Courant*

$14.50 ($19.95 Canada)

AFFORDABLE FLORIDA
AFFORDABLE CARIBBEAN

"Concentrates on life's basics...without skimping on literary luxuries."
—*New York Daily News*

"Extremely useful books, even if you forget their promise to help you find ways to save money while you travel."
—*Houston Post*

"Travelers with champagne tastes and beer budgets will welcome this series from Fodor's." —*Hartford Courant*

"Budget travelers tired of roughing it get all the maps and sightseeing ideas of Fodor's established Gold Guides with a bonus— shortcuts to savings." —*USA Today*

Priced from $16.00 ($21.95 Canada)

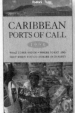

CARIBBEAN PORTS OF CALL

Here is a compact, fact-filled guide designed especially for Caribbean cruisers looking for all their ports have to offer, from dining and shopping to sightseeing.

$9.00 ($12.50 Canada)

CRUISES AND PORTS OF CALL

"A gold mine of information." —*New York Post*

"The most detailed of any of the standard cruise guidebooks...superb." —*Cruise Travel*

$18.50 ($25.50 Canada)

At bookstores, or call **1-800-533-6478**

Fodor's
The name that means smart travel.™